THE STUDY OF ANTHROPOLOGY

THE STUDY OF ANTHROPOLOGY

Morton H. Fried
Columbia University

Thomas Y. Crowell Company

New York   Established 1834

To *My Teacher, Julian H. Steward,*
and
To the Members of the Mundial Upheaval Society
(MUS)
(you know who you are)

L. C. Card 78–179769
ISBN 0–690–78986–6

Manufactured in the United States of America

PREFACE

There is an ancient Chinese custom called 圍 晬 chou-sui (the whole year), or sometimes 晬盤 之 期 sui-p'an chih ch'i (the time for examining the year), which provides a test whereby, on the first birthday, a child is confronted by an array of diverse objects, each symbolizing a different profession. The child's selection is thought to foreshadow his future career. So it may be with this book. The student who reads it may be electing to follow the path of anthropology as a lifelong vocation. That being a possibility, this book can be seen as an effort to 和盤 托 出 ho-pan t'o-ch'u (assemble the dishes and set them out), which is to say, to tell it like it is, to give the details about this particular field of endeavor.

I didn't think of doing this book by myself. Tom Simpson, then anthropology editor of the college department at Thomas Y. Crowell Company, spent a few hours convincing me that the idea had merit. I can only hope that most readers will agree. Actually, I have few illusions about it. There is too much polarization to permit any book of this kind to appeal to all readers.

Nonetheless, anthropology has come very far in a couple of decades. Before World War II, it is said, the American Anthropological Association could have held its annual convention in a phone booth. Now there are thousands of anthropologists and tens of thousands of students who take at least an introductory course in the discipline. There are so many majors and graduate students that a book like this fills a need—to tell as levelly and honestly as its author can what the field is about, not in terms of its subject matter, but with regard to its nuts and bolts as a way of life and study. Actually, the title it bears is somewhat arrogant, or at least hyperbolic; a more precise one would have indicated that the book is pretty much limited to anthropology in the United States. (For a time I thought of calling it *Skeletons in the Closet: A Study of Anthropology,* but why antagonize people who are looking for detective stories?)

Anyway, the main purpose of this preface is to thank various people who helped me along the way, explaining that they are responsible for nothing except whatever good may be found in these pages. Let me begin, therefore, by mentioning Nathalie F. S. Woodbury, editor of the Bulletins of the American Anthropological Association. The annual *Guide to Departments of Anthropology* is the source of much of the data that have been used in various chapters, and the

Newsletter will be found much quoted. Without the work put in by Mrs. Woodbury and her staff, this book would have been immeasurably poorer. It is for the same reason that I must also single out Edward J. Lehman, Executive Director of the American Anthropological Association, for thanks.

I am particularly indebted to Professors William S. Willis, Jr., and Marvin Harris, friends as well as colleagues, for penetrating suggestions and criticisms, some of which I accepted. Needless to say, as the cliché goes, neither of these scholars is responsible for any of the views expressed in the pages that follow, or the errors that may be therein contained. On the other hand, Robert F. Murphy may fairly be held responsible for whatever blemishes may be uncovered, since he failed to read the manuscript when he had the opportunity, thereby forfeiting his chance for immortality.

Grateful praise is due also to Mrs. Amelia Hess, whose sharp editorial eye and superb grasp of the administrative aspects of academic anthropology were placed at the service of the manuscript, with much appreciated results. Nancy Jillard did a most professional copy editing. Peggy Barlett helped with some data analysis on women in anthropology. Martha Fried and Nancy Fried put up with me during the writing and did what they could to improve the prose. Charles H. McNutt of the Anthropological Research Center, Memphis State University, pointed out an error in Chapter XII, which is now corrected, thanks to him. Most of the typing was done at Columbia's East Asian Institute and I am grateful for that hospitality, especially to Mrs. Mary Schoch, and to the people who did most of the labor, Gail Klement and Grace Gattuso. The final indispensable touches were supplied by Anne Margaret Birrell, who is primarily interested in Chinese studies and, I think, looks at anthropology with amused tolerance. Jim Bergin and Susan Bass at the Thomas Y. Crowell Company have been particularly helpful, and Robert L. Crowell very encouraging and supportive.

There is, however, a very special kind of gratitude that I must express. It is to the many, many students who helped to prepare me for the writing of this book. It is to Julian Steward and my own cohort of graduate students, to whom this book is dedicated, who shaped my views of the discipline. It is to my colleagues, from whom I continue to learn. All of the foregoing will find bits and pieces of themselves in these pages.

Thank you, all.

Morton H. Fried
Leonia, New Jersey
Spring, 1971

CONTENTS

By the time you hear of it, things will be changed.

—Peter Marin

part one

BEGINNING IN ANTHROPOLOGY

1

THE FACES OF ANTHROPOLOGY

If the profession is small, the subject matter
of anthropology is enormous . . .
—A. L. Kroeber

When I told my parents that I was thinking of going into anthropology as a career, my father was pleased, but I could tell that my mother was stunned and unhappy. My father had passed from a difficult childhood to what he considered an intellectually unrewarding adult life. His father, an immigrant widower with eight children, had made a pitiful living as a butcher and regarded the elementary educational system as a frivolous plot threatening his traditional right to determine his children's roles and daily behavior. Each child, upon reaching the age at which regular employment could be obtained (there were no child labor laws then), dutifully took a job. The wages went into the scant family budget but the standard of living did not improve; each addition was swallowed in the requirements for survival. My father's turn came as he approached his twelfth birthday. The sixth grade was his last. He had been a good student, but the excellence of his grades apparently made no impression on his father. Although pleading to remain in school, he was forced to leave and enter the first of a succession of mindless, often menial, positions. Bitterly exploited at work and at home, my father never relinquished a personal view of himself as a frustrated scholar. Throughout his life he read with ferocious hunger, storing up fantastic amounts of often unrelated information which he managed somehow to keep in order.

I was his only child and through me, in the kindest sense (though not always without strain and conflict), he set about living a second, vicarious life in which his childhood dreams might be realized. My announcement about anthropology filled him with pleasure; he began to focus our discussions and arguments, until then largely political, on what he conceived to be anthropological topics.

My mother's response was different. Partly because of her desire to please my father, partly because she was always extremely indulgent with her "one and only," she strove to conceal her deep dismay and anxiety. It was not that she opposed an intellectual career; her own mother had battled through life to produce two lawyer sons. Indeed,

3

she hoped I would follow my uncles' road or go into medicine, or perhaps become a school teacher. But an anthropologist? What was that? One thing was sure. You couldn't make a living at it. She worried about what she would tell her "family," the numerous brothers and sisters to whom she often seemed most attached.

Years later, when I was a graduate student, my wife was asked by the grocer what her husband did. Overlooking the fact that it would still be several years before I became a true professional, my wife replied, "He's an anthropologist." "What in hell's that?" asked the grocer. "Can he make a living at it?"

The emphasis on the relationship between anthropology and income that appears in these anecdotes may puzzle some readers and offend others. The current generation of students includes many who have shown a very interesting contempt for the material considerations long admired, if not worshiped, by those in the middle class or eager to enter it. But the purpose of my anecdotes is not merely to celebrate the fact that anthropology provides a viable career in terms of financial rewards. Readers who express an interest in the study of anthropology and with ambitions beyond the amateur certainly have a right to know if they can maintain themselves should they enter the field. Let us simply say that the present supply of trained anthropologists in our society, despite conditions of economic recession, does not yet exceed demand. Usually attributed to the exceptionally rapid expansion of higher education facilities, this situation is also related to the adoption of anthropological concepts and information by the general culture. This has been accompanied by the steady penetration of anthropology into curricula at lower and lower levels of the formal educational process. Even where not given as a distinct subject, anthropology is often included in some kind of "social studies" package. Training teachers for such courses has required increasing use of anthropologists in normal schools and other parts of the educational process. Anthropologists are also employed in small but probably growing numbers in industry, for example, as advisors on the conduct of interpersonal relations in cross-cultural situations, or in management relations. In areas such as the last, but particularly in the growing employment of anthropologists by government, deep and sometimes difficult questions of ethics must be faced. (See Chapters 2 and 13.)

Anthropological ideas have passed from the relatively esoteric world of the academy to society at large. For example, among the most widespread themes in the contemporary youth outlook, particularly in a vocal segment of high school and college students, is moral relativism —the avoidance of absolute moral imperatives and judgments—and the existential feeling that public morality is best served by those who are honest and true to themselves. The present vogue of such concepts can be associated with the evolution and diffusion of specific philosophical and religious ideas and related to the great leap forward in technology and communications that has occurred in the past couple of decades. But it also seems that anthropology played a role through its prior dissemination of the concept of cultural relativism, which recommended that different cultures be judged in the light of their own standards. At the same time, the concept of culture itself has been taken over by the larger society. A few decades ago, most people used the word *culture* to refer to arts of high cultivation and their appreciation, but the primary sense in which the word is now used is very close to the anthropological: at its core is the notion that culture comprises all symbolically learned and transmitted patterns of behavior.

As important anthropological conceptions have caught on in society at large, familiarity with anthropology as a discipline has increased, although some confusions and errors remain very common. We rarely hear, "Anthropology, what's that?" any more; but we do hear such things as "An anthropologist? Isn't that someone who digs up old bones?" Or, "You mean like Margaret Mead?" Or, "What are anthropologists going to do for a living now that all 'primitive people' have guns, transistors, and clothes?"

The tendency to identify anthropology with the work of an outstanding scientist in the field is anything but new. For many years, educated people in the United States tended to link anthropology with the work of Franz Boas, even after his death. Then there was a period when the reading public identified the field with Earnest Hooton, a Harvard physical anthropologist who produced several popular books about human evolution. Similarly, when *Patterns of Culture* was a best seller, Ruth Benedict was considered a symbol of all anthropology by a large public, just as Margaret Mead is today. In other countries, the same fashion exists although perhaps not on quite the same scale. In any case, the attempt to characterize anthropology in terms of the work or personality of a single contributor, no matter how outstanding, is doomed to failure because the discipline is simply too large for any one person to encompass. This is a simple consequence of the growth of technical sophistication in the various subfields. In later chapters we will consider some of the effects of this developing complexity, the concomitant centrifugal effects on the discipline as a whole, and the involvement of such currents in the present student situation in the discipline.

ANTHROPOLOGY: BIOLOGY AND BEHAVIOR

One of its main attributes makes anthropology difficult to characterize briefly and accurately, namely, that anthropology relates simultaneously to the study of human biology and human ethology, the science of human behavior. Merely to make this statement raises many problems and difficulties. To begin with, the field of biology, particularly as it has developed in recent years, straddles such traditional concerns as represented by anatomy, physiology, growth, variation, and evolution on the one hand, and ethology on the other. In other words, biology is taking an increasingly intensive and penetrating view of its subjects as behaving organisms. If we consider man[1] as an animal, then all of anthropology may be incorporated under the rubric of biology. There are at least two good reasons, however, why this has not occurred.

The first has to do with the fact that the studies are carried out by men and women. Historically, as we are all much aware, humanity has considered itself very special and to a considerable degree separate in the history of the planet, if not the universe. Indeed, the easy acceptance of man as an animal and of his evolution from primate ancestors is a recent feature of intellectual life. (Despite a generally humorous attitude toward such anti-evolution-teaching laws as became notorious in the wake of the Tennessee Scopes trial, it was only in December 1970 that Mississippi, the last state in the union to have a law forbidding the teaching of evolution, finally saw it overturned in the courts.) What is important to the present argument is that our own culture has long regarded man as a special creation, requiring that he be approached as the subject of special study. Since the organization of intellectual and academic studies is in every way part of a broader continuum of social and cultural phenomena, that organization must conform to the rules governing such phenomena. The emergence of a new idea does not instantly alter the social world but is part of a lengthy process of testing and selection. The outcome may be rejection of the idea, or its transformation; on the other hand, its acceptance can force additional changes in social structure. Before these changes occur there is usually a fairly lengthy delay, sometimes referred to as *lag,* or *culture lag.*

This is not, as may appear to some, a metaphysical attribute of sociocultural systems, an inherent, primordial, and obstinate resistance to change, but, as social scientists have shown, a functional derivative and concomitant of structure itself. The articulation of parts to form a whole requires certain relations among these parts. Change in one or more parts requires change in others, even if nothing more than adjustment to the event of substitution. But the continuation of un-

---

[1] *Anthropology is often referred to as "the study of man," when it is obviously the study of* people. *In a similar vein, I tried, but failed, in writing this book, to avoid the use of the pronoun "he." Let me state, therefore, that in the sense given by David Hume (1776), I refer to "all men, both male and female," and regard the pronoun "he" as asexual for most of the purposes of this volume.*

changed parts also has positive effects in the system, and these are frequently experienced as "conservative" or "reactionary" forces. In any event, they qualify the diagnosis of lag by presenting functional bases for the continuation of old traits and rejection of new ones. What is of moment to us is the clear indication that there is nothing divine or of absolute logical necessity about the existence or definition of any particular discipline or field of knowledge. The point has been neatly stated by Joseph Featherstone:

> One difficulty in imagining alternatives to the way the professions are organized is the sheer complexity of so much of our social machinery. Education, for example, is an intricate apparatus of historical accident, neglect, and professional greed, loosely bound together by haywire and red tape. Since most people seldom question the supposed necessities under which they labor, it is not odd that in the past few wondered whether things had to be the way they were.　[1969:19]

To some extent, all disciplines represent arbitrary delimitations of subject matter. The fact that other delineations are not only possible but sometimes desirable and preferable does not suffice to bring them into existence or sustain them after they have appeared. The conventional divisions of knowledge possess enormous staying power; indeed, some of them may well have outlasted their peak of utility. To change them, however, requires so much concomitant alteration elsewhere in the sociocultural system that individual or even collective efforts at reform fail, simply on the basis of inadequate energy. This phenomenon is of more than passing interest to the present generation of students because it has already witnessed sharp challenges to existing organization of colleges and curricula. Some students may be aware of the fact that the anthropology they visualize is to greater or lesser degree at odds with the discipline they discover as they take up its study in its major centers, the outstanding graduate departments and museums. Whether such students agitate for the transformation of anthropology to something closer to their dream, whether they grow to accept it as it is and gradually enter the "establishment" that perpetuates it, or whether they seek to accomplish individual aims by manipulating programs and curricula to achieve their own interdisciplinary balance of courses, it is clear that serious problems exist. Concerns such as these are given greater attention in later parts of this book.

Historical considerations do not fully account for the present location of anthropology within the academic scene. It is readily demonstrated that, behaviorally, man displays a level of complexity quantitatively so different from other animals that it is necessary for simple efficiency to set his behavior apart qualitatively. This has been done conventionally for about a century through the formal use of the concept of culture. Yet the use of the culture concept has been jeopardized in recent years by growth of knowledge. As ethologists have contributed more accurate and sophisticated observations, it has become evident that much larger portions of the behavioral repertories of many animals are comprised of learned action sequences than previously were thought possible. Conversely, some anthropologists have been able to throw into doubt the degree to which formal and even informal social rules govern human behavior. Since many anthropologists tend to place such rules at the very core of their definition of culture, the logical structures they have erected now display certain weaknesses. I argue, however, that these threats to the concept of culture necessitate its refinement; they do not require us to throw it away.

The problem can be resolved, it seems to me, by distinguishing three different kinds of learning processes. The first is virtually coterminous with life. Almost all living things known to us can be shown to acquire new behavioral responses through experience; hence, the simplest and most widespread form of learning is *situational*. An organism encounters a novel situation and behaves in a novel way (although the novelty may be tiny indeed). When the novel situation recurs, so does the new behavior; the organism has learned. The analytically significant aspect of situational learning is that it is exclusive to the organism experiencing the stimulus of the new situation; furthermore, the situation-stimulus must be encountered directly. It follows that situational learning is nontransferable—it cannot be communicated. The sole contrary possibility is that the novel response is somehow recorded in the genetic matter of the organism and thus is passed on to the descendants of the initiating organism through purely biogenetic means. The degree to which such a process operates, indeed, whether such a process truly exists, is not yet known for sure but is the subject of continuing debate. There is no question of the importance of situational learning among all the more complex animals, including man. In the course of individual isolated play, human infants and children make innumerable homely discoveries leading to greater or lesser changes in their behavioral repertory. Adults continue to learn this way throughout their lives and our culture has taken formal notice of this; we often say, "Experience is the best teacher." It may not in fact be "best," but it is very important.

Simple organisms display no means of learning other than situational, but more complex animals have a second process, *social learning*. Basically, this is simply the act of imitation. One animal observes another encountering a stimulus and emitting an appropriate behavioral response and adds the new behavioral item to its own repertory. The literature of ethology is becoming richer in carefully documented sequences of this kind. Analytically, the crucial aspect of this kind of learning is that its possibility for transmission is limited and strictly controlled by the real and immediate presence of the concrete stimulus and the equally concrete response. Any variation or substitution whatsoever, and this kind of learning will not take place. Once again, it is clear that this kind of learning is of inestimable importance to human beings. A major portion of the learning of children derives from imitative actions in social settings; such learning continues throughout the lifetime of all of us. Despite its importance, however, social learning takes second place to the only type of learning process that, as far as we know, makes massive cultural activity possible, that of *symbolic learning*.

In Leslie A. White's neat culture-oriented definition, the symbol is something without implicit meaning that is made to represent something else. Within the curious concatenation of sounds there is no reason why I am represented by the phonemic formula mɔ:tn frid. It just so happens that my society dictated that my "last name," or "family name," should be that carried by my father; while, for reasons never made clear to me, my parents gave me Morton as a personal name. There is no more inevitable connection between a certain large carnivorous quadruped and the word *tiger,* or our most adjacent star and the designation sun. There is no reason why green shouldn't mean stop, and red, go. The analytical significance of this remarkable ability to make some things represent completely different other things lies in its transformation of the learning process as it is completely freed of dependence upon the key situation. As we have seen, both situational and social learning require the real, physical presence of the original stimulus, reaction to which is the essence of the learning process. But in symbolic learning, the key situation is represented by something else, usually by a string of sounds or even by visual representations of those sounds. You, of course, are at this very second looking at precisely such symbols, and you are engaged in symbolic learning.

Three correlates of symbolic learning must be mentioned, although they are implicit, perhaps even obvious, in the previous discussion. First, symbols are indefinitely cumulative. Hence the learning process based upon them is of virtually unlimited flexibility, due to the endless possibilities of combining and recombining each and every individual element in the system. Second, combinations and recombinations do not merely repeat old situations but are capable of generating new ones. Symbolic learning makes it possible for human beings to learn how to go to the moon before they can actually go there. Such a feat is absolutely impossible when learning is of only the situational or social kind. Third, and most obvious of all, symbolic learning is not only capable of communication, of transmission of information, but can exist only in the presence of communication.

What emerges from the process of symbolic learning is a behavior so rich as to make its recording a matter of despair. Primate ethologists find the behavior of animals quite complex and the job of observation extremely rigorous. The animals stop and go and move unexpectedly in unpredictable directions. They interact and break off, enter combinations, form cliques and alliances. Behavior changes with age and varies with sex and social rank. For all of this, the behavior of the most complexly acting primates in the most complexly organized primate society is of another, incomparably simpler, order compared with that of the humans living in the simplest cultures ever studied. Such a human society has a kinship terminology with concomitant behavioral distinctions. It has a technology with a variety of implements and weapons, and knowledge of their manufacture and differential use. It has an exchange system that lacks even a rudimentary precursor on the simpler primate level. Beyond the kinship system, it has a means of socially categorizing all people ever encountered, and without necessarily regarding all aliens as enemies or worse. It also has an ideology that includes notions about the meaning of life and death and the place of human beings in the world, probably also deals with the supernatural, and provides concepts of proper conduct.

As cultures have grown in complexity, so there has developed increasing elaboration of different institutional sectors. Though these continue to overlap in life, they can and must be distinguished to facilitate their analysis. So far has separation of institutional complexes gone that special fields of knowledge, disciplines, have long since appeared merely for their separate study. The kind of specialization implied in even the most partial list of disciplines dealing directly with human behavior and its products—linguistics, sociology, economics, history, political science, mathematics, engineering, literature, art, medicine, and law, merely to scratch the surface—is inconceivable in dealing with the behavior of any other known species, not because the student is so closely identified with his subject but because only human behavior has the complexity requiring such an elaborate division of labor for its proper study.

This matter of the qualitative gap between the behavior of cultured and noncultured animals can be put another way. Cultured animals are bound by all biological laws, but no merely biological description of a cultured animal, no matter how thorough and complete, can encapsulate its range of possible behaviors. As we well know, technology is the means whereby biological incapacities of culture bearers are redressed. For example, having no biological means of flight, a cultured species can develop mechanical substitutes which rival and exceed the efficiency of biologically evolved features. Such a species can also develop and perfect life-support systems which enable it to conform to all applicable biological laws and rules under extraordinary circumstances: to breathe an artificial atmosphere where no natural one exists, to provide nutrients where none are otherwise available, to create a life-sustaining temperature in the presence of incredible cold or fantastic heat—these are some of the adaptations that can be provided by culture, enabling a bioform to exist far beyond its "natural" range.

This means that to a degree not possible with man, the behavior of other animals can, by available knowledge and techniques, be understood and accounted for on the biological level. Comparable reduction of human behavior, which is to say cultural behavior, to biological laws and rules is not possible within the framework of presently available knowledge. That it may become possible to engage in complete reductionism on such a scale is theoretically and methodologically improbable. Conversely, it must be pointed out that some reductionism is both possible and desirable. For example, analysis of culture must always be informed with knowledge of the biological setting of the cultural behavior. (A few brief and gross illustrations: no understanding of human social organization is possible without comprehension of sexual reproduction; no useful picture of economic institutions can be constructed without recognition of biological dependence on access to certain life essentials, such as food and water; no culturally structured society can be adequately comprehended without the inclusion of such biological phenomena as birth and death, growth, maturation, health and disease, although we are now deeply aware that all of these fundamentally biological processes respond to cultural factors.) Growing realization of the need for simultaneous study of biological and cultural factors in human ethology is a major factor in the recent revitalization of the field of physical anthropology, which, like some ruin-dotted desert given intensive irrigation, has begun to bloom with fascinating and important intellectual contributions. But this pious recognition of the desirability of simultaneous study of biological and cultural aspects of human ethology returns us to the dilemma we began with. The cultural aspects of that ethology are too numerous to enable anthropology to become simply an extension of biology. Anthropology, then, is placed by its fundamental nature in the difficult position of straddling a number of major disciplines pointed in different directions.

The consequences of this strategic location of anthropology have an immediate effect on all students of the subject, whether they take only an introductory course and no others, or whether they become graduate students in the field and make it their profession. Problems arise concerning the organization of introductory courses: Shall they run a single term or longer? Shall they try to survey all major branches of anthropology or concentrate on either human evolution or culture? In fact, there is no single solution to these problems, and a variety of alternatives exist. The question is discussed at greater length in Chapter 4; the reader who is taking an introductory course or has previously taken one may get some insight into the problems faced by the teacher or the staff that made up the course.

ANTHROPOLOGY AND THE HUMANITIES

If anthropology cannot turn itself over to biology, neither can it relinquish its field of inquiry to any other social science, still less to the humanities. A congeries of fields of learning, the humanities usually includes philosophy, aesthetics, linguistics (with philology sometimes listed separately), musicology, and history. Of all these, the most uncertainly classified is the last; history is often considered a social science and in the hands of some of its practitioners clearly warrants recognition as such. Other historians treat their materials so as to justify precisely the dictionary definition of the humanities: "The branches of polite learning, esp. the ancient classics and belles-lettres" (Merriam-Webster 1961: 402).

Clearly, the main thrust of the humanities is compatible with the definition of culture in terms of some conception of high development, not in terms of the anthropologically favored emphasis on all behavior patterns symbolically acquired and structured. Accordingly, it is obvious that many things of prime interest to anthropologists hold little attraction for colleagues in the humanities. How shall the latter react, for example, to problems dealing with regularities of kinship terminology among Plains Indians, marriage-class systems among indigenous cultures in Australia, or the exact methods used by Chinese peasants in fertilizing their fields? Yet there are many junctures at which the interests of scholars in the humanities and in anthropology do coincide or overlap. As enumeration of the humanities indicates, there are certain fields common to both. Linguistics is one of these, as are musicology and the study of folk literature, while the deep interest of anthropologists in graphic and plastic art and material culture (i.e., the material artifacts produced within the context of culture) stimulates exchanges with the field of aesthetics.

In many ways anthropology and philosophy overlap as technical fields of study; let us simply consider three. For one, both have a common interest in the third discipline of linguistics, with all that implies: understanding and criticism of the fundamental concept of the symbol, the nature of languages as grammatical and logical systems, and the very structure of language learning itself. Both also share a profound concern with the comparative study of values and ethical systems, as well as the philosophical problems of the application of ethical concepts within the discipline of anthropology, a matter considered at length in our final chapter. Finally, it is a highly appropriate task for philosophers to consider the place of anthropology within the sciences and equally important for philosophers of science to contemplate and criticize the methods of anthropology, the anthropological concepts of problem and solution, and the relations between anthropologists and their data.

Among the humanities, no field is in broader, deeper, and more continuous touch with anthropology than history. In some measure this merely acknowledges that history as a discipline is perhaps as much a part of the social sciences as of the humanities. What materials the social sciences do not receive from history, social scientists present to historians as data. Indeed, the earliest mention of the English word *anthropology* is attributed by the Oxford Dictionary to one R. Harvey who, in 1593, wrote that anthropology was the part of history dealing with genealogy, the arts, and "acts" (the brief citation leaving the reader quite uncertain about the constitution of the last). More recently, one anthropologist paraphrased a famous dictum and announced that "cultural evolution," a central theme of all anthropology, "will be history, or nothing" (Goldman 1955:680).

Recognizing that history and anthropology are extensively intertwined, sometimes leading to specializations wedding the two, such as culture history and ethnohistory, we shall find it useful to dwell briefly on certain distinctions between them. One of the most commonly noted is rendered increasingly inaccurate by recent developments in both fields, that is, history's disciplinary preoccupation with written source material. Unfortunately for those who appreciate sharp differences, this concern is being reduced on one side by increasing ventures into "oral history" and on the other by anthropologists' increasing tendency to make as extensive use as possible of written records. More serious is the extent of anthropological interest far beyond either written records or human memory, into the remote past when species and perhaps even genuses ancestral to our own were taking the adaptive steps leading to human physique and to culture. Most important, perhaps, is a theoretical distinction that separates the products of most historians from those of most anthropologists. The former show a marked preference for idiographic works; the latter for nomothetic. Historians delight in particulars and emphasize the uniqueness of the events they study and recount. Anthropologists are disposed to seek regularities and are much more prone to generalize their data and attempt the formulation of rules, if not laws, of cultural phenomena.

Put this way, the differences between history and anthropology appear in sharpest relief, but the picture conveyed is too definite, even in intention. That many eminent historians—Ibn Khaldun, Turgot, Gibbon, Buckle, Toynbee, among others—have sought nomothetic interpretations must be balanced against very strong tendencies among anthropologists to seek out and highlight the strange, the exotic, the anomalous, all in the service of exploring idiosyncrasies in the cultural process. Much anthropology has been dedicated to the negation of lawful statements explaining that process. In concluding the most detailed and critical examination of these tendencies, which have often virtually controlled schools and long periods of anthropological theorizing, Marvin Harris (1968:687) looks forward to the ultimate triumph of nomothetic anthropology. If and when it comes, says Harris, it will be the result of "a long hard struggle all the way." It will produce "a science of history . . . equally capable of explaining the most generalized features of universal history and the most exotic specialties of particular cultures."

ANTHROPOLOGY AND THE SOCIAL SCIENCES

No less an authority than David L. Sills, the editor of the *International Encyclopedia of the Social Sciences* (1968), has declared that "the question 'What are the social sciences?' is one to which no final answer can be given" (1968 I:xxi). Finding that the contents of the social sciences differ not only from generation to generation but even within a single generation, he begins his enumeration of disputes with the problem of classifying the discipline of history.

In a sense, one answer to the question of defining social science is contained in the seventeen massive volumes of the encyclopedia (to which might be added the fifteen volumes of its predecessor, the *Encyclopedia of the Social Sciences,* published between 1930 and 1935). For the new encyclopedia the decision was made to include ten disciplines: anthropology, economics, geography (exclusive of physical geography), history, law (i.e., jurisprudence, legal systems, and theory), political science, psychiatry, psychology, sociology, and statistics.

Anthropology is rarely confounded with geography, yet the two disciplines have extensive congruence, particularly between cultural geography and cultural anthropology, the former having been defined by two geographers as "the application of the idea of culture to geographic problems" (Wagner and Mikesell 1962:1). The history of theory in the two disciplines is shared to some extent, and some of the great geographers have been taken for professional anthropologists, Friedrich Ratzel being a noted example. On the other hand, some outstanding scientists, Franz Boas for one, moved into anthropology from geography.

Relations between geography and anthropology have been clouded by notions of a monolithic "geographical determinism." Mention of the theory, actually espoused by few acute scholars, has sometimes been enough to frighten off whole generations of students, not only from geographical but from any determinism. At times it has seemed as if the very notion of a science of culture were jeopardized. Strongly cyclical and modish, the influence of antideterminism seems to be on the wane, at least temporarily. Concomitantly, new interest in geographical environment is being expressed by anthropologists. Calling itself ecological, the approach is not really novel except in the intensity of its scrutiny of the environmental component in cultural studies. Of course, even during the dominant days of anti-environmental determinism, numerous major currents of geography coursed through and nourished anthropology. Examples include themes such as culture area, particularly as expounded by Clark Wissler (1917) and Alfred Kroeber (1939); the "hydraulic hypothesis," relating one of two major civilizational building tendencies to the problems of labor mobilization and manpower control associated with irrigation and flood control (Wittfogel 1958); or the early and rather imprecise ecological approach of Evans-Pritchard (1940). Some of these currents mingled, producing the efflorescence of the approach known as cultural ecology, in the vanguard of which was Julian H. Steward (1955). Although different versions have developed, most anthropologist-ecologists share the idea that causation is complex and protean but also regular and discoverable. Dealing in functional relationships, effects, and feedback processes, ecologists see environmental conditions not only as a factor in cultural developments but also as an active cause. Simultanously, the effects of cultural and other systems upon the environment are noted and taken into account. It is assumed that different weightings of factors will yield different historical results; hence one expects to find that even minute environmental differences may occasion cultural variability, while different cultures may occupy somewhat similar environments.

Since every culture is situated in a physical environment with which it is in sensitive interaction, some ethnographers and ethnologists must deal extensively with geographical and related data. As studies of environment become more sophisticated, awareness of the extent of variation is heightened and large scale discriminations give way to more precise delineations of microzones. Despite feedback, physical environment exists apart from and to a considerable extent independent of culture. This is not true of economics, law, or political institutions, for all of these are part of culture and have no existence independent of it. The application of terms such as economics, government, or law to noncultural societies is essentially analogic or metaphoric. Certainly this is the case with regard to the latter two. Apart from certain insect populations, the closest approach to political structure is found in one or another form of pecking order. Such hierarchies, however, are devoid of symbolic offices, loci of decision-making and administration, and chains of command. Basically, there is very little evidence of power not immediately correlated with the product of the equation that determines the capability of an individual or small coalition to exert physical force.

Still less is law (in the jurisprudence sense) visible, congruent with the fact that the general concept of legality and all its specifics are completely symbolic in nature. Indeed, the present author believes that law, as such, is a relatively late cultural acquisition, one that is not found in truly primitive cultures (cf. Fried 1967: 90–94; 144–53; 235–40).

Economics is somewhat more difficult to dispose of on the noncultural level; the major problems are presented by certain social insects. Defining economics as the behavioral subsystem that carries out the production, distribution, and consumption activities of a society, we can take refuge in the fact that few species other than those associated with culture have anything like a system of distribution. This assertion is weakened by the existence of fairly widespread activities of food sharing associated with rearing young. It is a matter of observation, however, that in noncultured species the period of such dependence is universally of short duration, and distribution is mainly limited to that short period and transient status.

Few economists are likely to become interested in whether the concept of economics can be applied to nonhuman society. Those who might be attracted are the mavericks, like Kenneth Boulding or the late Karl Polanyi. Anthropologists, by contrast, tend to be fascinated by questions like these. Recently this interest has been linked to the reaction in contemporary theory against notions of cataclysmic emergence, that is, against theories of change in terms of sudden irreversible movements that produce completely different phenomena not connected to past forms by a series of infinitesimally small changes. Such thinking was common in biology at the end of the nineteenth century, for example, when some philosophers wished to keep the concept of a divine hand in evolution. It led to such discarded notions as Henri Bergson's élan vital, according to which a divine creator's intervention was needed to instill the spark separating the living from the dead. A similar notion appears, quite ironically, in the work of Leslie A. White, since in his view the symbol radically transforms its environment and constitutes a quantum change. But such notions have had to be revised because of the success of biochemists in revealing the nature of life and the genetic materials that comprise and transmit it. Just so, it is felt that the transition from noncultural to cultural behavior was as gradual as it was inevitable in the species that sustained it. This brings us again to such questions as whether economic behavior exists prior to the emergence of culture—questions that are much more attractive to anthropologists than to economists.

Regarding the intellectual relations between anthropology and economics, their common interests include much more than pertains to pre- or protocultural activities of the economic type. Anthropology has deep and continuous interests in the whole gamut of economic theory and substance. Indeed, some cultural anthropologists identify their particular specialty as economic anthropology. For better or worse, the embrace tends to be one-sided: few economists show professional interest in the theory or data of anthropology. The reasons for this are many and must be differently weighted to explain different cases. One of the most profound of conditioning circumstances is the usually implicit, but sometimes directly stated, assumption of economists that their science is essentially not culture-bound, which is to say they believe that economic models are closer in most significant aspects to natural laws than to the more subjective statements of other social sciences. To put it somewhat vulgarly, it is believed that statements concerning the determination of value by the intersection of supply and demand are logically equivalent to such things as Boyle's law and other generalizations concerned with the kinetic theory of matter in physics. The historical fact that the most prestigious developments in economics have been associated with econometric theory and generalized model building, while there has been almost inverse minimization of more localized "area" models and theory, correlates with extensive formal lack of interest in anthropology among outstanding economists.

Until very recently, those economists who showed real interest in anthropology were associated mainly with problems of what some call the "third" or "developing" world. Even at their most energetic, however, such economists showed far more reliance upon Marxist theory and extrapolations from such theory than upon ethnographic and ethnological data. (Of course, these things are not necessarily contradictory; one can easily build simultaneously on both. But even areally oriented economists have shown little interest in the latter.) In very recent years, the situation has grown more complex. There has been a systematic attack within economic anthropology on some of the main contributions to the florescence of that field, particularly the notion that non-market economies require analytical treatment different from the market economies which produced classical economic theory. What is more, at least one economist specializing in the third world, Latin America to be precise, has derided anthropologists for their work. The main thrust of the attack is both substantive and ethical as questions have been raised about unwitting bias and about the use of data and analysis mainly for preservation of the economic status quo of imperialism and neocolonialism. We will see more of this in the next chapter; here it is sufficient merely to make sure the reader knows that something is going on, that it is hotly controversial and of keen interest to many people, some of whom are anthropologists. Yet there is light on the economic side, as bright young economists, capable of handling econometric approaches but neither dominated nor cowed by computers, have at last discovered means of socializing portions of their discipline.

Just as economics provides a rubric for professional anthropological interest by virtue of constituting a portion of culture, so the phenomena of political activity constitute a similar focus of anthropological interest (as well as the subject of a discipline called by various names, the most fashionable currently being *political science*). Once again we are in the presence of specialization inspired by the fact that we are simultaneously human beings and scientists studying human beings. We are studying ourselves, our own behavior, and its products. However defined, political relations are part of a larger category, social relations. (The astute reader is quite right who at this juncture may mutter, "What about economics? Isn't economics part of the same larger category of social relations?" Economics can well be defined as the study of the relations among members of society with respect to production, distribution, and consumption of goods and services.) My favorite definition of political science is a paraphrase of the aphorism offered by Harold Lasswell as the title of one of his books: who gets what, when, and how. But every time I mention this pithy postulation of political science, I have to add hastily that it works almost as well as a definition of economics, at least in its descriptive aspects.

The problem of separating economics and political science probably bothers anthropologists much more than it does either economists or political scientists. Thus it furnishes another insight into anthropology by showing us one more aspect of the question "What is culture?" Meanwhile, we note that most academic citizens are quite content to recognize that the study of economics revolves about objects of value, while political science concentrates on decision-making that affects most, if not all, members of a society. Personally, I can imagine no economic activity devoid of political significance and no political action without some economic connotation, however remote. It is a matter of emphasis: we are caught in the act of dividing a continuum that in life is undivided. Even the most extensively specialized cultures known show tremendous areas of overlap among internal segments: the United States military force carrying out a politically determined economic policy in Southeast Asia relies in part on a corps of religious practitioners, chaplains, to achieve its goals;[2] the government of the People's Republic of China assiduously attempted to transform Mao Tse-tung into

[2] *Consider the demand of the Roman Catholic Bishop Antulio Parilla Bonilla of Puerto Rico, who, after visiting nineteen military and civil prisons, called on January 13, 1970, for the abolition of the military chaplaincy on the grounds that "chaplains are Army men first and churchmen second"* (The New York Times, *14 January 1970: 10*).

a god to achieve its political and economic goals. Cases are easily multiplied.

Just as some anthropologists specialize in economic analysis and call their field *economic anthropology,* so others have developed *political anthropology.* The parallel goes further. As we have indicated, all too briefly, the economic anthropologists are in conflict on some major, basic issues, and this has caused some fragmentation of the field between "substantivists," who follow the late Karl Polanyi's lead and seek separate analysis of nonmarket- and market-oriented economies, and "formalists," who would analyze all economies on the basis of abstract theory derived from a scarcity-based concept of economic value. A similar division appears in the ranks of the political anthropologists. Some organize informally around the banner of what has been labeled "the behavioral approach to politics." The essence of this approach is a drive to see political phenomena as a cultural universal, found in all cultures although taking different forms and leading to diverse institutional arrangements (cf. Almond and Coleman 1960). Opposed in varying degrees are those who seek to preserve an evolutionary view and describe certain institutions, including formal government, law, and the state, as emergents dependent on prerequisite events and processes.

Unlike economists, substantial numbers of political scientists pay serious attention to anthropological methods, theory, and data. Even those who deal almost exclusively with the political systems of the United States, the Soviet Union, or other complex powers show the influences of anthropology in some of their work, as well as elements derived from other disciplines. Sociology and psychology in particular have had marked effect on the development of political anthropology, the former in too many ways to summarize here even briefly, the latter largely through the achievements of social psychology, as in recent interest in controlled experiments on interaction in small groups. Finally, all of these have developed to varying degrees special interests in the essentially mathematical approach known as game theory, one aspect of which is simulation, the representation of hypothetical situations and structures in terms of mathematical models.

The separation of jurisprudence from political science is a further example of specialization in our own culture affecting the development and organization of learning. Within anthropology, however, problems of legal analysis are invariably associated with investigations of political phenomena. This does not obscure one of the basic differences between the work of political scientists and that of political anthropologists: Political scientists display varying degrees of awareness of the phenomena into which politics merges; anthropologists remain primarily concerned with culture as a whole system, in this case approaching the totality through emphasis on phenomena defined as political.

ANTHROPOLOGY AND SOCIOLOGY

One of the more common questions put to an anthropologist is how his discipline differs from sociology. The answer will certainly vary somewhat with his nationality, which is a misleading way of saying that it depends to a degree on where he received his training. (For example, Americans trained in British departments of social anthropology respond like English colleagues and not like American compatriots.) Actually, though quite sensible, the question opens so many possibilities that the same respondent may give different answers at different times without being incorrect. In any case, the answer may well stress the great and basically irreducible overlap between the subject matters and the approaches of the two fields.

It is possible, however, to narrow the question somewhat by showing that large portions of anthropology are of little or absolutely no concern to sociologists. Physical anthropology, with few exceptions, can be eliminated; most of the content of anthropological linguistics is remarkably remote; and archeology bears slight interest for most professional sociologists. Even within cultural anthropology, extensive areas concern only rare, eccentric sociologists. On the other hand, there is little or nothing of professional interest to sociologists that does not cut across the professional interests of some anthropologists. One can say, therefore, however it may offend sociologists, that anthropology as a discipline includes all of sociology, but sociology is congruent with only a relatively small portion of the subject matter of anthropology.

There is an important point here, albeit one that is periodically subject to debate within anthropology and never more so than at present. It is not merely a question of anthropology's extending its intellectual interests over a great range of topics—this is accomplished by including a wide variety of specialists with highly particularized training. But surmounting this assemblage of individual specializations is an ideological commitment of the discipline itself, a commitment to holistic study which has two intertwined and at least partially integrated themes: (1) an insistence upon approaching man, the prime culture-bearing animal, simultaneously as a biological organism and a culture participant, and (2) a similar insistence upon considering any particular aspect of culture in its larger setting, which means studying it in the context of its natural environment and what has been called its "superorganic environment"—all other impinging aspects of culture.

Both of these commitments have theoretical and methodological consequences that better enable us to distinguish between anthropology and sociology. Sociology is more likely to accept the biological nature of man as given and constant, and not to take it into account in explaining any phenomena. Consequently, scientific generalizations from sociologists are likely to be stated entirely in terms of social phenomena—there will be no reductionism, no attempt to link the regularities of sociological phenomena with rules and laws applicable to other levels. Furthermore, the tendency of sociology to avoid the holistic ideal with which anthropology is pervaded means that sociological analysis may be better suited to attacking specific problems of a given society. For example, it is sociologists who look most explicitly into relations between poverty and crime, divorce and social mobility, or educational levels and use of contraceptive devices. Methodologically, sociology has been primarily responsible for the development of techniques of mass observation, the questionnaire being perhaps the most important single instrument. By contrast, anthropology has preferred the smaller and much more intimate study, based upon observation-participation.

What is involved is not to be passed off lightly with the judgment that one orientation and method is better than the other. Each is suited to different conceptions of problem, and both are necessary to arrive at reasonable understanding. The typical sociological method involves much more sophisticated conceptions of statistical sampling than characterize most anthropological studies. But the anthropological study offers data in depth unrivaled by even the best sociologically obtained materials. Obviously the advancement of science depends upon culling the best of the two approaches in considering any particular problematic interest, though other factors may intervene, making one approach more feasible than the other. It is also important to be aware of the methods of obtaining and analyzing any body of data. The reader of this book, whether he takes one anthropology course or several or goes on to develop professional goals in the discipline, should at all times maintain an awareness of the methodological aspects of the material being offered to him. Remote from the events and phenomena being described and analyzed, the student has the best chance of gauging the reliability of the presentations, whether written or verbal, by determining the means used to obtain the data originally, as well as the operations performed in bringing these data to some useful state.

Sociologists tend to gather much of their data by using broadcast measures, that is, they cast a wide net but seldom have the opportunity to go deep. Their classic tools are surveys and questionnaires. Even when they interview, they tend to do so with respondents previously unknown to them, whom they do not observe in action, so to speak. On the other hand, anthropologists emphasize intimacy with the people whose society and culture they are studying. Interviews and questionnaires may be an important part of an anthropologist's work but usually play a special role within it, enhancing rather than supplying the main body of data. It is important to note these different methodological tendencies between anthropology and sociology, for they can supply a basis for an informed career choice. The student who wants to do research on problems of human life and its organization must be aware that performance of such research may not be compatible with his own personality. The person who is shy about approaching people, especially strangers, or is unduly wary about maintaining intimate communications and relations with people, is probably better advised to think of going into sociology, where the approach to the collection of data is usually more formally structured. Students are often distressed to find no courses in the curriculum in field-work technique in cultural anthropology. If courses are given, students may be disappointed to find them somewhat amorphous, more anecdotal than "how to." They may be upset to hear the technique of anthropological field work referred to as an art rather than a science. Having said this much about field work, I will place the subject in the background until Chapter 6. It has been worth mentioning at this point to stimulate thoughts about the fit between career objectives and personal resources and abilities.

Another difference between sociology and anthropology that relates subtly to career choice is the greater tendency of the latter to make use of what is known as the comparative method, that is, simply the insistence upon utilizing the data of several cultures at once, wherever possible, to elucidate a variety of problems. While the comparative method has often been associated with the attempt to fill in blanks in the historical or evolutionary record, it has equal value for efforts to determine structural and functional regularities of society and the properties and features of culture. Since it is such an important tool, its use has been recurrent in sociology, but only rarely to the degree that anthropology finds commonplace. To some extent the anthropologist has used his experiences in exotic sociocultural frames better to see his own society. Well-known examples are furnished in the work of Margaret Mead, who gained insight into the cultural nature of adolescence by comparing the treatment of that age period in the United States and Samoa; or the late Jules Henry, whose experiences among Indians in Brazil enabled him to analyze child rearing in our own culture, and the subculture of our high school system in particular, with a sharp and coruscating intelligence.

One reason for anthropologists' tendency to emphasize the comparative viewpoint is that it provides a rationale and excuse for commitment to other cultures. Many anthropologists have seemed to be at odds in some ways with their own societies. At the very least, most anthropologists have looked askance at their own society, not accepting its assumptions without reservation and frequently aware of alternatives at crucial points where the society insists there is only one right way. Yet, despite the rise of repression in several areas of contemporary American society, certain institutional sectors are now much more open to the expression of alternatives. Concomitantly, apart from military situations, it is no longer necessary and certainly not fashionable to seek a form of escape from one's dislikes in this culture by taking intellectual and sometimes physical refuge in another. Indeed, as I write this, I am aware of the personal turmoil of some fine graduate students of anthropology who display deep concern for problems of their own society and fear that giving way to long-cherished drives to learn about one or more alien cultures is a "finking out," to use their own idiom. The next chapter presents my reasons for thinking that this fear may not be justified.

Before leaving this mention of the comparative method as something of a divider between sociology and anthropology, let us note very briefly that the method has its drawbacks as well as its advantages. The main difficulty has to do with the establishment of the comparison. Are the things being juxtaposed really comparable? This may sound like a nonsense question, so consider an example. The "typical" family in United States society, certainly middle-class society, is nuclear. It is sometimes known in anthropological literature as the "Eskimo-type" family, this usage constituting an implicit comparative statement. But the question can be raised, despite superficial structural resemblances, whether these two family types are similar, considering their respective sociocultural contexts. To take another instance, some decades ago anthropologists used to write blithely about "totemism," or "animism," as if all examples were part of a single universal creed. As a matter of fact, books were written in which illustrations were taken helter-skelter without regard to their fuller cultural settings. Now, just as we have become suspicious of the single informant view of the whole culture, or the approach to culture through the generation of idealized rules, so we are no longer impressed with numerous comparative examples drawn without regard to the broader comparability of the cultures from which they were extracted.

Returning to the differences between anthropology and sociology, we note that some claimed differences are simply fabrications while others are exaggerations of tendencies that are really not profound. It was never completely true that anthropologists were interested only in simple and exotic cultures while sociologists toiled exclusively in their own complex societies. Émile Durkheim devoted much energy to the analysis of the aboriginal cultures of Australia, and Max Weber was deeply concerned with non-European society and influenced the study of Chinese culture. Lewis Henry Morgan and Edward Tylor concentrated on the simpler stages in the evolution of culture but were concerned about social problems in their own societies, the latter going so far as to identify anthropology as a "reformer's science" (Tylor 1871:529). Yet it is correct to see the two fields oriented in general in the respective directions described, at least until a couple of decades ago. The more extensive changes were those in anthropology, forced in large measure by the shrinking of the field as primitive cultures were extinguished or came increasingly under the influence of complex outside forces. At the same time, confidence grew in the feasibility and utility of applying intensive anthropological field methods to the study of complex modern cultures. The result was the emergence of new formal subfields in anthropology, urban anthropology being conspicuous. Any attempt to differentiate urban anthropology from urban sociology would be an exercise very much like those practiced by the medieval scholastics; what is more, such an attempt would be regarded with impatience and contempt by most of the competent scholars in those fields. Why, then, call the "new" field urban anthropology when the designation urban sociology has been around so much longer? The explanation would take more space than we can give it here and would venture into such topics as the social and economic structure of academia, as well as problems of occupation identification, association, and loyalty. The important thing is not the designations given lines of inquiry but the information-producing, problem-solving capacities that are mobilized and realized. To accomplish that end, few participants will hesitate to cross arbitrary disciplinary boundaries. Far more painful and difficult is the question of judging the utility of the work—to answer the question of whether this or that investigation (research) is necessary or even of any use whatsoever, not to mention its possible social harm; but this is a problem to which we turn in the second chapter.

It is frequently said that the main separation between sociology and anthropology parallels the concern of the former with society and the latter with culture. I find this generalization to be virtually without merit, save for the considerations implied earlier about relative breadth and depth of inquiry between the two disciplines. To be sure, the holistic orientation of most anthropologists results in a finished product that is easily distinguished from the work of most sociologists. But the differences do not lie in the presence or absence of technical concern for problems of society, whether concrete or abstract. Indeed, it is the anthropologist rather than the sociologist who interests himself in problems of noncultural society and the emergence of cultural society. Once culture is upon the scene as a massive phenomenon, however, questions about the distinction between culture and society (among culture bearers) are at best scholastic and perhaps nonsensical, since all social forms among culture bearers are ipso facto cultural.

It bears reiteration that those recognized as the finest scholars in both fields spend very little if any time worrying whether what they are doing is sociology or anthropology. C. Wright Mills (1961:4ff.), for example, defined "the sociological imagination" as a view of phenomena that enables one to relate one's own life and the life of other individuals to larger and larger historical scenes. Having thus defined sociological imagination, Mills made his frame of reference not sociology but social science. For Mills the vital imagination was not exclusively academic but had to help rouse people to awareness of social problems, assisting them in focusing upon and perhaps solving them. Many anthropologists would have no hesitation in accepting Mills' concept as entirely applicable to their own discipline conventionally defined (cf. Berreman 1968); others, Leslie White, for one, might object, not on moral but scientific grounds, arguing that problem solving, to the extent that it implies human intervention in the cultural process, is impossible (cf. White 1948). Still others do object on what they declare to be ethical grounds, and demand "value-free" social science. More about this in subsequent chapters.

A final word on the topic of the relation of anthropology to other academic disciplines and particularly other social sciences. Having learned that the boundaries are artificial and that the brightest people in the discipline and some of its neighbors show little or no concern in their own work for such boundaries, some readers may be shocked to discover that such and such a topic is ruled off-limits for a doctoral dissertation or even for a term paper, on the ground that it is "not sufficiently anthropological." Similarly, a student may be discouraged from electing nonanthropological courses. Both of these problems are discussed along the way.

THE FIELDS OF ANTHROPOLOGY

It is not difficult to see that the most important division within anthropology is that paralleling the distinction between the biological and cultural levels. Yet that division, however in the past it tended to produce distinct bodies of knowledge, is presently bridged by the work of many scholars applying themselves to intermediate problems and devoting attention simultaneously to biological and cultural factors.

At its point of greatest divergence from the subfields of cultural anthropology, *physical anthropology* deals in precise detail with the biological evolution of genus *Homo,* the only bioform known to be massively engaged in cultural behavior. It is also concerned with contemporary physical variation in *H. sapiens,* the one extant species of the genus, as well as with its reproductive and growth patterns, health, and disease.

Physical anthropology also plays more mundane contemporary roles. Anthropometry, the subdivision concerned with human measurement in its broadest terms, has a variety of practical applications, from assistance in the manufacture of better-fitting mass-produced clothing and athletic equipment to the furnishing of buses, railway cars, and aircraft with more comfortable seats; from the manufacturing of machinery to accommodate human operators to the production of equipment and life-support apparatus for the astronaut in space.

Physical anthropologists, studying human evolution, rely on information exchanged with paleontologists, physiologists, and anatomists. The link with dentistry is especially interesting. Because teeth are probably the most commonly recovered fossil evidence and because some major evolutionary steps are most clearly revealed in changes in dentition, dental studies have made significant contributions to our understanding of the development of man. In recent years, geneticists have made increasingly important contributions. They in turn have implicated astronomers, astrophysicists, chemists, biochemists, and geologists, whose evidence of major physical changes in the earth's environment, sometimes produced in conjunction with data on changes in orbital attitude, radiation from space, or global variations, may have had profound effect on the mutation rate in and the selection pressures acting upon our ancient ancestors.

To some extent, the interest in physical anthropological study of the evolution of man is a direct descendant of an ancient and widespread human desire, namely, to comprehend our origin. In part this seems almost an intrinsic aspect of human nature, but it must remain "almost intrinsic" because some cultures, and vast numbers of individuals, show no interest in the problem. However, a great many cultures offer fairly extensive explanations of the origin of man. One such treatment is well known in our own culture—the biblical account of Genesis. The ancient Egyptians and Greeks, the Chinese, the Pawnee, the Nuer, the Thonga, the Polynesians, the Maya, the Hindus, the Arunta, and innumerable others have or had their own extensively articulated views of man's origin. Like most of these views, our present attempt to unravel the problem scientifically is only in part made to satisfy what seems to be a deeply implanted curiosity. These explanations also provide some basis for a culture's orientation to its present and therefore to its future. For most cultures, explorations of origin have simultaneously offered interpretations of why men are what they are at that period in history. Some cultures use these explanations to justify the present and to project it endlessly into the future; others incorporate change and predict major shifts in the future. In Western culture, most conspicuously in the United States and the Soviet Union, the view of man as an evolving animal came dramatically to the fore in the placing of man on the moon. More than one commentator has seen the human penetration of space as the beginning of the ultimate answer to the problem of expansion of human population beyond the sustaining capacity of the earth's resources.

Physical anthropology is well known to a wide public for its studies of collective human variation, or race. For decades, however, the physical anthropological study of this topic has been complicated by the fact that a sociocultural phenomenon called by the same name, "race," has been at the center of some of the most violently expressed and unhappy problems of our own and other societies. The cultural matrix of this problem is so complicated that it can merely be indicated at this point; fuller analysis would usurp the rest of this book. In brief, it is my view that biological race is a generally inconsequential feature of human variation. Fundamentally, I find that assignment of an individual to a conventional racial category tells less about that individual than is revealed by analysis of the society in which he lives. To say that a person is a "Negro" or "black" tells little or nothing about his physical makeup; in different parts of the United States, the existential and sometimes even the legal definition of "Negroness" is different. When the frame is a comparative one and we consider the varying definitions of "blackness" (or "whiteness") in other sociocultural systems, such as Brazil, Cuba, South Africa, China, or India, the concept dissolves in the face of major variation.

It would be myopic to conclude that physical anthropology as a discipline is free of racism, here defined as the belief that certain statistically aggregated physical features of man define large human populations characterized also by fundamentally different levels of intelligence and types of behavioral orientation.[3] Superficially curious is the anomalous use of "science" in the service of such racism. The charge is leveled that "liberal" scientists are choking off research into the vital matter of racial differences. A number of scientists, including a few physical anthropologists and a much greater number whose specialization is in other, often remote, fields, such as crystalography, continue to urge us to consider racially based theories of differential intelligence and other traits. Although the vast majority of scientists have turned away from theories of race as a determinant of culture, it is a matter of profound interest to anthropology that a handful of scientists continue to persevere in the defense or elaboration of racist theories. There are substantial reasons why such attempts continue, and their explanation has everything to do with our understanding of social systems, culture, and the causes operating in this realm.

Contemporary physical anthropologists attempt to understand the interaction of biological and cultural factors in the development, mainte-

---

[3] This definition of racism differs from the one currently in vogue in certain political circles, one that finds its essential criterion in the exploitation of individuals or populations under the cover of asserted biological differences. It is not a question of conflict between these definitions, but of determining which is to be used at what time and for what purpose.

nance, and change of the human species. Specialists in the evolution of man are deeply concerned with the effects of culture at critical junctures. They ask, for example, how the adaptation of our ancestors was affected by a dentition that made it difficult for them to take on powerful carnivores in direct conflict. They inquire into the significance of the fact that our ancestors of australopithecine (and probably immediately pre-australopithecine) grade lived not in forests but in savanna regions, where they could not readily take to trees as a defense against predators. As in various other instances, it seems that cultural or protocultural adaptations came to the fore when these animals learned to use weapons and tools and new forms of social organization. Venturing far beyond such examples, physical anthropologists employ dimensions of culture in interpreting the evolution of man.

Among the most culturally oriented of the physical anthropological studies are those dealing with the contemporary study of health and pathology. Earlier physical anthropologists manifested some interest in the topic; in a sense they were compelled to do so because fossil evidence often reflected information of a medical nature. Fossils frequently show pathology: badly formed or caried dentition, bone tumors, crippling conditions of various kinds. Ancient evidence indicates that our ancestors did not live in a Hobbesian world of "war of all against all," but kept alive a variety of fellows who had debilitating injuries or diseases. Eugenicists take note: it is not an invention of modern society that keeps alive those who, unassisted, might perish. It seems to be a trait as old as human society, and possibly older.

Interest in the history of human illness persists, and the scope of this subfield has now greatly widened. It has been overtaken by the new field of medical anthropology, which concerns itself with health and illness as part of a cultural field. Starting with empirical data on different conceptions of "health," and with widely varying notions of disease, diagnosis, therapy, and recovery, the medical anthropologist seeks to comprehend the interaction of biological and cultural factors in debility and death. At times such work is primarily biological, as when investigating recurrent and nonchangeable effects of germs, viruses, and parasites; at other times it is primarily cultural, as when observing the interaction between a sick person and other members of his society, or between a patient and the (medical) practitioner.

Many archeological anthropologists (archeologists) are equally close to physical anthropologists in problem interest, method, and theory. On the other hand, the archeologist is sometimes called an ethnographer of past societies, precisely because the main focus of archeological interest is on cultural reconstruction; archeology thus may be considered a variant of cultural anthropology.

During the past several decades of anthropological development, the position of archeologists has not always been clear with reference to the aims and objectives of the larger field of anthropology. In part this may be attributed to the division, now much less acute, between archeological investigation of certain classical civilizations and all other archeological work. Curiously, it was not long ago that little connection or communication existed between those who specialized in the investigation of Paleolithic, Mesolithic, and Neolithic sites, and those who were interested in the origins and development of civilizations in Southwest Asia, Northeast Africa, and Southern Europe. Major contributions, however, have begun to link the earliest florescent stages of these cultures with earlier developmental periods going back to Paleolithic levels.

When sites yield the remains of ancient man as well as some of his products, archeologists are most likely to share their work with physical anthropologists. Yet mutuality of interest is not confined to these earliest periods. Wherever the archeologist works, he may discover skeletal (very rarely mummified) remains of the population that carried the cultural tradition represented at the site. When such materials are found, they are analyzed in a variety of ways and attempts are made to discover the biological relationships of that population with others, whether earlier, contemporaneous, or much more recent. At times the evidence may throw light on problems of certain diseases, their origins, and distributions, or on the state of medical arts in the culture at the time.

In recent years the collaboration of archeologists and physical anthropologists on the analysis and classification of human remains has been carried out with generally increasing restraint. There is less haste now in pronouncing racial judgments. (Nonetheless there are still some scholars who are prone to project a picture of a neat and homogeneous population on the basis of relatively little physical evidence. Such extrapolations may be harmless enough in themselves, but they represent an abuse of scientific method and should be avoided on that ground alone.)

Hasty associations of certain cultures with particular and narrowly defined racial types are frequently erroneous and contribute to certain inflammatory themes in a biased and racist ideology. An excellent illustration is offered by a widespread interpretation of the so-called neanderthal fossils. According to theories developed in the late nineteenth century and still popularly held despite mounting repudiation by the specialists closest to the data, neanderthals were markedly different from other *Homo sapiens* and were driven to extinction by such clean-cut rivals as so-called Cro-Magnon man. Actually the evidence, long available, supports a totally different picture. The neanderthals were thoroughly *sapiens* and differed from their contemporaries probably less than some individuals vary from others in the present world. Furthermore, the population designated neanderthal was no more driven to extinction than any other human population that lived at that time. Instead, it is probable that at least part of the genetic material of the neanderthals continues to exist in a substantial portion of the present human race.

When anthropology scrutinizes itself, it discovers that it too is part of a sociocultural system and that its products serve that system. The neanderthal myth was nothing less than the projection into the distant past of the nightmare of racist genocide that was intrinsic to colonialism, imperialism, and fascism. The history of European expansion is replete with such events as the hunting of "natives" for sport and enslavement, and whole populations, such as that of Tasmania, were extinguished. It is not difficult, then, to see the development of the neanderthal myth in the nineteenth century as the mistaken interpretation of the past in terms of the present, an implicit justification of that present on the grounds that history had always been so. Thus was social Darwinism, the concept of the survival of the fittest (i.e., the ruling elite), confirmed.

It is very difficult to root out erroneous notions and procedures. There are still numerous archeologists who rely upon fairly rigid assumptions of correlation among physical type, language, and culture. In the Soviet Union, for example, archeologists continue to speak about the presence of certain cultural groups or linguistic groups where the remains of the past are only skeletal. Or it is asserted with equal probable error that where only certain cultural evidence has been recovered, such as particular tool or weapon types or indigenous art forms, that such and such a human "race" must have been present. But if there is anything that anthropology as a general field of knowledge has learned and is able to prove, it is that language, culture, and physical type can vary totally independently of each other. Furthermore, archeological evidence itself shows that such independent variation is not a new phenomenon brought on by modern rapid transportation but is a widespread feature of culture extending into the remote Paleolithic past.

The errors discussed in the previous paragraphs can be lumped together under the general heading of "archetyping." While it is true that one of the aims of science is generalization, scientists must take great pains to avoid the creation of a series of narrow pigeonholes into which their data must be fitted. Just as unwary travelers seeking rest on the bed of Procrustes were stretched to fit if too short and brutally cut down if too long, so a system of archetypes suppresses variation to fit the ideal construct, the archetype. In recent years archeologists have been turning emphatically and in increasing numbers away from the archetypical approach to site and culture classification. They have developed techniques for describing their results statistically, presenting a profile of their findings instead of concentrating on a few "typical" details. The restoration of living complexity to analysis has many beneficial by-products, not the least of which is a view of culture as a subtle congeries of adaptive processes embedded in a larger ecological framework. It allows consideration of cultural traits as elements that can undergo great change and that can move from place to place without requiring large-scale human migrations or population shifts. Unless actual biological remains substantiate a theory of population change, we should not assume that even drastic cultural changes in a particular area represent the replacement of an older population by a new and biologically different one. We should not permit anything to obscure the central goal of archeology, which is to discover sufficient evidence of past cultures to enable us to reconstruct them with as high a degree of accuracy as possible.

Locating sites and properly exploiting them is the basic task of all archeologists. The fact that the process of excavation is precisely equivalent to the process of destroying the site complicates the work enormously. There are really no second chances; there are only new sites to destroy. It is for this reason that most professional archeologists fear the amateurs and despise incompetents in their own ranks. Furthermore, rarely if ever do things come labeled; objects do not themselves proclaim their nature, use, provenience, age, or anything else. It takes hard scientific work to deduce these things. Nonetheless, fundamental to archeological interpretation is the logical stricture known as Occam's razor, which its author, William of Occam, stated in the words, "a plurality is not to be posited without necessity"—the simplest explanation is the best. In archeology this is accomplished by assuming that similar things in different societies tend to have similar functions, contextual associations, and consequences. On simpler levels, this principle leads to the classification of manufactured objects on the basis of probable use—such an object is a "knife," because it has a long cutting edge, while another object is a "burin," because it has a sharp point, and so forth. On more complex levels it justifies more intricate assumptions, for example, that differential burials, in which some corpses are found in small holes without accompanying goods, while others are found to have been interred in massive tombs with much treasure and perhaps animal skeletons or remains of persons killed at the time of the original burial, are evidence of sharp socioeconomic distinctions in the society, with a host of probable correlates.

The ties between archeology and cultural anthropology have been growing closer after many years of relatively little exchange of anything but data. Younger archeologists in particular are taking seriously problems related to the structures of societies known largely or even

entirely through "the testimony of the spade." This is not to say that
only the present generation of archeologists has discovered cultural
anthropology. Each generation has had some brilliant synthesizers who
wedded the two approaches. But after a period when archeology was
virtually dominated by the "potsherd" approach, the pendulum is swing-
ing in favor of a more freely interpretive posture (cf. Binford 1968).

Just as archeology has two aspects, "classical" or "fine-arts"
archeology and "dirt" or anthropological archeology, so *linguistics* is
divided between linguistics proper and anthropological linguistics. Part
of the dichotomy rests in the historical structure of fields of learning,
universities, and payrolls, although the work performed may show little
or no significant differences of content or method. On the other hand,
over the long run there are differences of frequency that offer some basis
for distinguishing the two interpenetrating parts of linguistics. Linguistics as a whole, of course, is the science of language, which strives to
comprehend the general principles behind the formation and development of any and all languages, as well as relationships among languages
and the analysis of any particular language's structure and operation.
Although exceptions are not at all unusual, most "general" linguists
work on what may be called, somewhat awkwardly, nonexotic languages. They are highly likely, for example, to work on Indo-European
languages. Anthropological linguists, however, are more likely to work
on languages spoken by only a few survivors of cultures on the verge of
extinction, such as Hupa (a California Indian language), or languages
found in still remote parts of the world, such as New Guinea. As a
consequence of this divergence there is some difference of method. To
the extent that anthropological linguists deal with "rare" languages and
speech that have never been put into writing, they have the problem of
obtaining their own textual materials for analysis and study. Even with
modern recording equipment, ultimately there comes the time when the
raw sound must be transcribed phonetically. While general linguists are
also dependent on textual materials and sometimes concentrate on
problems of dialect geography requiring the extensive collection of
original materials, much of their work is accomplished with available
materials, sometimes of a documentary nature.

The role of the anthropological linguist in the study of culture has
always been strategic, for language represents the most common as well
as the most massive and tightly organized of symbolic systems. Even
greater significance is attributed to linguistics today, particularly in such
areas of cultural anthropology as the "new ethnography," which is
partly derived from earlier techniques and theoretical considerations in
anthropological linguistics—concepts having to do with set theory,
componential analysis, and generational grammar. In mastering such
concepts and the techniques of analysis they are associated with, the

student should pay cautious attention to the controversy that these concepts are embedded in. At present, it does not seem possible to develop a neutral approach, or pursue a syncretism of one's own; each of these positions is associated with a dialectical opposition, which the student might well approach with care. The componential approach, for example, is an attempt to specify culturally bound rules of logical classification for various kinds of sets in a cultural system, such as kinship terms (and associated behavior), color categories (and perception), the assignment of plants and animals to taxonomic categories, and so on. In dealing with human relations, the result has usually been a projection of behavior in terms of a priori rules, a consequence that, in turn, has been severely criticized as a profound error of philosophical idealism.

For those who may fail to see the immediate and intense connections between the foregoing and anthropological linguistics, consideration of one particular subfield of the latter may help. Psycholinguistics begins with the assumption of the strongest interrelations of language and culture. Although recognizing a condition of mutual feedback between the two, psycholinguists tend to emphasize the initiating role of language. They remind us that each child entering a culture acquires its language, which is exactly equivalent to acquiring a certain view of the world that is implicit in the grammar and the vocabulary of that language. It is a relatively short theoretical step from such a view to those indicated in the previous paragraphs, and with that step conflict ensues between idealists and materialists.

This whirlwind tour of the fields of anthropology now brings us to *cultural anthropology,* which is the redundantly named heartland of the discipline, since it may include anthropological linguistics and archeology and has much to say about physical anthropology as well. Cultural anthropology has been subdivided in a variety of ways by different national traditions of scientific development and management. For example, in Great Britain and certain societies deeply influenced by the British, the term "cultural anthropology" is understood, but rarely used. "Social anthropology" is much preferred there. Indeed, that term better reflects the comparative sociology that has been the mainstay of British anthropology, with its heavy concentration on functional analysis of the structure of societies, mainly nonindustrial and frequently part of its recent colonial empire. In the United States, the term social anthropology is not infrequently heard, particularly at places which have been subjected to British influence, such as the department of anthropology at the University of Chicago, which continues after more than a generation to reflect the teachings of A. R. Radcliffe-Brown. Students are warned, however, not to seek to make too sharp and mechanical a distinction between cultural and social anthropology, for the boundaries between them are even hazier and more permeable than between those of sociology and anthropology, as the preceding reference to "comparative sociology" should indicate.

A generally if not universally recognized distinction within cultural anthropology separates ethnography and ethnology. Ethnography employs descriptive and analytical study of specific sociocultural aggregates, such as France, Bathonga, China, Navajo, Baganda, and Gilyak. Ethnology is the comparative study of culture utilizing ethnographic monographs or other ethnographic materials as its raw material. Contributions to ethnography are invariably bound to original field work in the subject culture. Ethnological studies, by contrast, may sometimes be enriched by ethnographic work but are usually on such a scale that they must be based upon secondary experience of the subject cultures.

Sooner or later in this book we are going to have to deal with anthropology in terms of some of the mystiques it has generated and with which many, perhaps most, of its practitioners like to see it surrounded. I have already mentioned the relationship between anthropologists and field work. Many graduate departments of anthropology predicate successful attainment of the doctorate, and some even the master's degree, on the accomplishment of field research, usually in an alien culture. Students whose propensities and talents lie in the direction of library research often undergo severe pressure until they agree to undertake field work. And the same professors who engage in these subtle pressure tactics are known to say that they are amazed about the strange lack of library dissertations in the discipline! Why, it is asked, don't we have more solid biographical and history-of-science studies of significant past contributors? Why not more ethnohistory? Why not more probing into our own culture?

Most cultural anthropologists' feelings on the significance of field work in an exotic culture resemble other people's religious beliefs. In comparative ethnological terms, a deep experience of "culture shock" is worth the ecstasy of conversion, but may be closer to the old Plains Indian vision quest. Briefly, culture shock, for those who may never have experienced it, is the deep-seated feeling of anxiety or euphoria that takes command when one's cultural milieu is suddenly changed. Some travelers get culture shock very easily; they show its signs when they find they can't drink the water for fear of parasitic invasions of their inner organs, or they find the plumbing quaint or (real shock) nonexistent, or when none of the food seems edible or adequate in previously understood terms. Although many fledgling anthropologists succumb to culture shock on the foregoing level, sophistication has increased, partly because of improvements in travel facilities and partly because our own culture has become more cosmopolitan. Nonetheless, culture shock still arises with the sudden realization that the assumptions on one side of an interaction are regularly failing to be met by those on the other. Major behavioral cues are being missed. Wanting to signal camaraderie and friendship, the interloper is standing too close (or too far off), he is smiling (or not smiling), he is talking when he should be silent (or silent when he should be talking), his costume is wrong for the occasion (and perhaps for all time), his facial expression conveys anything but what he expects, his gait is wrong, his body is being held in a tense and hostile posture (but he doesn't know it). Inadvertently he is making a supremely obscene gesture in front of his host's wife and kiddies and there is a very strong taboo against making that kind of gesture in front of women and children. In short, Murphy's law, which states that everything that can possibly go wrong will do so, is in fullest operation, although the person in culture shock does not know why. At precisely such a moment he comprehends that culture is indeed real, that people are not necessarily bound by common denominators of "human nature" into patterns of mutual understanding.

Thus it can be readily understood why so many anthropologists insist on field work in an alien culture as part of the training for the discipline. It is for this reason that some instructors of anthropology at the most introductory levels attempt to confront their students with some kind of experience that will give an electrifying feeling of the reality of culture. I have attempted this myself by opening cans of (Japanese) fried grasshoppers or (Mexican) agave worms. Ostentatiously eating the first one, I pass the cans around the classroom urging everyone to try some. I don't think I've ever gotten more than about a third of the class to indulge themselves, although the items are carried in many ordinary supermarkets and the students approached have been quite cosmopolitan. Sometimes the reasons given for not partaking are quite interesting. One student insisted it had nothing to do with his cultural background but said it was entirely due to his religion, which forbade eating such things!

Students are frequently prone to pay lip service to the concept of cultural differences. Speaking very generally, previous generations of students maintained a posture of acceptance of the propriety of strange cultures for only a brief span until their ethnocentrism and culture-boundness became manifest. Although far from homogeneous, the present generation of students can hold a position of cultural relativism for longer periods, staving off more temptations to relapse into ethnocentrism. This is due partly to the spread of the ideological themes of "doing one's thing" and toleration of others. There is ample evidence that this value has strictly limited distribution in the society as a whole, but undoubtedly its main locus is to be found among youth, particularly students. Yet this group shows very interesting limitations, which can be related to a culture-boundness that it would indignantly deny but that is manifested in its dialectical opposition to precisely those things it believes most typical and diagnostic of its own culture (cf. Hitchcock 1969). Another way in which ethnocentrism is shown and the reality of culture denied is through imputation of common desires for peace, equality, and personal fulfillment to all mankind, irrespective of culture. Unfortunately, anthropologists can make similar errors. At the 1966 annual meeting of the American Anthropological Association, I joined a majority of my professional colleagues in voting for a resolution that declared warfare to be inconsistent with "human nature." Several of our associates tried vainly to call us to professional attention, urging us to consider the overwhelming evidence that war is supremely associated with human beings and their cultures (although not with all of them). The resolution was intended to convey that war need not necessarily be an aspect of a sociocultural system. The actual wording, however, violated basic precepts of the discipline.

There may be some readers who will be upset or angered by the foregoing, or who will wish to question the desirability of cultural relativism run rampant. If the proposition is accepted that cultures vary, often in tremendously significant ways, and if it further is acknowledged that cultures should be judged only in their own terms, then it will have to be concluded that even the harshest treatment afforded one segment of a society's population by the remainder of that population cannot be criticized or negatively sanctioned by the population of another sociocultural unit. In other words, it would be wrong to condemn the Aztec culture of some five hundred years ago for its elaborate cult of human sacrifice, the Roman for its use of the arena, the German for its murder of millions of Jews, and the American for systematic mistreatment of nonwhites. Put this way, emotional responses are likely to be aroused and, as we have been told continually, emotion has no place in science. Does this mean that anthropology can never be scientific? I have no intention of teasing the reader, but the question cannot be pursued here. I will come back to it, however, in the next chapter.

2

SOME VITAL ISSUES

. . . a morality which places the welfare of science
above the welfare of people must be rejected.
—Ralph L. Beals

Reflecting contemporary life, anthropology is beset with problems of
identity and purpose. Befitting an upstart science with a tradition of
iconoclasm, anthropology has always been concerned with its own
definition and nature; but until quite recently, inquiries tended to be
bland and philosophical, or esoteric, devoted to narrow questions and
carried out in such ways as to be of interest mainly to anthropologists
and only a small segment of them at that. Now anthropology, like other
forms of occupational specialization, is being scrutinized in terms of
social utility, or what is usually called *relevance*.

It seems to me that the questions of use and identity or relevance
when applied to a field of knowledge, a discipline, or an occupation are
rooted in the social question of whether the activity's yield is of equal
value to the labor put into it. Whatever else may be said about this
problem, it is superbly anthropological. Although our first steps toward
an answer will be logical and philosophical, we will quickly discover
that the crucial elements, far from being fixed and immutable, are embedded in kaleidoscopically varied sociocultural settings.

In a symposium on social responsibility in anthropology, the Nor-
wegian anthropologist Gutorm Gjessing recalls Leo Tolstoy's remark to
the effect that historians are like the deaf, answering questions that no
one has asked them. Gjessing wonders if anthropologists are not doing
the same thing. Are they involved in intellectual games of interest to
only a tiny ingroup? Gjessing makes it clear that if that is the case, it is
reprehensible because "science for science's sake" is irresponsible in
the face of a holocaust that threatens to annihilate all mankind (1968:
397). In the same symposium, another commentator, Andre Gunder
Frank, forces the issue in his opening statement:

Che Guevara, upon being asked what, as a writer, one could
do for the Revolution, answered that he used to be a doctor.
[1968:412]

If that is not sufficiently explicit, Frank spells it out:

> [The anthropologist's] responsibility is to use anthropology
> only as far as it is sufficient, while doing whatever is neces-
> sary to replace the nearly world-wide violent, exploitative,
> racist, alienative capitalist class system which embraces most
> anthropologists and the people they study.   [Ibid.: 412]

While we are about it, we may as well put all the fat in the fire. Frank
quotes with approval the suggestions of Barbara and Alan Haber. They
advise the radical professional to repudiate "loyalty . . . to the profession, or institution in which he works." They call instead for loyalty to
"political comrades and to . . . political aims." The next step is inevitable for the Habers: "We are not intellectuals above it all who say the
truth to whomever will listen or asks: we are *partisans*" (Haber 1967:
95–96, as quoted in Frank 1968:413. Emphasis in Frank does not appear
in original). The consequence is faced with equal equanimity: the Habers
advise selective rejection of "the code of ethics and responsibility of
their professions," wherever "[c]onventional ethics entrap us into support of things which we do not support politically and into loyalties
which conflict with our own values and politics . . ." (*ibid.*). In brief, we
can see that at one pole relevance is narrowed to a revolutionary prag-
matism. It is worth pursuing the matter a few steps further.

It can already be seen that the definition of *use, value, relevance,*
or any related concept is inextricably linked to the individual or social
group performing the activity of definition. In the views expressed in
the citations from Frank and from the Habers, the central concept is
declared to be furtherance of revolution against capitalism and its associated political systems. But it is now clear to almost everybody who
has any interest in the question that there is not a monolithic camp
opposed to the political and economic dominance of the bourgeoisie;
there are many parties, factions, and splinter groups. Each proclaims its
own revealed truth and has the "objective" analyses to prove its own
correctness as well as the falseness of all opponents. Apart from occasional short-lived ventures into popular front movements, the revolutionary sects display perhaps more hatred for each other than for the
enemy they proclaim in common. To the extent that each integral
political group comprises a social structure complete with a discrete
ideology, it may be said to be a subculture, and the comparative analysis of its concepts of "use," "value," and "relevance" becomes a conspicuously anthropological problem.

All this is preliminary to noting that relativism applies to all concepts of value. This in turn means that at some point in the analysis we
are forced to consider the source and basis of the evaluation. Often it
is necessary to go to the beneficiary of the activity being evaluated.

This is not so simple. There may be many "beneficiaries": the producer (who perhaps engaged in the activity as a temporary expedient to maintain subsistence, while hating the activity); or the distributor (perhaps an entrepreneur whose action set the formally recognized "value" of the product of the activity and even the price of the labor producing it); or the consumer. But this barely begins to suggest the complexity of the problem. As a sample activity, consider some bit of research in ethnography. At a minimum this confronts us with a cast of potential beneficiaries: the researcher; the sponsor; the social order which includes sponsor and researcher; the society studied in the course of research; and the specific informants whose responses furnished the data. Which among these is to be considered prime beneficiary? Which interests are to be used to set the value of the activity in the sense of determining if it is worth doing? Is it the researcher, who may be working in the spirit of an artistic or intellectual innovator, seeking his return in the satisfaction of doing a skillful and aesthetically pleasing job? Of course, the researcher may enjoy other rewards for his activity: money, job security, fame, status, travel, or ego fulfillment. He may also have the individual satisfaction of having brought to light and forced consideration of the phenomena he has described and analyzed, perhaps even bringing about amelioration of some horrible condition. In any case, the precise kinds of return an individual may have from such activity are many and varied. Until recently, personal satisfaction was almost the only return openly acknowledged and considered. Others existed, of course, but were either handled implicitly, or ignored, or denied. Among those handled implicitly were the returns to the society that sponsored the research. Until perhaps as recently as World War II, most research of this kind was carried out with private funding or with very limited grants from private foundations, such as the Guggenheim, or from the Social Science Research Council, or through museums, most of which were entirely private in funding. The amount of public support such activities could muster was minimal. Although usually unspoken and unanalyzed, the ideological assumption linking work and support seems to have been that the society would inevitably be served as the result of the anthropologist's serving himself. Explicit was the notion that knowledge and learning were intrinsically good; that any addition to the store of knowledge was good; that society benefited from any activity increasing information and understanding.

That this message could be explicit is readily shown. When I was a young assistant professor, my own university made it the theme of its bicentennial year. It was president Grayson Kirk who proclaimed the belief of Columbia University in "Man's Right to Knowledge and the Free Use Thereof." The year was 1954. With an irony that was not lost on the university, the country was still in the throes of emergence from the threat to academic freedom and intellect posed by McCarthyism. But, as it was not the last time that conflict would exist between the slogan and reality, so it was not the first. Long before Columbia's bicentennial, the same conflict had existed. It was manifest in the repression of Marxist ideas going back to the turn of the century and before, not to mention the university's racism, antifeminism, and anti-Semitism. So pervasive was the racism that the total absence of Negro professors and virtual absence of black students was accepted as naturally and inevitably as the inability of women to gain tenure seats. And the struggle between the ideology of the pure quest for knowledge and the true state of affairs surfaced openly when a distinguished professor of economics was forced to leave Columbia because of his political views. The victim was Daniel DeLeon, an articulate supporter of the International Workers of the World, and the founder of the Socialist Labor Party. And it yet remained for thousands of students, over a half century later—by their actions of protest over Columbia's participation in secret research—to raise a question of the disjuncture between Columbia's stated aims and its social reality.

I am less interested in details of repression of knowledge and science in our democratic society than in recognizing that such repression has existed, does so at present, and gives indication of persisting. I will admit that much of this repression has been self-inflicted in that both faculty members and students have at times censored themselves either for fear of possible retaliation or in pursuit of favorable recognition and rewards. Indeed, this is one of several grounds for the present climate of distrust among students for their teachers. I have not personally felt the whip of repression; on the other hand, I am well aware that most of the work I do, the teaching I am engaged in, some of the books and articles I have already produced, would not be permitted in certain societies, including Nazi Germany, contemporary Greece, the People's Republic of China, the Soviet Union (never at certain periods, questionable in others), and a long list of others.

Given so difficult a political stage, why should anyone study anthropology or make the discipline a profession? We have already seen that there are many reasons why participation in anthropological research should be attractive to individuals. There are also reasons why significant portions of the anthropologist's society should wish to support such activity. Beyond the motivations already suggested or implied, there are others of more equivocal nature. For example, there is a germ of truth in the notion that where "the old formula for successful counter-insurgency used to be ten troops for every guerilla . . . [n]ow the formula is ten anthropologists for each guerilla" (Braestrud 1967; quoted in Berreman 1968:427). The case has been made in various contexts; one of the clearest was the attempt by the Department of Defense to undertake a social science counterinsurgency project in Chile, the project called Camelot (cf. Horowitz 1965; Horowitz 1967).

I do not mean to suggest by this that our present society tolerates only those activities that perform directly to its advantage. Quite to the contrary, a wide range of things go on that are clearly out of step with the main thrust of events as defined by reigning ideology. Nonetheless, the structure of our society is conducive to certain kinds of contradiction and dissonance, while at the same time it actively encourages increasing homogenization of behaviors. One manifestation of this conflict is the degree to which intellectuals are troubled about the problem of whose interest in an activity shall be paramount in determining whether or not that activity should be encouraged or even permitted. There is widespread uncertainty about the problem of individualism, despite frequent expressions of pride at being the culture most closely identified historically (although perhaps ethnocentrically and erroneously) with the rise and florescence of individualism. Rather than involving ourselves in that philosophical discussion, let us take our departure in the observation that our society, particularly its young adult and adolescent generations, is now asserting, perhaps more loudly than ever before, that individuals should be free to "do their thing," while many who approve this slogan wholeheartedly quickly add the proviso, so reminiscent of utilitarian philosophy, that "the thing" should not be harmful to others. It is here precisely that permissiveness itself splits, and separate, sometimes warring camps appear.

Our culture has long flirted with the notion that service to society is the paramount good. Usually this does not require the sacrifice of individualism—although generations of our philosophers have argued the point. Our ideology either attempts to wed individual success and social contribution or ignores the conflict between them. Contrast this with the official position put forward in the People's Republic of China. According to Mao Tsetung Thought the notion of individualism is associated with "ultra-democracy," the source of which "consists in the petty bourgeoisie's individualistic aversion to discipline" (Mao 1964:108). The Maoist ideology takes care to analyze the conflict between the individual and the social group and insists on something approaching the total suppression of the interests of the former on behalf of the latter. One must "fight self and criticize revisionism." Those most successful become "Shining Models for Youth," like twenty-year-old Chin Hsun-hua, graduate of Woosung No. 2 Middle School in Shanghai and a member of the Standing Committee of the Congress of Red Guards of Shanghai Middle Schools. Comrade Chin died in August 1969, attempting to fight a serious flood. His canonization depended not alone on his sacrificing his life for society, but on his behavior up to that supreme moment. As he stated in his much reproduced diary:

> We've come [to the countryside] for re-education by the poor and lower-middle peasants; we seek neither fame nor gain, nor "official" posts. Our sole purpose is to become ordinary peasants with socialist consciousness. (Peking Review 23 January 1970:12)

What has all this got to do with problems of identity and relevance in contemporary anthropology? Everything! Before anyone mocks the ideas surrounding Chin Hsun-hua's martyrdom and elevation, consider the parallels in our own society. Although certainly not identical, there is a powerful bond between Chin's activity and such things as participation in VISTA or the Peace Corps, or the Black Panthers' or Young Lords' attempts to develop children's feeding programs in the slums, or, perhaps closer in spirit, the attempt by black students to maintain and reinforce their ties with the black ghettos from which their individual educational advancement could probably free them, if they desired.

Beyond such general symptoms of positive protest and disaffection are many specific areas of concern, narrowing to the interests of trainees in a wide range of special subjects. This quickly devolves into a quest for meaning, identity, and relevance. Let us look at the student community in general, before turning specifically to anthropology. Ron Karenga, black activist, community organizer, and linguist, stated the problem well when he said:

> [Students] come [to college] only because their parents sent them or to escape the draft or for five other reasons that we have developed in a syndrome to communicate to them. They never really understand why they come, and so they ask the questions, "Why should I go to school?" If they were inspired, that would never be the question. Sterile data has nothing to do with real life, so change the curricula and change the methodology. [Robinson 1969:46]

Although casting these sentences in the form of a universal constitutes obvious hyperbole, there is sufficient truth in Karenga's criticism to bring quite conservative educators to attention. Sterile data (or sterile classes) and real life—what a deadening contrast! It brings us dramatically to the problem of relevance.

The word *relevance* has two meanings. The current dictionary definition has to do with pertinency—something is relevant when it bears upon or contributes to the case at hand. There is an older meaning that fell into disuse but seems to have returned, precisely through its application to problems of contemporary education. I refer to the relevance that is remedial or relieving. Both of these meanings of relevance seem applicable to what is going on today in the colleges and universities (and many high schools, too). On one side, relevance reflects the backgrounds and real life expectations of the students. On the other side, it involves the identification of social problems and the attempts to solve them.

With regard to the former, it has been pointed out many times that the concept of cultural lag applies nowhere more beautifully than in higher education. The structure of that education remains substantially as it was when college-level and postgraduate students were few in number, predominantly male, and from the upper social classes. As the system went through transition to mass education, the cracking of the elitist wall was delayed because lower-class students accepted the goals of their socioeconomic superiors; the need to succeed by entering "the Establishment" was paramount. But changes in the recruitment of students started after World War II as a by-product of the G.I. Bill, continued through radical alterations in the scope and nature of fellowship and scholarship programs, and culminated in actual changes in the philosophy of the offices of admissions and escalating demands for "open admissions" from some sectors. What this produced, in turn, was a student population considerably different from that which had preceded it. I believe that this had a further consequence, of course, in association with other factors. Previously, when lower-class students were only a small part of the total, it was much easier for individual students to assimilate to the prevailing ethic of education at the expense of the ethic in which they had been raised. It was never difficult for the lower-middle-class student to associate his petty bourgeois aspirations with the more elevated ambitions of his social betters at school; the process was facilitated by the then popular denial of significant class differences in American society, and even the Depression failed to damage the American myth of universal social mobility. Now that the absolute numbers of students of lower-class and minority background have greatly increased, it is possible for them to attempt to reject the success values of the Establishment. What is more, a reverse phenomenon is seen, as students of much higher social status, including sons and daughters of members of the economic and political elite, attempt, however transiently or unsuccessfully in some instances, to associate themselves with elements of lower-class and minority origin. Although the starting places are different, convergence occurs, usually at the point of rejection of some of the most explicitly held values of the middle and upper classes. A consequent demand arises for the content of learning to resemble more the experience of those who have been the outs, rather than of those who have been in. How else can we understand the cries arising around us, or the angry demands, none more vociferous than those of black activists, for a relevant curriculum? Take, for example, the view of the sociologist Nathan Hare, a pioneer in the Black Studies movement:

> *Other things being equal, when . . . students [having had a relevant education] get out into the black community . . . once they have been graduated, they will be more effective, because first of all, other things being equal again, they would be more committed to the black community, rather than trying to escape it as educational exposure now teaches them to do, where you learn about Shakespeare and Beethoven's Fifth Symphony and so forth. . . . These are the things that we're going to have to start questioning, because even the white student, too, is beginning to grow dissatisfied with that kind of thing. At the same time as we transform the course content, our new educational process can, so to speak, help transform the community.   [Robinson 1969:121–22]*

When we turn to relevance in terms of social problems and attempts to remedy them, the first task is to determine whose problems are to be tackled and what kinds of solutions are to be sought. Using the notorious project Camelot as an example, it matters whether the problem of revolutionary potential is viewed from the perspective of those controlling the government apparatus in Washington or by those desirous of accomplishing sweeping social and economic changes in Chile. It is of the essence whether the solution sought will stabilize conditions at current levels, making those in inferior positions and situations more accepting of their lot, or whether the solutions being considered extend to changes so far-reaching as to revise the existing system drastically.

Closer to home, the same questions have been asked, with a modicum of success, by students and faculty who have forced changes at many institutions involved in attempts at problem solving on behalf of one or another self-anointed agency or division of the United States government. Under contracts that were sometimes secret themselves, secret research has been carried out for the Institute for Defense Analyses (IDA), the Department of Defense, the Army, the Navy, the Air Force, and so on. Some projects concern the development of military hardware, including new weapons such as bacteriologicals; others pertain to psychology and the social sciences and entail manipulation and control of people, including Americans. It is precisely in conjunction with such programs that a number of anthropologists are employed, confronting us with an individual as well as a professional problem.

Unfortunately, questions cannot be resolved merely by turning from them. When dealing with contending parties, one of which is in power, "neutrality" is support of the incumbent. Actually, the kind of neutrality that involves total aloofness is a conspicuous rarity. The Cox Commission report on the disturbances at Columbia says:

> When students see work being done at a university on the application of science to spreading death and destruction in Vietnam, but little evidence of similar work on eliminating poverty and racial injustice, they are naturally concerned. . . . [1968:21]

The effect may be enormously disturbing but proceeds with logical inevitability as the conclusion is reached that "the university is not basically an educational institution—it's a *political* institution . . . it seeks to maintain the power base of American society" (Ron Karenga in Robinson 1969:38–39. Emphasis in original).

The second qualification that must be made to the notion of student demand summed up in the phrase "solve my problems" concerns radical students other than those tabbed "black" by themselves or others. They are fragmented into many groups with variously divergent philosophies and programs.[1] The white student radicals certainly have problems and much interest in dealing with them, but the central concerns that they most avidly advance pertain primarily to other social sectors. Thus in addition to opposing the Indochinese war and the draft, they push forward demands on behalf of the weak, the dispossessed, and the exploited. To some extent, then, the white student radical seems to be altruistic in pursuit of the problems he defines as relevant. Yet to leave it at that would be somewhat romantic. Behind the selection of problems lies a tactical sense that is sometimes sharp, sometimes naïve or distorted. Issues are sought that can produce mass support, but sometimes only alienation is achieved. There is a gamut of issues, from spot reform to a spectrum of revolutionary demands. These ultimatums for the drastic reform or abolition of capitalism, for support of efforts to achieve international peace, and for the elimination of pollution are seen as the means of improving life for all.

[1] *The black aggregate is not monolithic either, but almost seems so in contrast to the divisions among nonblack students. The fact of division in the black aggregate, however, must qualify anything said about leaders. As a matter of fact, astute black leaders tend to be very cagey about defining their constituencies. Furthermore, because of limits of space, a false dichotomy may seem to be presented between "blacks" and "whites." Of course, there are many other aggregates on the scene, of great importance in different localities: Indians, Chicanos, Chinese-Americans, to name only a few.*

There remain, however, certain perennial sources of student discontent which tend to cut across differences of "race," socioeconomic class, and political alignment. I refer to such issues as academic requirements, prerequisites, and hierarchically structured curricula.

Since the crux of relevance seems to be located in attempts to deal with real problems, certain disciplines experience immediate crises. A "real problem" is one or another of the ills of contemporary society —poverty, war, alienation, injustice, discrimination, racism, crime, addiction, exploitation—the list is long and some of its items murky (except to the sufferer). Quite often the opposition is roused to fury because many items are included that have plagued societies for as long as we have knowledge of them. The demand of youth that these ills be cured now, immediately, seems to most of their elders and many of their peers to be nothing but another display of adolescent utopianism, or sabotage of already ongoing ameliorative efforts, or even nihilism. It was on April 12, 1968, only eleven days before the "disturbances" at Columbia leaped into the nation's headlines, that Grayson Kirk, then president of that university, remarked in a public speech:

> *Our young people, in disturbing numbers, appear to reject all*
> *forms of authority, from whatever source derived, and they*
> *have taken refuge in a turbulent and inchoate nihilism whose*
> *sole objects are destruction.   [Avorn 1969:25]*

Just before the Columbia rebellion this remark was specifically challenged in a letter addressed "Dear Grayson," and signed "Mark." The letter presented Mark Rudd's views, speaking then for a unified Students for a Democratic Society (SDS) and a growing horde of sympathizers, denouncing and ridiculing the charge. Rudd asserted that it was Grayson Kirk who lived in "a very tight self-created dream world," and he enumerated some of the painful realities that were motivating student protest: the Vietnam war as an example of the lengths to which the Establishment would go to maintain control over its empire; the ghettos and slums; the exploitation of labor. "We can point," he wrote, "to our own meaningless studies, our identity crises, and our revulsion with being cogs in your corporate machines . . ." (*ibid.*:26). Rudd made it clear that the struggle he was prepared to wage would not be nonviolent. "We will have to destroy at times, even violently, in order to end your power and your system," he stated, "but that is a far cry from nihilism." For him there was one criterion of relevance and that was pertinence to the victory of a "war of liberation" that would bring "justice, freedom, and socialism" (*ibid.*:26–27).

One does not have to be either cynic or cultural anthropologist to realize that justice and freedom have been in demand just about as long as the political institution known as the state. They have been promised to the people by the very tyrants who, by any definition, were least prepared to grant them. It is highly appropriate to note at this point that the question of the universality of the concepts of freedom and justice, and their definitions, comprise a highly proper research topic for the anthropologist. One who pursued such an inquiry would be expected to detach himself to as great an extent as possible from currently fashionable slogans and contentions and to work comparatively. The questions involved are exceptionally tricky: in all cultures there are considerable gaps between normative or idealized statements and social reality. It is one of the commonest tactics of political argument to contrast the squalid actuality of one society with the goals of another.

Most radical anthropologists have attempted to take a broader point of view in this matter, trying to distinguish between dream and reality, although not going so far, perhaps, as to admit relativism. A good example is offered by Kathleen Gough. Accused by a senior anthropologist of attempting to surmount the dilemma of cultural bias "by surrendering wholly to . . . the systematic dialectic of one side of the Cold War, with all its weary cliches" (Beals 1968:408), Gough replies:

> Which "side" does Beals mean? Cuba, China, the Soviet Union, or possibly the Students for a Democratic Society? Surely Beals knows that their "dialectics" differ and at some points are deeply opposed? . . . There is no widely acceptable, unified dialectic for socialists of the Western world. . . . Unmodified, the theories of Marx and Lenin are outmoded. Stalinism produced its own somber lessons, and the socialism of poverty-stricken new nations struggling against present imperial powers cannot offer more than flashes of understanding for those who would build post-imperial, post-national society. A theoretical system has to be formed out of the old ones. That is the task of socialist intellectuals; I think it is also consonant with my role as an anthropologist interested in contemporary society. As theories do develop, the pace of events makes it unlikely that they will remain closed or rigid.   [1968:429–30]

Gough proclaims herself "a revolutionary socialist" (ibid.:429) as well as an anthropologist, and she attempts to confront the problem of what she can do to best combine the two roles. Admittedly, as we have just seen in the quoted paragraph, the task is complicated by the absence of a uniform, common theory. It is also troubled by some of the suggestions and countersuggestions already proliferating on the left. Take those of Gunder Frank, for example. He urges anthropologists to redirect themselves and "pursue the research and develop the theory required and requested by the liberation movement at home" [Frank 1968:413]. To put it bluntly, "West European and North American anthropologists can best fulfill this responsibility [to support the struggle against imperialism] by working in their own societies" (ibid.). Gough is forced to equivocate before such harsh logic. On one hand, she tends to agree: "If [the radical anthropologists'] purpose is primarily to aid revolution, most may find it necessary to work at home, and some, for various reasons, will prefer to do so" (Gough 1968:431). On the other hand, Gough continues:

> It seems to me, however, too early to lay down rules for the settings and creative activities in which revolutionary anthropologists can best engage. Presumably several roles will emerge, some more contemplative, theoretical, and global, others more local or more activist.   [Ibid.]

The reader may wonder at this point why I am so concerned with the agonized and agonizing analyses made by a few social scientists of their own roles in revolution. It has to be admitted, for example, that these precise concerns are of immediate and conscious importance to what seems to be a decided minority. On second thought, however, one might wish to query the population out of which the apparent minority is drawn. I think there is no quibble if it is limited to the fully professional, defined, let us say, by the holding of a doctorate in anthropology, or evidence of a commensurate degree of experience and professional productivity. Such people tend to be those already substantially employed in the discipline. Under most circumstances such professionals tend to represent older age sets and higher incomes. While some radicals can be found even in these circles, their numbers are not great. On the other side, if we include in our reckoning all the graduate students and go beyond to get the undergraduate majors as well, I am not at all sure that we would not find a majority. No one can predict how this young generation will age, how far right it will swing in the course of assuming the dominant statuses in the society, but an unusually high proportion of its members are displaying active concern about precisely the questions we have been raising.

If the professional anthropologist may be driven in the course of his research to wonder how he came to be there, why and to what purpose, so the student of anthropology, sometime during his exposure to the discipline, may ask the identical questions. For those who prefer promoting social change to studying it, the answer may well be chilling and negative: they may be in the wrong place, doing the wrong thing.

The trouble may lie in certain inherent difficulties in the concept of an "advocacy anthropology." So far as I know, this is the first time this term has been used; it is coined for this occasion out of the current use of such terms as *advocacy journalism,* and the idea *of advocacy jurisprudence.* A few words about these will show what is intended and also give a basis for pessimism about extending the concept of advocacy to anthropology. Advocacy journalism is new in name only. Basically, it rests on the belief that the reporter should not be merely a disinterested observer and recounter but the engaged advocate of social doctrine, pursuing a position by selective reportage. Similarly, advocacy on the part of a trained lawyer means not that he exercises his skills as energetically as possible on behalf of whoever happens to be his client, but that he plunges into the trouble spots of his society, deliberately seeking his cases there, or bringing his knowledge of the law to those who previously had been concerned only with avoiding courts, judges, policemen, and all other apparatuses of that law. It is significant that journalism was almost born in such advocacy, and that the figure of the lawyer as champion is deeply embedded in our culture. By contrast, the image of the anthropologist is neatly split between the pedantic professor and the exploring adventurer.

Anthropology has also long been split in the argument about its general social role. One of the great pioneers of modern anthropology, Edward B. Tylor, believed that one of the important lessons taught by anthropology was that

> *we civilized moderns . . . [ac]quainted with events and their consequences far and wide over the world . . . are able to direct our own course with more confidence toward improvement. In a word, mankind is passing from the age of unconscious to that of conscious progress.* [1881:439]

To which may be added the final sentence of what is perhaps Tylor's most important work:

> *Thus, active at once in aiding progress and in removing hindrance, the science of culture is essentially a reformer's science.* [Tylor 1871:529]

Even Leslie A. White, whose work is known for its emphasis on cultural determinism, has offered a voluntaristic view of the cultural condition. A couple of years before the outbreak of the Second World War, White lectured at Yenching University in (then) Peiping, China, and contributed an article to a journal published at that university. The piece speaks optimistically of the prospect for culture change in China, although White noted with remarkable prescience the likelihood that the changes would "be difficult, . . . and costly in labor and even lives" (1937–38:133). Although the problems facing China were monumental, the Chinese people would be aided in overcoming them not only because of "the vast resources of the Chinese people, their courage and their ability" (ibid.:120), but because of their "spirit and determination" as well. As with some voices heard since, White viewed the matter as a "struggle for freedom and progress," in which the application of science would be decisive. After all, he commented, "Through the philosophy and techniques of science man has increased his control over his environment and his vital processes immeasurably" (ibid.:133). He readily admitted that the social sciences had not advanced so quickly or so far, but he was sanguine enough to express his belief that "enough has been accomplished to assure us that in this direction lies our most substantial hope of a rational conduct of social life" (ibid.).

If White at one time acknowledged the possibility that man might tamper with his destiny, he has been the spokesman most of his life for that group of anthropologists who believe that man's control over culture is merely an anthropocentric illusion, to slightly paraphrase the title of one of White's provocative articles on the topic (White 1948). White, more than any other anthropologist, insists that "understanding culture will not . . . alter its course or change the 'fate' that it has in store for us, any more than understanding the weather or the tides will change them" (White 1948:247). Rather than wondering if White has chosen poorly in mentioning the weather, which to a limited degree has succumbed to planned control, let us raise the question so often thrust at that complete determinist: Why should anyone with such a view bother to do anything at all, not to mention studying culture? To this, the culturologist generally makes two replies. First, in his view determinism is truly determining; it establishes not merely what the bearers of culture will do, but how they will do it, and when. Determined by their culture, neither the culturologist nor the revolutionist, the anarchist or the conservative, the activist or the recluse, can avoid doing what the culture has prescribed for them. White's second reply to the question may bring a smile to those who take him at his own word as a committed antireductionist. White says, "As long as man remains an inquiring primate he will crave understanding. And a growing Science of Culture will provide him with it" (ibid.).

Fundamental as White's problem is, this is not the context in which to argue it. The epistemological complexities alone would take us far afield. It is sufficient to note that at least one camp in the field of anthropological theory denies all possibility of significantly changing the course of history by spontaneous acts of human will. For that camp, as previously indicated, there are no spontaneous acts of will. Thus, this school offers no comfort to those who seek to end war, negate racism, abolish capitalism, establish a new program for women's rights, or achieve any other sociocultural goal through demonstrations, strikes, boycotts, terrorism, or any other mechanism. Conversely, this version of cultural determinism offers no support to the other side, either. All cultures change, and the changes cannot be prevented by cordoning off Cuba or China, or having the police beat up protesters, or jailing people for smoking pot, or legislating against pornography. In the view of the strictest cultural determinists, then, any attempt to tamper with the cultural process is illusory and doomed, like the fabled attempt of the real King Canute to stop the tides from rising on the Thames.

Many anthropologists who do not agree with a virtually unqualified cultural determinism are still loath to tamper with the cultural process on a somewhat different ground. Culture is so complex, it is argued, that the unanticipated consequences of any program for change, any specific bit of social engineering, may bring conditions more fearsome than those that were to be removed. We are reminded that one of the earliest attempts made by a United States anthropologist to influence legislation in order to bring about favorable sociocultural change was that of Alice Fletcher, almost a century ago. To assist the Omaha Indians, among whom she had done some of the finest ethnographic work known to the discipline, she "played an important role in the adoption by the United States Congress of the Dawes Severalty Act of 1887" (Beals 1968:407, citing Helm 1966). The resulting legislation, intended to help the Omaha protect their homes and lands, had such disastrous consequences that it has been called "probably . . . the single most damaging act of legislation for the American Indian ever adopted" (Beals 1968:407).

Although the attempt to influence the fate of the American Indian through legislation may be considered a special case, it has aspects of remarkable generality. Those, for example, who would argue that the last disastrous century of American Indian history was simply the result of failings inherent in capitalism must deal with parallel histories of expropriation, colonial war, and exploitation in situations remote from capitalist economic organization, polity, or ideology, as in China's historic policy toward certain of its minorities (cf. Fried 1952), as well as Chinese policy toward and treatment of certain minorities since 1949. This should be compared in turn with events in the Soviet Union since the 1920's, in Burma, and in various other nation states containing discrete ethnic minorities while not subscribing to capitalism, at least in its Euro-American guise. It is interesting to note that in the Soviet, as well as in some, but not all, of the other cases listed, anthropologists have played critical roles in determining and implementing the policies pursued by their governments in relation to ethnic minorities.

In the United States, perhaps the most exposed wing of the anthropological profession with regard to the problem of the ethical evaluation of attempts at social engineering is that engaged in what is sometimes also known as *applied anthropology*. I will note only a few salient points here. First, applied anthropologists are not usually distinguished from the general run of anthropologists; those who designate themselves as applied anthropologists will invariably think of themselves at the same time, and with complete justification, as cultural anthropologists. Second, those who consider themselves applied anthropologists have been concerned about ethical problems almost since they banded together to form a distinct society. Indeed, the Society for Applied Anthropology adopted an explicit code of ethics before the question arose in the American Anthropological Association. Third, despite the code of ethics, there has been an air of questioning suspicion about some of the activities carried out in the name of applied anthropology. Nothing that has occurred recently has dispelled such suspicion. On the contrary, particularly among younger professionals and a substantial cross-section of students, the climate has worsened, largely as the result of the employment of persons and concepts identified with applied anthropology in such projects as the ill-fated Camelot, or in counterinsurgency in Vietnam, Thailand, and elsewhere.

Now, against this background, what can be said for undertaking the study of anthropology in these conscience-ridden, guilt-racked closing decades of the twentieth century? To begin with many will be capable of maintaining attitudes of unconcern throughout the epoch. There is a variety of roles in anthropology available to those who detach themselves from the political events of their time. Indeed, there remains a substantial segment of the profession, perhaps even a numerical majority, that feels more or less strongly that the profession as such must conscientiously adopt a neutral position regarding all political matters. The basis of this view has less to do with attitudes about the substantive issues at stake and everything to do with the fear that taking a political position will threaten the authority of professional pronouncement. It is argued that the public, confronted by anthropologists talking sometimes as scientists, sometimes as moralizing citizens, will be confused, if not angry, and come to distrust both (cf. Richards 1968). The issue is a real one. In recent years it has enlivened the annual business meetings of the American Anthropological Association, as floor fights have taken place over resolutions about the Vietnam war, genocide, and a variety of problems concerning professional ethics. However, as indicated before, there seems to be an important generational split over these problems such as to make it probable that passing years will see proportionally greater increase in the radical camp. On the other hand, those over thirty-five can easily recall the phenomenon of alternating generations in campus political activity. Although we now have an outstandingly radical generation of university students, there is no guarantee that another few years will not see the virtual disappearance of radical campus activism, so that chapters such as these may appear as curious historical debris to the younger reader.

Not to resume the entire argument again—I may have already abused the patience of some—let us note that opposition to the "neutralists" appears from both ends of the political spectrum. On one side there are those who thrust the profession into action by carrying out specific tasks in support of the present policies of the government. Whatever may be said of their politics or their ethics, or even of their anthropology, it has never been denied that they are quite professional in their theory and method. Indeed, that is precisely the trouble. The problem of what to do about such involvement is recognized and legitimate. It raises questions of professional ethics that we return to in the final chapter.

On the other side, the opposition to "neutralism" comes from a spectrum including radical and "liberal" elements. The most radical, as we have seen, really have little to recommend to anthropologists short of sublimating their disciplinary goals and activities in favor of revolutionary ones. If there is any area in which these things merge, it is not spelled out. What is more disconcerting, it is not likely to reach such a point of specificity for the simple reason that the focus becomes terribly narrow as the action orientation increases. Each such increase comes closer to requiring that the recruit identify with the ideology and program of a particular action group. Mere general support for "the left" becomes contemptible and is regarded as a means of avoiding the basic question of revolution itself. Once again, it is Mao Tse-tung who states it quite succinctly. In one context he quotes Stalin with favor: ". . . theory becomes purposeless if it is not connected with revolutionary practice" (Mao 1965:13, quoting Stalin 1954:31). Perhaps more to the point is Mao's statement that:

> People who are liberals look upon the principles of Marxism
> as abstract dogma. They approve of Marxism, but are not pre-
> pared to practice it or to practice it in full . . . they talk Marx-
> ism but practice liberalism; they apply Marxism to others but
> liberalism to themselves.   [1965b:32–33]

It need only be said that liberalism is regarded by Mao as a major evil; he says that "there should be no place for it in the ranks of the revolution" (ibid.:33).

What does this mean for the seemingly large aggregate of anthropologists, especially younger professionals and students, who want to see extensive changes in the fabric of their own society and in contingent portions of the world scene but who cannot accept Maoist politics? Unfortunately, I have no satisfactory reply. Fried's sixteenth law states humbly that "all problems do not have solutions." (There may be a little cheer in the first corollary: "some minor problems can be solved," and perhaps even in the second: "most problems ultimately go away." However, the final corollary states darkly, "Problems that are solved or that go away are replaced by bigger and more difficult problems.") Resisting the tendency to succumb to despair, it can be noted that whatever its liberal, bourgeois origins (see the next chapter), anthropology has made contributions to enlightenment that may help produce a better world. No matter how obscured at present, it has been this discipline above all others that has made intellectual nonsense of racism. Ironically, the overwhelming evidence amassed by anthropologists showing that belief in racial distributions of individual intellect and ability is a cultural artifact reflecting social conditions has had only limited effect on that belief. Nonetheless, the way has been prepared for a rational assault on the problems of prejudice and discrimination with the diffusion of this information and point of view to growing numbers of young people both within and without the academic milieu.

Another major contribution deserves repetition at this point. It is the anthropologist who bears the main burden of spreading simultaneously our knowledge of the universal aspects of human nature on one hand, and the idiosyncratic diversity of cultures on the other. These concepts, particularly the latter one, are very badly handled in the world at large. Attack comes from several political directions. The radical right hypostatizes a United States culture and social organization out of historically invalid idealizations and would make this the universal goal of cultural evolution. The radical left is no less ethnocentric when it does not hesitate to speak universalistically for the oppressed, downtrodden, and exploited regardless of cultural variations. Mounting difficulties within the so-called socialist camp reveal that this error has bitter consequences regardless of the ideology of the perpetrators.

It remains to be seen how this kind of information will be used as the young assume dominant social roles. Everything we know conditions us to avoid undue optimism. Thus, it is with a nagging sense of failure that I will bring this tormented chapter to a close.

Theodore Roszak, in the introduction to *The Dissenting Academy*, complains that the values of academia place a premium on the application of skills to "mindless specialization and irrelevant pedantry" (Roszak 1968:36). He presents a number of hypothetical alternatives. Shall a teacher of American history receive more intellectual and professional credit for an obscure study than for organizing a "well-conceived campaign against capital punishment"? How about a teacher of psychology running for public office and thereby stimulating an excellent discussion of vital issues, even if it means forgoing "an exhaustive study of olfaction in the unrestrained rat"? Or, to abridge his examples, how about having an anthropologist turn his energies to anti-Vietnam war activities, rather than to some "study of unity and diversity in the celebration of cattle-curing rites in a north Indian village" (ibid.: 33–34)?

For once I find no difficulty coming to grips with a problem. Roszak's attack of self-hatred and anti-intellectualism succeeds only in presenting us with a straw man. For one thing, most of my own professional colleagues who have taken active roles in precisely those nonacademic activities which he endorses have also maintained serious productive roles in their disciplines, including teaching, research, and even writing.

Perhaps more serious is Roszak's delusion that equates the kind of nonacademic activity mentioned with the sorts of demands raised by the activists. At best they will pigeonhole him with other bourgeois liberal reformists. As for the demands of the activists, to truly pursue them requires a complete break with all academies as we know them and a negation of every shred of elitism such as is inherent in specialization. This places such activists to the left of reality in the USSR and Cuba, too. It even places them well beyond events in the People's Republic of China, where at the time of writing the academies were again being activated after a lapse of about five years.

Short of making such a break, it remains for the individual to decide the content of his work. The individual must also conduct that work so as to make it lie within a socially responsible concept of ethical obligation. To the problems inherent in the individual's grappling with such burdens we return in the final chapter.

3

LOOKING BACKWARD

... all that is new in anthropological theory
begins with the Enlightenment.
                                                        —Marvin Harris

Although anthropology is quite young as a formally organized scientific discipline, its history in terms of concepts of man and differing patterns of human behavior extends into the distant past. In this
chapter, however, we are not concerned with anything like a full picture of the development of the various portions of the discipline. The
primary purpose is to place anthropology and some of its current
strengths and weaknesses in some kind of historical perspective, with
special attention given to certain crucial issues.

Several questions emerge from the discussion in the previous
chapter. For example, has anthropology since its formal inception and
in its subsequent development been essentially a bourgeois field of
knowledge? Can anthropology be identified with a racist or an antiracist
orientation? Has anthropology been placed in the service of colonialism
and imperialism? What about Tylor's view of anthropology as a reformer's science—has it been justified in action? Having seen some of
the arguments relating to theories of culture change, we will now try
to relate the development of these theories to their political consequences, and discuss the integration of anthropology as a historical
accumulation of subjects.

At the outset it is possible to offer one important distinction concerning the interpretation of history. George W. Stocking, Jr., reminds
us of the contrast posed by Herbert Butterfield between "historicism"
and "presentism." The former may be characterized as an effort "to
understand the past for the sake of the past," while presentism studies
"the past for the sake of the present" (1965:211). Avoiding some of the
major epistemological problems that beset such a distinction, let us
regard it simply as a warning to avoid oversimple criticism of figures
in the past who spoke or wrote in ignorance of the wisdom that was
to follow them. As Stocking has put it, giving the example of Tylor,
contemporary anthropologists will better understand that work of perhaps a century ago "if they are able to distinguish between the ques-

tions that he asked that have long since been answered, the questions which are still open, and the questions which we would no longer even recognize as such" (*ibid.*:217). Stocking notes that Tylor's main concern was to "fill the gap between Brixham Cave[1] and European Civilization without introducing the hand of God!" (*ibid.*). Stocking goes on to note that the view of culture as an evolutionary product of natural development is so widely accepted as to be considered an answered question. However, the precise details of this evolution are often vague and sometimes still unknown, so this much remains open. Finally, "the question of the hand of God . . . we would not even regard as a question" (*ibid.*). It is equally appropriate to keep in mind that the political conceptions of the last part of the twentieth century are not those of the nineteenth, still less of earlier centuries. Yet even this remark makes it seem that the object must be to patronize the spokesmen of the past, when it is properly to understand them.

Convention usually begins historical treatments of anthropology with sweeping references to the distant past. Greek and Roman poets, geographers and historians, Chinese philosophers and commentators, Indian wise men, have their words cited to show that some kind of anthropology was known in the ancient world. Sol Tax, for example, tells us:

> *Men have always been interested in studying themselves . . .*
> *a people provides itself with myths; nations write their his-*
> *tories. Therefore it is futile to speak of the beginning of the*
> *study of man. We usually refer back to classical Greece . . .*
> *but the study is world-wide . . . and it goes back anywhere*
> *that records carry us back.   [1964:15]*

With that, Tax takes an enormous leap and picks up his narrative in the nineteenth century with the founding in 1800 of the Society of the Observers of Man, an assembly of medical doctors and naturalists in Paris. He then jumps to 1838, when the Society for the Protection of Aborigines was formed in London, more for political and social than for scientific purposes, with its avowed aim an attack on slavery. Out of the same milieu came the Ethnological Society of Paris and, shortly thereafter, societies of like name and enterprise in London and New York.

---

[1] *Brixham Cave (Windmill Hill Cavern) was discovered in 1858 in Devonshire. It contained an interesting geological stratification series, many fossilized animal bones of essentially modern type, although of species not presently considered native to England, such as elephant, lion, and rhinoceros, plus numerous tools of man dated to the Mousterian culture.*

Before considering the rush of events in anthropology during the nineteenth century, however, a few words are in order about anthropology before that time. It is usually readily conceded that the real forerunner to the development of scientific anthropology was the increase of knowledge in the age of exploration. A dramatic quickening of interests properly anthropological is associated with the commercial expansion of Europe, and further bloom took place in conjunction with the flowering of European imperialism. This is certainly too pat; we wish to know if there is a relationship between anthropology and the ideology of colonialism and imperialism, and we discover that the congruence is usually granted without question. Hallowell tells us:

> As a scientific discipline, anthropology as we know it is a recent and highly distinctive achievement of modern western civilization. . . . It is only with the revolution in world-view that has occurred in western culture that the level of folk-anthropology has been transcended.   [1960:1]

The message is to be found even in popular accounts of the history of anthropology:

> It would be a waste of time to pick details from Herodotus or Marco Polo in order to prove them precursors of the modern social scientist. The historical process that truly fathered social anthropology was Europe's gradual domination of the world through successive waves of exploration and colonization.   [Hays 1958:ix]

I am aware that Hays, in the quoted passage, refers to social anthropology, yet this qualification is scarcely necessary. Much that went by the name of anthropology between the fifteenth and twentieth centuries was a very fuzzy mélange of observations on biology and culture, having as its major goal an understanding of the difference between Europeans and those the Europeans encountered in their expansion. The understandings that developed might better be called rationalizations; for they usually served to justify the kinds of social relations which were involved in contact, whether these were racial, religious, or ethnic. Somewhat later these rationalizations were used to explain even domestic relations between groups of demonstrably common descent but even more obvious socioeconomic class difference; zenith was reached in the view known as social Darwinism.

Similar goals seem to have inspired the anthropology of the classical world, whether of the Greeks, the Romans, or the Chinese, and perhaps others, throwing light on the problem of the necessity of association between anthropology and capitalism. Greek society for much of its history, of course, was based on slavery. Although Greeks themselves could become slaves (indeed, were prized as such by Romans in later periods), most slaves were from elsewhere, particularly Asia Minor and points further east. It is not surprising, then, that Greek anthropology, so to speak, rationalized this situation, as in the famous statement of Aristotle:

> Those who live in a cold climate and in Europe are full of
> spirit, but wanting in intelligence and skill; and therefore
> they retain comparative freedom, but have no political or-
> ganization, and are incapable of ruling over others. Whereas,
> the natives of Asia are intelligent and inventive, but they are
> wanting in spirit, and therefore they are always in a state of
> subjection and slavery.   [Aristotle 1941:1286]

Hippocrates can be quoted to the same effect (Gossett 1963:7).

At the same time, the Chinese were noting the differences between themselves and various "barbarian" peoples with whom they were in contact. The Chinese made such distinctions very early in their history and have continued to make them. These distinctions, accomplished by varying the ideograph for a particular ethnic group, have reflected the quality of relations between the Chinese government and specific peoples. Chinese ideographs, usually called characters, are composed of various design elements. The most important element helps establish the meaning and in complex characters frequently comprises the left-hand side or the top part of the character. There are 214 such radicals, including number 9, jen, the radical that stands for "human being," number 94, ch'üan for "dog," and 142, ch'ung, "insect." When relations were excellent, the character usually included the human radical. When relations were not very good, a dog radical was used; and when things were really bad, it was the insect radical. More seriously, Chinese histories and geographical writings dating back 2000 years and more are well supplied with ethnographic descriptions and analyses of various non-Chinese societies. It is through such examples that it is known with some confidence that people resembling the modern "Negritos" of the Philippines and Southeast Asia used to live in what is now central China. It can be said that much of ancient Chinese anthropology was pejorative and supported a system of social relations in which hostility played a significant part.

Roman ethnography was more widely known when most high school students had to read Caesar's account of the Gallic Wars and some went on to Tacitus. In both these instances and others, it is not difficult to see that the accounts of the Germanic tribes and other non-Roman ethnic groups played a considerable function in Roman statecraft, facilitating Roman rule of a far-flung empire.

Europeans for a long time believed that there were races of men lacking heads, going about on four limbs, or possessing tails. Early in the age of exploration, Europeans believed that the people living in Patagonia, at the tip of South America, were all giants. Those that spread the story had not been there; but when travelers who had actually returned from Patagonia tried to set the record right, it was they who were disbelieved. While it is not surprising that ideas about the people in faraway places should have sometimes been weird, fairly close observation did not necessarily produce accuracy. Jews, from about the eleventh century, were cooped up in walled ghettos in many of the countries of Europe. Though locked in after sunset and all day on Sunday and Christian holidays, they were otherwise familiar sights in most cities. Nonetheless, a few hundred years ago popularly held beliefs about Jews included such curiosities as male menstruation, the birth of children with right hands affixed to their heads requiring surgical separation, horns on the head, and the possibility of giving birth to animals (Gossett 1963:11–12). Of course, we are now completely familiar with the notion that people living in close physical proximity can be separated by chasms of social distance and may believe the most horrendous nonsense about each other. Such unfounded and outrageous beliefs are particularly manifest about people of color. Thus, the English physician John Hunter, although not an anthropologist, asserted in 1775 that all Negroes were born white, turning black from the action of sun and air (*ibid.:37*)

It is an inescapable fact that flagrant racism is purveyed in the name of science in our own time. The language of the professionals like Audrey Shuey, Henry Garrett, and the more recently recruited Arthur Jenson is more sophisticated than that of the amateurs, such as William Shockeley, Dwight Ingle, and lesser fry, but the message is boringly the same. All of them are reminiscent of, or repeat, the nonsense of such crude but dedicated "scientific" racists as Robert Bennett Bean, medical doctor and anatomist, who held forth in the 1920's and 1930's. Typical of Bean's "anthropology" was the assertion, based on quite limited and carelessly selected and controlled data, that the size of the brain among members of the "Black Race" was smaller than among the members of the other two races he recognized, the "White" and the "Yellow-Brown." This "datum" was used to introduce a series of assertions about Negroes:

> The psychic activities of the Black Race are a careless, jolly vivacity, emotions and passions of short duration, and a strong and somewhat irrational egoism. Idealism, ambition, and the cooperative faculties are weak. They love amusement and sport, but have little initiative and adventurous

*spirit. Within limits the Blacks are rather artistic in music,
but not intellectually so. . . . They have poetry of a low order,
are rather free from lasting worries, are cursed with super-
stitious fears, and have much emotionalism in religion. . . .
[1932:95]*

Although most scientific concepts seem fairly obvious once they
have been accepted, much of the actual current of scientific work is
anti-common sense. Common sense tells us that the earth is flat, that
the sun orbits Earth, that heavier objects will fall faster than lighter
ones. Commonsense assumptions about race and behavior are equally
"obvious" and erroneous. Thus one of the outstanding anthropologists
who helped shape the discipline as it is presently constituted, Franz
Boas, several times reiterated the commonsense opinion that

> *. . . it would be erroneous to assume that there are no differ-
> ences in the mental make-up of the negro race and of other
> races, and that their activities should run in the same lines.
> On the contrary, if there is any meaning in correlation of
> anatomical structure and physiological function, we must ex-
> pect that differences exist.   (1911a:271–72)*

It is interesting to compare this with the phrasing Boas supplied
for the revised edition of the same work, published twenty-seven years
after the appearance of the original:

> *. . . it would be erroneous to claim as proved that there are
> no differences in the mental make-up of the Negro race taken
> as a whole and of any other race taken as a whole, and that
> their activities should run in exactly the same lines. This
> would be a result of the varying frequency of personalities
> of various types. It may be that the bodily build of the Negro
> race taken as a whole tends to give a direction to its activities
> somewhat different from those of other races. An answer to
> this question cannot be given.   [1938:270]*

Actually, Boas went through a most interesting personal evolution
with regard to this question. His earliest statement under the title "The
Mind of Primitive Man" was an article in which he stated:

> *A number of anatomical facts point to the conclusion that the
> races of Africa, Australia, and Melanesia are to a certain ex-
> tent inferior to the races of Asia, America, and Europe. . . .
> [We] are justified in assuming a certain correlation between
> their mental ability and the increased size of brain in the
> latter.   [1901:453]*

Even in his early pieces, Boas consciously sought to mitigate his assumption of inferiority of certain races by noting the evidence that variation within races was at least as great, if not greater, than between races. He also gave theoretical warning that there was a major distinction beween the development of individual mental capacity and the development of culture (*ibid.:460*). Yet, such mitigations notwithstanding, the adoption by many anthropologists of the commonsense position with regard to racial inferiority in the last decades of the nineteenth and early decades of the twentieth century represented a thoroughly reactionary step, scientifically as well as politically. The ground had already been well laid, a century and more before, for the elimination of racial differences as an effective explanation of the development of cultural differences. Rather than repeat the excellent review and analysis of this matter presented by Marvin Harris (1968:9–16, 76–79, 80–107), it is sufficient for our purposes to summarize his main findings. As he clearly shows, the Enlightenment thinkers of the eighteenth century shared an "egalitarian environmentalism" as a basic point of view. For them race counted little or not at all. Decisive was the cultural and educational environment in which children were reared. Why then did racism come not merely to the fore but into a dominant position? Harris tells us that racism combines easily with war and commercial competition. In the prevalent nineteenth-century view, the economic order was governed by immutable laws; capitalism was a self-regulating machine whose mainspring was competition. The sequel proceeded inexorably:

> The fiction of common descent enshrined in the metaphor of fatherland and motherland, and applied indiscriminately to the overwhelmingly hybrid populations of Europe, improved the tone of civil and military organization. The racial interpretation of nationhood imparted to the physical, cultural, and linguistic hodgepodges known as England, France, Germany, etc., a sense of community based on the illusion of a common origin and the mirage of common destiny. . . . Racism also had its uses as a justification for class and caste hierarchies; it was a splendid explanation of both national and class privilege. It helped to maintain slavery and serfdom; it smoothed the way for the rape of Africa and the slaughter of the American Indian; it steeled the nerves of the Manchester captains of industry as they lowered wages, lengthened the working day, and hired more women and children. [1968:106]

The deadly point of all of this is that the rise of modern anthropology as a discipline parallels and is inextricably entangled in the growth of the modern phenomenon of racism. Many have come to this realization, not the least Claude Lévi-Strauss:

> *Anthropology . . . is the outcome of a historical process which has made the larger part of mankind subservient to the other, and during which millions of innocent human beings have had their resources plundered and their institutions and beliefs destroyed, whilst they themselves were ruthlessly killed, thrown into bondage, and contaminated by diseases they were unable to resist. Anthropology is daughter to this era of violence.*   *[1966:126]*

On the other hand, this kind of recognition conflicts, sometimes in the same individual, with the maintenance of attitudes that members of reprobated ethnic and racial groups can only consider implicitly racist. Such, we saw, was the case with Franz Boas. But Lévi-Strauss is another inadvertent victim of this game. In the article just quoted he bemoans the loss of opportunity to carry out the traditional and fundamental research of anthropology, primitive ethnography, because of "the high rate of extinction afflicting primitive tribes the world over" (*ibid.:125*). He itemizes part of the toll—the population of Australian aborigines down from perhaps 225,000 to about 40,000 since 1800, with the survivors threatened by hunger, disease, and such encroachments as nuclear weapons testing grounds. The notorious reduction among Brazilian Indians is also mentioned, as are other examples, which, says Lévi-Strauss, are only a fraction of such cases. It is Lévi-Strauss's next sentence, all unconscious, that provides the shock: "Yet, this is no reason to be discouraged" (*ibid.*). He explains what he means: while original material pertaining to primitive ethnography must become rarer, we can put it to better and better use! Of course, Lévi-Strauss is not to be taken as a simple Philistine; he does not eschew the new wave in anthropology, the emphasis on "the problems of developing countries and the pathological aspects of our own society" (*ibid.*), but he does wish absolute priority to be given to the study of remaining primitives.

Lévi-Strauss would justifiably be outraged to be called a racist. Certainly he cannot be put into the same category with those who, despite all epistemological warnings to the contrary, continue to call for "value-free science." A particularly illuminating example of how one man's "value-free" stance is another's hopeless bias is provided by the comments of one reviewer, Werner Cohn, of a recent book about race relations. Cohn congratulates the author, Michael Banton, for not being a "do-gooder," but deplores Banton's "moralistic anti-racism." Although this is said to be manifested in "such tell-tale language as 'silly and unscientific theories of racial superiority,' and 'social pathology of stereotyping,' " Cohn's "value-free" objections go deeper:

> As far as American Negroes are concerned, there is good reason to believe that white people, together with all their prejudice and irrational racism, also experience physical fear of Negroes, and that this fear, if one is to judge by murder rates, is related to the Negroes' much greater propensity to kill. In general, the Negro murder rate is perhaps eight times that of whites. It is fashionable to "explain" this difference by reference to socioeconomic conditions, but this type of "explanation" is traditionally no more than apologetics. A decent social science would have to free itself of the moralistic notion that murder is "bad" before it could honestly and scientifically investigate this area of Negro-white relations. Banton speaks of many things, but not of Negro murder rates. Why doesn't he?   [1969:203]

I cannot refrain from commenting on the content of Cohn's statement. First, his contrast of "Negro" and "white" is in the great pseudo-scientific tradition and can be thrown into relief by his own criticism of Banton for not having a firmer idea of what is meant by "race." Second, there are no statistics worthy of the name on which Cohn can base his remarkable statement. As already indicated, the concept of racial "blackness" varies widely from country to country and, within the United States, it varies considerably from state to state. Furthermore, are we to place credence in the skill and ability of arresting officers and perhaps officers of the court to make complex anthropological discriminations? Shame on you, Mr. Cohn! Finally, to really savor the blend of moral opacity and stupidity that makes such a position, consider its implicit bowdlerization of the definition of murder. If Cohn included such events as the slaughters of war, concentration camp exterminations, and the killing effects of exploitation, his category of "whites" would hold the world's murder record for a long time to come.

Ostensibly historical, this chapter may remind the reader of the concept of time displayed in the novel of former anthropology student Kurt Vonnegut, Jr., *Slaughterhouse-Five*, summed up, somewhat earlier, by T. S. Eliot: "Time present and time past/Are both perhaps present in time future, /And time future contained in time past" (1935:213. I was reminded of the passage by coming across it in Mering 1968:421). The crux of the matter lies for me in the painful and drawn-out discovery that the history of anthropology is less pure and romantic than I might wish. Of course, as Ralph Beals remarks, "Social scientists everywhere are the products of their culture" (1969:67). That helps to explain not only what they have been and are, but what they would be.

For example, if Edward Tylor identified anthropology as a reformer's science, Lewis Henry Morgan (1818–81) raised the possibility that it might be a revolutionary one. Morgan's life was anything but revolutionary. Few could have been less likely to be associated with such a view than the first anthropologist to become president of the American Association for the Advancement of Science (1879). Born into comfort, Morgan himself made a tidy fortune as a corporation lawyer and capitalist. From his mid-twenties Morgan spent much time studying American Indian society and later broadened his interests to the entire globe. He virtually initiated the scientific study of kinship nomenclatural systems, published an ethnographic account of the Iroquois, and produced a grand theory of cultural evolution that attracted the attention of Karl Marx and inspired a book by Friedrich Engels. The treatment of evolution occurred in *Ancient Society;* on the third page from the end of that book Morgan deplored the immense growth of property "since the advent of civilization." He believed that property had become "an unmanageable power." But he was confident about the future:

> *The time will come, nevertheless, when human intelligence will rise to the mastery over property, and define the relations of the state to the property it protects, as well as the obligations and the limits of the rights of its owners. The interests of society are paramount to individual interests, and the two must be brought into just and harmonious relations.* [1877:561]

Judging from comments I have heard, Morgan's reputation as a reformer may be better than he deserves, at least among anthropologists. In the 1840's he helped start a campaign to gather funds for the education of individual Indians as a means to facilitate integration of the Indians into American life (Resek 1960:31); he had become friendly with a Seneca, Ely Parker, and much of what he was to learn about the Iroquois came to him through Parker or a contact with whom Parker had acquainted him. As early as 1846 the United States Senate had a Committee on Indian Affairs, which held hearings on various injustices suffered by the Indians. Henry R. Schoolcraft (1793–1864), an expert on Indian culture who assisted in the negotiations that transferred millions of acres in the Great Lakes area from Indian to white control, apparently regretted some aspects of the transactions and testified on behalf of the Indians. He emphasized that decision making among the Indians was based on consensus rather than majority vote, hence urged abrogation of various treaties on the ground that many Indians who should have consented to them were not even apprised of their making. Interestingly enough, Schoolcraft argued on behalf of the Seneca in terms of an ecological understanding of their agriculture. He saw clearly that they could not use their accustomed methods to till the Kansas prairie, nor could they survive back East, where their lands were now too small (Resek 1960:32). Morgan came upon this scene as one sent to Washington to present a memorial to President Polk and to the Senate urging consideration for the rights of the Seneca. As reconstructed by Carl Resek (1960:33–35), Morgan's trip had no favorable outcome for the Indians but provided the anthropologist-to-be with an educational tour of the national capital. Later in his life Morgan, who made several attempts to be appointed Commissioner of Indian Affairs, continued to petition presidents and legislators on behalf of the Indians, apparently to no avail.

The theme of anthropologist as reformer is only one important strand of the history of anthropology that can help the reader understand the present position of the discipline and its practitioners. In lieu of a detailed rendition of the themes of American anthropology, it is useful to look to the contents of its most representative journal for evidence. In the first volume of the *American Anthropologist* (1888), a wide range of articles marks several focuses of interest. The first paper was devoted to a criticism of Malthusian population theory and presented a generally optimistic view, indicating its author's belief that productive capacity had always previously enlarged in response to population increase (Welling 1888), although leaving the question open in the future. The first volume also displayed anthropological interest not only in Indian culture, language, and archeology but also in discussions of the classical world, with sweeping statements about the evolution of practically everything.

Leading the field in general pronouncements at that time was John W. Powell (1834–1902), a Civil War hero who served as the director of the U.S. Geological Survey and as the first director of the Bureau of Ethnology. The first volume of the *American Anthropologist* contained Powell's speech, given as President of the Anthropological Society of Washington, the forerunner of the American Anthropological Association. In his speech, entitled "Competition as a Factor in Human Evolution," Powell offered a variety of opinions having a nice contemporary feeling. He approved of competition but was careful to distinguish "antagonistic competition," which he considered antisocial, from "emulative," which he said redounded to the profit of the entire human race. The wounded veteran took a harsh view of war, declaring, "In organized warfare the processes of natural selection are reversed; the fittest to live are killed, the fittest to die are preserved . . ." (1888:303). Powell was also anti-Malthusian and expressed himself succinctly on the problem, declaring: ". . . if some hunger it is not because of the lack

of the world's food, but because of the imperfect distribution of that
food to all." Indeed, he went out of his way to derogate social Darwinism, although not by name. He castigated the capitalists of England for
pleading that competition forced an iron law of low wages, and implied
that strikes and riots were a proper means of compelling employers "to
yield a greater share of justice." Of the use of the theory of the survival
of the fittest to justify oppression, he wrote bitterly:

> Then let the poor fall into deeper degradation, then let the
> hungry starve, then let the unfortunate perish, then let the
> ignorant remain in his ignorance—he who does not seek
> knowledge himself is not worthy to possess knowledge, and
> the very children of the ignorant should remain untaught, that
> the sins of the fathers may be visited upon the children. Let
> your government cease to regulate industries, and instead of
> carrying the mails let them erect prisons; let government dis-
> charge their state-employed teachers and enlist more police-
> men. . . .   [Ibid.:322]

Powell did not know how the social problems, the grave injustices of
his day, could be conquered, but he had faith in his fellow-man, "in
human endeavor . . . in the genius for invention among mankind," and
for the love of justice which he thought a universal human characteristic, albeit one under sometime eclipse. In all of this he was consistent
to his anthropology, for like most of his contemporaries and many of
his predecessors, he conceived of the motive force of cultural evolution
as the evolving capacity for thought of the human brain and the drive
for higher and higher degrees of rationality in behavior and institutions.[2]

When attention is paid to the range of available historical material, it becomes clear that the development of anthropology has not
been entirely dark. It has had its share and more of honest devotees
whose ideas were somewhat ahead of their time. It is patent, and not
to be obscured by revisionist presentism, that a rather high quotient of
social-mindedness is characteristic of many anthropological pioneers.
Nonetheless, for the most part anthropology was not out of phase with
the dominant ideologies of those societies that supported it as a legitimate intellectual activity. In the words of the biologist J. B. S. Haldane:

> Modern cultural anthropology is a by-product of colonialism.
> It consists of accounts given by persons almost all of Euro-
> pean origin of the behaviour of members of other cultural
> groups over which they exerted their dominance, largely
> through the greater efficiency of their weapons.   [1956:8]

[2] Compare this with Marvin Harris's comment on Tylor's Primitive
Culture: "The basic point . . . seems to be that the human mind has
the ability to perfect itself by thinking more clearly" (1968:203).

This theme, still rare if not totally absent from textbooks, is beginning to percolate through the profession. Moreover, some of its implications are beginning to be raised for closer examination. In an essay that is as interesting as it is pertinent, William S. Willis, Jr., repeats the theme but goes on to a significant variation:

> To a large extent, modern Western anthropology is a by-product of capitalism and especially of capitalism in its imperialistic phase. This sad fact is beginning to be recognized, and anthropology is described increasingly as "the child of conquest" and "the child of colonialism." [1970:36]

The variation, however, concerns the American Negro and raises two questions. First, why has anthropology, particularly in the United States, paid so little attention to blacks until fairly recently? Second, why has the discipline produced so few black professional anthropologists, the number enlarging in recent years but still remaining fairly low in absolute terms? According to Willis, "[e]ven today there are no more than ten Negroes holding the Ph.D. degree in anthropology in the United States" (ibid.:38).

Willis's charge, that anthropologists have neglected the study of the American Negro, should jolt the smug professional. Any attempt to refute it will likely lead to increased embarrassment. Before World War II the number of actual field studies carried out in black communities in the United States could be counted on the fingers of one hand with some left over. Melville Herskovits had done prodigious labor to demonstrate that despite an overwhelming myth to the contrary, American blacks had a very extensive African cultural past (Herskovits 1941). But Herskovits had no field-work experience in the United States, although he had done field work in the Caribbean and in Dahomey, West Africa. Willis is entirely correct to call to our attention the fact that "Why anthropologists selected Indians instead of Negroes for study is an intriguing and important problem that has not been investigated" (Willis 1970:34). The reasons tentatively suggested by Willis in answer to his own question are too complex to summarize here. They range over considerable areas of theory, touching on the tradition of the young anthropological discipline as well as on conditions of imperialism and colonialism. Additional ethnohistorical work must be done, however, before we really understand "the intricate racism and escapism that led anthropologists to prefer reservation Indians to shantytown blacks" (ibid.:38).

That Willis has a case is apparent from what is already known about the history of anthropology in the United States. According to A. Irving Hallowell, one of the most respected specialists on this topic, it was Thomas Jefferson who helped set the course. Although opposed to slavery, Jefferson was a thoroughgoing racist who set down his prejudices against blacks in unmistakable terms. Starting by finding Negroes ugly, he proceeded to exhaust the list of stereotypes (cf. "On Negro Ability" in Ruchames 1969:162–69). Jefferson did not approach the Indians in the same way; the same *Notes on the State of Virginia* (1784–85), in which he laid bare his antipathy to Negroes, shows his anthropological interest in the Indians in the form of his own observations and statistical data. He collected vocabularies of Indian languages and was interested in Indian archeology, even to digging an Indian mound himself (Hallowell 1960:16. Also see Lehmann-Hartleben 1943). Perhaps most important were the instructions Jefferson gave to Lewis and Clark for their expedition into the Northwest Territory—"full directions for the recording of ethnographic data, surprisingly modern in tone, which might even now serve as a guide to a field worker," according to Clark Wissler, an anthropologist specializing in American Indian cultures (Wissler 1943:196, cited in Hallowell 1960:17). The sophistication of Jefferson's concept of ethnographic method may be debated; less equivocal are the motives behind his interest in Indian culture. Certainly there was more to it than the Jeffersonian thirst for knowledge for its own sake. As Hallowell saw it:

> During [Jefferson's] lifetime a shift from decentralization to centralization of our responsibility for our formal relations with the Indians came about. By the late seventeen eighties the new American government had developed a policy which recognized Indian titles to Western lands which had to be extinguished before the whites moved in. It was of great practical importance, then, for the government to have reliable knowledge about the western tribes. . . . Jefferson . . . saw the need for ethnographic information in relation to guiding the administration of Indian affairs. . . . [1960:18]

Clark Wissler says that Jefferson realized that "the acculturation of the Indians would be more effective if based upon knowledge of the aboriginal tribal culture" (Wissler 1943:197, quoted in Hallowell 1960:18). The exact wording of the instructions issued by Jefferson is very interesting:

> considering the interest which every nation has in extending and strengthening the authority of reason and justice among the people around them, it will be useful to acquire what knowledge you can of the state of morality, religion and information among them, as it may better enable those who endeavor to civilize and instruct them, to adapt their measures to the existing nations and practices of those on whom they are to operate. [Hallowell 1960:18]

It is also worth noting, in view of the important question of whether the general conception of anthropology should continue to be linked with a "four-field" approach, that the connection of American anthropology with American Indians is implicated. Hallowell reflects upon this point:

> Perhaps the underlying unity implied in the study of the inhabitants of a single great continent . . . accounts, in part, for the traditional emphasis later given in the United States to anthropology as the unified study of man. [Ibid.:23]

Whatever may have flowed from the work on American Indians, the relations between anthropologists and Indians have not always been friendly. There are episodes in which non-Indian anthropologists have been rejected in the field. On the other hand, such incidents seem to have been relatively rare. Most fieldworkers have gotten on well with informants or at least have claimed so and continued to do their work. In recent years, however, there has been a shift in the picture. Shortly after World War II, the mounting number of graduate students in anthropology were involved in a similarly increasing number of field studies. In December 1948, the Commission on Human Rights of the Economic and Social Council of the United Nations (UNESCO) proclaimed a Universal Declaration of Human Rights. It was said among anthropologists, half in jest, that the Pueblo Indians were disappointed because a freedom they prized did not appear—freedom from anthropologists.

Actually, that Universal Declaration of Human Rights has a pertinent section devoted to the freedom of privacy, which is extended to both home and correspondence. There is, of course, no sanction behind such provisions. Subsequent years have seen more explicit statement of related themes by articulate members of various ethnic groups. For example, Vine Deloria, Jr., says in his book *Custer Died for Your Sins* that anthropologists are "ideological vultures. . . . Why," asks Deloria, "should we continue to be the private zoos for anthropologists?" (1969: 95). He suggests that anthropologists could change this negative role by donating to the group under study an amount equal to the cost of the project being conducted. When I recounted Deloria's request to a young anthropologist who was doing his work among the Mohawk, the non-Indian anthropologist laughed and told me that his informants, although poor, habitually offered him money. Although he acknowledged the possibility of change in keeping with the newly roused political consciousness of many young Indians, he thought his experience was more compatible with most Indian behaviors.

The contrast between Deloria's expression of outrage against anthropology and the behavioral realities of courtesy and cooperation shown to contemporary anthropologists working with American Indians may serve as the introduction to the final part of this chapter, in which I propose to attempt an artistic arrangement out of some of the wreckage. The earlier reference to the distinction between historicism and presentism must now come into use. To a considerable extent the framework of the preceding pages has been presentist—although mainly in an implicit assumption that many of the values involved in anthropological controversies of the past are still ahead of their time for the majority of citizens in our country. To condemn predecessors may bring emotional release to some, or provide tactical political weapons to others, but for the social scientist the primary obligation is to understand and to be able to explain why certain events occurred, why certain opinions were held, and why certain forms of social relations held sway. The goal of such understanding is precisely that toward which anthropology as a whole has long been tending, however devious its actual course.

Obviously, attainment of such a goal does not fall solely within the ambit of anthropology alone, no matter how broadly defined; all other social sciences and humanities must be implicated. Nonetheless, the role of anthropology in such an endeavor is clearly evident. It is anthropology that confronts simultaneously the biological basis of human behavior and its cultural manifestations. It is anthropology, as a consequence, that stands at the pivot of understanding of many current problems, in particular those having to do with the real or imagined consequences of racial definitions and differences.

Although problems of race are very much at the fore, they are not the only ones of special interest to anthropology because of their blending of biological and cultural factors. The momentous problems of population and ecology also cross similar disciplinary boundaries, as does the whole range of questions pertaining to health and disease. In each of these areas, anthropologists have already made substantial contributions to knowledge, even if the immediate practical utility of such contributions has not yet become apparent. Nonetheless, the role of anthropology in constantly and consistently holding before professional and public gaze the distinction between racial fact and fiction, between the concepts of social and biological race, between genetics and culture, stands out in the history of the discipline. Similarly, awareness of the significance of the ecological approach, although making its earliest appearance in biology, has been highly developed in anthropology, particularly during the last twenty-five years. The same is true of anthropological contributions to demography, nowhere more important than in the study of differential fertility as an aspect of varying sociopolitical and ideological settings.

There are various positive achievements to celebrate in the field of cultural anthropology. Some have to do with precisely the areas of inquiry judged relevant by most contemporary standards, including those of protest. Indeed, much of the content of contemporary social protest is the outgrowth of thematic interests that first appeared in the context of the academic discipline of anthropology: concepts such as culture, part-culture and subculture, cultural relativism, and the notion of alienation as independently discovered by Edward Sapir (1924). As indicated earlier, one of the problems of contemporary anthropology is that it feels itself in crisis. George Stocking, expressing the apprehensions of an anthropologist friend, tells us that it is "a crisis of identity within a host-culture which has appropriated important parts of anthropological thought into the cultural baggage of its intellectual 'common sense' " (1966:282).

It was Alfred Kroeber, father figure and doyen to more than a generation of American anthropologists, who described the ideal anthropological contribution to humanity as sounding "like a pipe dream." Nothing less was visualized than anthropology functioning as the ultimate coordinating science, forging together the vast array of knowledge about man and his culture, hammering it into a set of coherent interpretations, understanding it "as something entirely a part of nature, wholly an evolutionary development within nature" in all its unprecedented, unique, and richly ramified development (1953:xiv). It could aspire to this attempt because it did not shy away from the primitive, the alien, the obscure, the distasteful, or even the dangerous. As for the last, sometimes the hazard lay in conditions of sanitation or medical care that would make disease not probable but inevitable; at other times the hazard lay in making contact with strangers who had no reason to be friendly and every reason for hostility; and still more was there danger from one's own kind, resenting the messages with which one returned —the knowledge that cultures must be judged in their own light.

Whatever else anthropology may have contributed, the concept of cultural relativism, more than a generous impulse of the Enlightenment, must be considered. One of the most poignant expressions of this concept, although there have been many at different times, occurs in the letter-diary of the young Franz Boas, traveling among the Eskimo of Cumberland Sound almost a hundred years ago:

> *I often ask myself what advantages our "good society" possesses over that of the "savages." The more I see of their customs, the more I realize that we have no right to look down on them. . . . Here, without the least complaint people are willing to perform every task demanded of them. We have no right to blame them for their forms and superstitions. . . . We "highly educated people" are much worse, rela-*

*tively speaking. The fear of tradition and old customs is
deeply implanted in mankind . . . I believe it is a difficult
struggle for every individual and every people to give up
tradition and follow the path to truth. The Eskimo are sitting
around me, their mouths filled with raw seal liver (the spot
of blood on the back of the paper shows you how I joined
in). As a thinking person, for me the most important result of
this trip lies in the strengthening of my point of view that the
idea of a "cultured" individual is merely relative. . . . But now
I really must get back to the cold Eskimo land. [Stocking
1965a:61]*

Some readers will have the effect of this passage diluted for them
when they learn that Boas traveled through that cold and difficult landscape with a servant named Wilhelm, and a guide, sometimes referred
to in the accounts as " 'his' Eskimo Sigma." It reminds me of Kathleen
Gough's objection, that "while Boas and his students did invaluable
work on race differences and race prejudices, they did not systematically explore the relationship of race prejudice to the worldwide historical and structural development of White nations' imperialism"
(1968:428). Gough has placed such an objection on several occasions,
but she too has yet to present a systematic exploration. It is a task that
many of her colleagues look forward to seeing done, and some are
helping to train the generation of scholars most likely to do it. I think
the name of the course is anthropology.

It is worth noting that the actual teaching of anthropology in the
United States is less than a century old. If the subject seems frozen into
the curriculum and into certain modes of presentation, fossilization has
occurred with preternatural rapidity. Although the matter is not entirely
clear, it seems that Harvard and the University of Pennsylvania acted
at approximately the same time, about 1885–86, to add professorships
in anthropology. Both shared similar motivations; they had acquired
museums and needed competent persons to take charge of their anthropological collections—teaching, ironically enough for contemporary
students, was not really considered important. Not until 1895 was a
general anthropology course carrying credit given in the United States.
The course was at Harvard, and the teacher was George A. Dorsey, who
had received his doctorate at Harvard the previous year and was a
specialist on the American Indian (Freeman 1965:80).

The addition of anthropology to the university structure in Great
Britain closely paralleled events in the United States in time and spirit.
E. B. Tylor, who was to become Oxford's first professor of anthro-
pology, was first appointed Keeper of the University Museum in 1883,

where, with the title of Reader in 1884, he started to lecture on a regular basis. It was in 1896 that he carried his work into Oxford proper with his appointment as Professor. As Stocking remarks:

> However much Tylor may have helped prepare the accep-
> tance of anthropology, he actually trained few anthropol-
> ogists, and only at the very end of his tenure at Oxford did
> anthropology as an organized discipline achieve more than
> nominal status.   [1968:175.]

In France, the efforts of a medical doctor and surgeon, Paul Broca, an amateur of physical anthropology, were influential in starting the independent École d'Anthropologie, which gave courses in anatomy, ethnology, archeology, demography, linguistics, and geography. The year was 1875. The course of development of the field was beset by hazards not faced by colleagues in the United States. As we have seen, developments in the United States quite early favored empirical work; the opportunity to work with American Indians was seized even before the formal appearance of the discipline. By the time anthropology was a recognized discipline, most of its major figures carried out field work as a matter of course, albeit in the context of isolated informants rather than in terms of ongoing cultures. In France, the tradition of field work, such as it was, was left to travelers, explorers, missionaries, and colonial administrators. The generation of Émile Durkheim (1858–1917) had no field experience whatsoever, and its successors raised the avoidance of field work to the level of a canon of method. Marcel Mauss (1872–1950) urged a division of labor between ethnography carried out by nonanthropologists, such as colonial administrators, and theory to be spun out by the social scientists. The rationale was aimed at the avoidance of bias; Mauss believed that the worst form of prejudice was that which might lead to the warping of observations to fit preconceived theories, a malady which he seemed not to believe pertinent to missionaries and government officials (cf. Bender 1965:146–47, citing Mauss 1913:834)!

As an anthropologist, I find the period of one hundred years a very short time. Anything less is like a moment. I am not at all sure that truly decisive trends can be determined for short periods, except for unusual leaps. What I am trying to say is that the formal subject of anthropology is terribly young and its teaching as a regular subject even younger. Thus we cannot take tradition too seriously. We should admit that there has not been enough time to experiment with different approaches in the lecture room or in seminars. All of our methods of teaching and learning this new subject matter have been inherited from other fields, as well as our ways of testing and grading. Further investigation would reveal, of course, that the subjects we have used as models, economics, political economy, and the like, are not much older. So why is everyone up-tight when students suggest changes? Of course there are reasons for apprehension, particularly when suggestions for obliterating some contemporary academic procedures are not coupled with ideas about what might take their place. But even the most outrageous challenges are directed at a tradition that is neither ancient nor proven, so extreme reaction does not seem to be in order. To this topic we return in later chapters.

ON "INTRODUCTORY" ANTHROPOLOGY

> In [some introductory courses] . . . anthropology
> appears as many kinds of contrastingly original powers
> addressing themselves in different, and somehow
> not entirely different, ways to a bewildering range
> and variety of facts about people . . . anthropology
> in this course is, as one student told me, very hard
> to get your teeth into.
>
> —Robert Redfield

You may remember that at one point during her adventures in *Through the Looking Glass* Alice fell in with the Lion and the Unicorn and had to cut up a cake. Every time she divided it, the slices only joined again. When she complained, the Unicorn remarked sharply, "You don't know how to manage Looking-glass cake. Hand it round first, and cut it afterward." Most instructors contemplating the content and organization of introductory anthropology courses feel the way Alice is described upon hearing this advice—"very much puzzled how to begin."

Since man is simultaneously an animal and a creature living in the context of massive cultural experience, a product of both biological and cultural evolution, should the instructor present the primarily biological, or the primarily cultural, materials first? This is only the beginning of a number of difficult questions that concern the organization of the general anthropology course. Perhaps currently most serious are those questions arising from the fact that many students come with the hope of contributing to the solution of critical social problems. They want to know immediately what anthropology has to say about such matters and are often impatient of what they feel are attempts to detour them from the paths of greatest relevance. Depending upon the student's vision, there is often resentment of any attempt to require learning that seems to promise little or no use. Why should the student interested in the sociology of imperialism learn anything about australopithecines and human evolution? Why should the student of comparative religion spend time on the sequence of cultures that once occupied the Viru Valley in Peru? Why should the future engineer be taught about medical anthropology, or one who would be a doctor or nurse learn about glottochronology and psycholinguistics? Why should those who want to bring a cultural perspective to the problems of the inner city be asked to spend time on primate ethology?

Some nonmajors are dissatisfied with introductory anthropology courses for completely different reasons. A common complaint is a "forest and trees" problem. Many nonmajor students are so busy memorizing the vocabulary of the field (Zinjanthropus, diastema, phoneme, Pliocene, Clactonian, kula, potlatch, kiva, Chuckchee, Hopi, Arapeshmundugumoraztecazandetrobriandaruntabagandahaida . . .) that they fail to get a larger vision. Usually they are encouraged in their misery by the harried instructor. Driven for material on which to base a test that will give meaningful intervals among otherwise indistinguishable examination performances, the teacher frequently turns to a relatively meaningless grab bag of "identifications." (That the abuses are worst where classes are in the hundreds says much, but doesn't alleviate matters.) I have found that when nonmajors are given a chance to overlook some of the particulars in favor of more general messages, there is much more enthusiasm and greater grasp of the really important things. Of course, students do show differential lack of interest or boredom in various parts of a survey course, but different individuals take exception to different parts. While one student approaches the instructor to complain that the pace has been too fast or treatment too superficial and couldn't more attention be given this topic, another student asks the instructor to go faster or drop this particular topic entirely.

There are also reasons why many nonmajors do enjoy the introduction to anthropology. Many see it as an intriguing field, although, like the millions who say of New York that it is a great place to visit, they have no intention of going much further with it. Sometimes the student is impressed with the zeal of the instructor, whether full professor or teaching assistant. The teacher obviously thinks that anthropology is one of the most exciting things in the world and is impelled to spread the word.

Even where such enthusiasm makes no professional converts, it enhances the interest of the student by making him feel that what he is getting in the classroom is not just musty academic folderol. Of course, some students may be threatened by some of the content of such a course. Those from families holding very conservative political opinions or certain religious views may experience a kind of intellectual culture shock, but this is now a rare occurrence due to the vast changes that have taken place in youth culture almost everywhere. More likely there will be some students in such a class who will regard it merely as so much bourgeois crap. At certain points in the work, however, even such students are likely to show great engrossment and may wish the instructor to go faster, deeper, or in certain directions rather than others.

It is worth looking at some of the things that nonmajors can derive from general introductory courses. Afterwards we will be in a better position to evaluate the design of the introductory course and consider alternatives and possible reforms.

One of the greatest things that geology gave the fledgling sciences of biology and anthropology in the late eighteenth and nineteenth centuries was time. The European savants who pioneered these fields were imprisoned in a chronology so restrictive that there was simply no time for anything to have happened in an evolutionary way. Archbishop Ussher (1581–1656) computed the date of creation to be 4004 B.C. Six thousand years was manifestly inadequate to permit the separation of man from his primate relatives, much less the emergence of all life from a primeval slime. Today, there are few people, perhaps none who would read a book such as this, who are cowed by the thought of intervals of billions of years during which the earth and its life forms evolved.[1] Most students come to anthropology already convinced that earth and the universe, and man, for that matter, have been around for a long, long time, so what is so special about the extended temporal view in an introductory anthropology course? It is precisely that this view is taken with regard to man and not galaxies, solar systems, or even planets. In no other course is the student forced to contemplate simultaneously what millions of years have meant for the evolution of the human form, the capacity for language, the kinds of behavior our type of animal indulges in, the institutions we build. While some students resent such an approach, not on theological grounds but as a form of antiradical defeatism (the emphasis on evolution to the detriment of revolution), other students find the active use of a deep time scale to be liberating. It affords a perspective in which even the gravest human problems can be approached somewhat more leisurely, while still permitting individual rage and revulsion over execrations such as the delay in achieving genuinely equal rights for black citizens. Such a panoramic view of time also helps to free us of one particularly burdensome set of racist shackles—the archetypal concept of race—and notions of the immutability of race can be seen for what they are, one of the last refuges of the pre-evolutionary concept of fixity of the species. In the place of the notion that such statistical abstractions as "Negroid," "Caucasoid," or "Mongoloid" existed in the dim past as pure types until improvements in travel led to mixing, we now are forced to recognize that the human

[1] *For perspective, however, consider the fact that the famous eleventh edition of the Encyclopaedia Britannica as recently as 1910 offered a table in which Ussher's chronology was compared with "probable real dates." Next to Ussher's 4004 B.C., Samuel R. Driver, author of the article and famous divine, noted that the real date of creation was "indeterminable, but much before 7000 B.C."*

race was always one continuous population with temporary local clustering and the most porous internal boundaries.

It is with respect to holding its students to the technical awareness of human biology that anthropology begins to fulfill its unique role among the disciplines. Even the most poorly prepared students now arrive in anthropology classes fully aware of or prepared to accept the fact that man is an animal by descent and in the functions and requirements he shares with other beasts. Despite routinization, this concept is continually enlightening. Man exists in a massive structure of culture; he lives in a daily world that has only indirect relation to genetic endowments and directives, yet all men must satisfy biological needs and conform to biological laws. The problems encountered in doing so have helped to shape his cultures. Realization of this must pervade and inform the anthropological approach, but the biology must not be permitted to overwhelm or obscure the culturology. As put by Mandelbaum, "the concept of culture should be presented early in a beginning course in physical anthropology in order to establish from the start the anthropologist's main concern with *human* biology rather than general biology, with *human* behavior rather than generalized animal behavior" (1963:52). True of the general course in physical anthropology, this applies even more emphatically to the course that introduces anthropology at large.

The counterdependence of human biology on culture, the latter in the guise of both technology and attitudinal systems, is conspicuous in contemporary developments in sexual behavior in our own culture. Indeed, anthropology seems to have played something of an active role in the shift that has taken place in sexual mores. Certainly I do not wish to suggest that anthropology has singlehandedly stimulated the change, but the knowledge that other cultures handle sexual relations differently has not been lost on an anxious public. It is not merely that the technology of contraception has undergone a great leap forward, tremendously important as that is, but the ideas of sexual pairing and its philosophy have gone through change too, so that willingness or desire to use contraception or to resort to abortion has fed back into the technology and stimulated its development.

Concomitant with the stress on the biological aspects of being human is the weighting of psychological factors. Of course, many students come with a preliminary understanding of psychology as a subject matter, or they have opportunities to pursue the inquiry in other courses. Significantly the student is forced in a good introductory anthropology course to deal simultaneously with psychological aspects of human behavior and institutions as he deals with a variety of other aspects, some directly related, some indirectly, some not at all, or related in ways that science has yet to discover. Incidentally, this sort of situation presents the student with an exciting but risky opportunity. He may be inspired to outrun his instructor in synthesizing the materials of the different fields. Unfortunately, many discoveries made under such circumstances turn out to be mistaken, useless, or old hat. But they are discoveries and the wise instructor treats them as such, seeing the possibility of better things ahead for the imaginative but yet not fully formed student.

Because linguistics remains for most students an arcane field, rarely if ever mentioned as such in high school and often unrepresented even in fairly large universities, it can be an exciting part of the general course. The miracle of language can be considered in itself, or equally significantly as the basis of much of our human cultural scene. In the former approach, most students at some point must consider the problem of biological evolution and the development of the several complex capacities on which the ability to use language must rest. Questions about how children learn language become inextricably tangled with questions of how children learn the cultures in which they live. This, in turn, raises other problems, such as the relations between language and culture, and variations of language associated with class or with social race, both of which have much to do with the kinds of educational problems that plague our country today.

The topics that occur in an introductory anthropology course are all intrinsically interesting—to somebody. They can be made interesting to larger and larger audiences as they illuminate problems of wide present concern, and I find that most of the material we take up in introductory anthropology courses *is,* for better or worse, close to the jugular of the human race at this point in its passage.

Introductory anthropology, more than any other course in the curriculum, has the potential for displaying the unity of mankind. Simultaneously, no other course has better opportunity to show how marvelously diverse is the behavior of man and the variety of his cultures. But this potential of the introductory anthropology course is present only when both the biological and the culturological aspects of man are included in the subject matter. Only the so-called four-field approach, that which includes some treatment of physical anthropology, linguistics, archeology, and cultural anthropology, takes on such a responsibility. It should be noted, incidentally, that the survey introduction to the social sciences found in some schools is in no way a substitute for the general anthropology course. The former invariably neglects or totally ignores the somatic character and evolution of man, pays scant attention to two million and more years of culture building, and has little or nothing to say about language.

Another means of exploring the potential of introductory anthropology for the student without professional interest in the discipline is to inquire into the role of anthropology in the concept of general education. This brings into question things we have already broached in earlier chapters, such as the increasing number of students taking higher degrees and their increasingly varied socioeconomic backgrounds. It is not merely the developing institutions of higher learning that are involved, but also the high school curriculum as it has evolved during the past century. To put the matter briefly, the preparatory school of the middle nineteenth century was devoted, as its name suggested, to graduating successive groups of upper- and middle-class "white" males into colleges. While dropouts were not unknown a century ago, there were relatively few who expected upon entering an academy of secondary education to be leaving it for work. This gave way to a broadened system of high schools with diverse programs, academic and nonacademic, with the latter turning out job-qualified young adults ready for the labor market. Until recently, however, only a minority of the graduates of the academic high schools entered college; of late the proportions have been rising and the projections indicate continued increases, particularly as the children of poor and otherwise disadvantaged parents win greater access to higher education facilities.

Whether in the academic high school program or in college, the problem defined by the supporters of general education involves the differentiation of three main elements in the curriculum and the desire to make sure that no one passes through the higher educational sequence without knowing something about each of the three realms—the sciences, the humanities (including the arts), and the social sciences. In a very real sense the argument popularly associated with novelist and British civil servant C. P. Snow, concerning the conflict between the "two cultures," is an older and broader one that really involves at least "three cultures." Placed in briefest compass, it is asked repeatedly whether the computer technician need be a literary imbecile, the social scientist a person to whom mathematics is a mystery, or the artist someone impervious to the knowledge of the hard and soft sciences alike. Since very few people would answer this question negatively, suggestions for improvement have come unsolicited.

Solutions may be offered wholesale, but basic questions still tend to be overlooked. Among the often-raised but rarely faced matters are (1) the problem of defining universally required areas of knowledge, (2) the problem of freeing time from specified requirements for general education use, and (3) quite apart from time, the question that concerns the social organization of learning itself: given the usual structure of colleges and universities, how to get departments to relinquish their usually self-centered views of the curriculum. This last has paradoxical elements. I know that my quest for the centrality of anthropology in a curriculum of general education may sound in other departments particularly egregious. On the other hand, there are now complications that a few decades ago were mere suspicions and speculations, for example, the problem of the legitimate interests of social groups associated with nonestablishment subcultures. The remarks of Nathan Hare (cf. p. 44) or similar statements questioning the value of understanding Shakespeare's plays, Beethoven's music, the Greek classics, Augustine's journals, or any other of the many treasures of Western culture are nothing less than an incendiary challenge to the educational establishment, or at least a powerful wing of that establishment.

Yet it is precisely here that anthropology comes to the fore. Without patronizing any non-Western culture, anthropology has been the discipline that, for decades, has been exclaiming at the narrowness of view of programs built on "Western" or "European" cultural foundations alone. It is no longer sufficient to make available to some students a course in "Oriental Civilizations" or humanities, thereby taking the edge of parochialism from an otherwise monolithic curriculum. (This is not to criticize such courses, often excellent and very much needed. It is rather to point out that they are invariably approached as electives and affect relatively few students.) We now face demands to truly expand the curriculum, introducing courses relating to the cultures of various ethnic groups—blacks, Puerto Ricans, Chicanos, and others—as well as crosscutting segments of the society, particularly the poor.

I must stress that the role of anthropology in this critical time in the history of higher education in America is not to act as a substitute all-purpose course that will take the heat off administrators who will be besieged for "relevant" courses. Anthropology can be one of the most relevant courses in any curriculum, but it cannot by itself satisfy the current demands. Indeed, it will not always be easy to keep the general anthropology course from being patronizing on the one hand or critical of certain political assumptions on the other. The former will be easiest to control. Anthropology as usually taught does not condescend to but relies upon the introduction of materials from Asia, Africa, Latin America, and other regions. Usually, as a matter of fact, that region gets greatest attention which was the site of the instructor's major field work. Even given this predilection, most teachers of anthropology pride themselves on achieving some breadth of coverage in giving ethnographic examples. Similarly, although anthropologists have an important running debate about the validity of "the culture of poverty" (cf. Lewis 1959, 1966; Valentine 1968), they are prepared to handle the concept as a normal part of the work of an introductory course. Admittedly, until quite recently there has been no introductory text, as such, making serious reference to these issues, but now that the ice has been broken by Marvin Harris (1971), others are likely to follow.

Another warning must be given about the use of anthropology in general education sequences adapted to demands of one or another ethnic minority. Particularly in the case of the demand for courses in "black culture," any anthropologist who becomes involved must decide how the content of such a course relates to one of the great discoveries of anthropology, namely that race and culture are not causally linked. But recognition of the causal dissociation between race and culture need not blunt the attempt to remedy in part by education the grievous harm that one portion of our social body has received over the course of centuries. It is anthropology that verifies that blacks, or Negroes, in the United States do not comprise a truly meaningful biological race but do constitute a most important social race. (It can do this, to some extent, by analyzing the words Negro and black, showing how their usage has little or no relevance to the sorting criteria of biological race, and certainly not to the genetics of skin color. What are involved in making such discriminations are social and political criteria, a fact well realized by such groups as the Black Panthers or some of their factions.) Once the meaning of the concept of social race has been established, the deeper problems can be faced.

Against this background I would argue that every student should be exposed to at least one course in general anthropology. Such a course necessarily includes materials from the four fields we have already discussed. I do not think that an introductory course confined to social or cultural anthropology answers the needs of general students. The reason for this grows organically from all the things already discussed: the pivotal value to students in general of an anthropology course is its potential for treating man biologically and culturally, thereby confronting common, settled views that students usually bring to the study of the subject of man.

It is only in such a course that students can deal with race and racism. The former, of course, is a concept that applies to biology and requires knowledge of the physical and chemical bases of life, the principles of systematics and classification, the discrimination of phenotypic traits and the means of dealing with them. And, too, while the phenomenon of racism has very little and sometimes nothing to do with the phenomenon of race, this message cannot be properly delivered until a minimum understanding of the biological facts has been appreciated. Today no justification is needed for insisting on the broadest treatment of problems of race and racism in classrooms at various levels. The presence of anthropology in a curriculum can be compared only to the acquisition of such basic skills as the control of literacy and the fundamentals of calculation. There may be a time when these basic messages will be so well disseminated at lower levels in the curriculum that there will be no need for them in higher education, but that day is still to come.

Beyond the area of racial biology lies the liberating knowledge of human evolution on the physical as well as the cultural side. We spoke earlier of the freedom for thought that is supplied by consideration of man in a geological time scale rather than a scale adapted from any more limited history. Similarly, the treatment of language as a natural phenomenon itself broadens horizons and prepares the way for the student's understanding of the independence of cultural phenomena. As we get more deeply into the realm of culture, we begin to see that the general course may need expansion and revision in order to respond to some of the requirements of contemporary students. Important as the study of simple cultures is to the anthropologist, such studies should not be approached as ends in themselves but be linked to other contexts. One of the oldest is still one of the best: to show in a simpler culture how different portions of the whole cohere and reinforce each other. One contemporary interest that can be served with particular cogency by the anthropologist is ecology, a major topic in anthropology long before it attracted widespread popular attention. The strategic position of anthropology astride biological, social, and cultural parameters enables the presentation of the most synthetic view. The subject may also be approached from the vantage point of simpler societies, thereby showing interrelations with greater clarity and with less emotional involvement than within the framework of our own immediate problems.

But the general anthropology course conceived here does not stick at the primitive; it must take the initiative to deal with current realities in our own society. Of course, two entries have already been mentioned —the analysis of racism and the study of ecological problems. Beyond lie many other fascinating subjects appropriately anthropological: problems of individual will versus cultural determinism; whether there are laws of sociocultural development and, if so, how they may be discovered and tested; the relation of individual personality to culture, to cite a few. Off in other directions lie questions of the integration of culture and the meshing of different institutional systems. Beyond such questions lies the area of alternative forms of economic systems and their relation to other aspects of culture, such as technology and social relations. This leads also to speculation on the nature and evolution of stratified society and the state, which can bring in some of the fascinating data of archeology. Still further on are problems of the maintenance of classes in stratified society; how the internal management of such a structure pivots on concepts such as slavery, wage labor, and, basically, exploitation. Externally we must deal with colonialism and imperialism, treating these phenomena in the socialist camp as well as in the capitalist world, linking these in turn to racism once again, and to problems of urban development and urban blight.

If it is argued that too much is sketched here for a beginning course in anthropology I must answer in two ways. First, what I have just been summarizing is not a beginning course for those who will go on to take additional courses in anthropology. If some students, however, are attracted by what they encounter in such a course and wish to enter upon a more detailed and prolonged study of anthropology, they are to be made welcome. But the course is designed rather to acquaint the person who will never again take a formal course in anthropology, or perhaps even in social science, with a sweeping view of what the discipline provides. Here, too, I had better be absolutely candid. The course I envision does not expend its main energies on factual content, nor on the methodologies which comprise the professional core of anthropology. Rather the emphasis is on the great conclusions that are regarded by a consensus of professional anthropologists as representative of the present state of anthropological knowledge. These "conclusions," of course, represent an ongoing consensus and are subject to change with new evidence. Second, it is incumbent upon students to master a portion of the evidence on which these concepts are based, just as they must be made critically aware of the methods by which the data were amassed, analyzed, and synthesized. While the introductory course does not equip students as anthropologists, it should make them appreciative of what it takes to "do" anthropology properly.

In any case, anthropology taught in this fashion brings together and imparts an essential portion of the knowledge that must be shared by the citizens of this shrinking and destruction-prone contemporary world. Whatever may be added to it, I believe it furnishes a fairly solid core well described by the phrase "general education." Having done, then, with pieties, let me conclude this chapter by offering some empirical data on the content of general anthropology courses throughout the United States.

A survey of the teaching of anthropology in the United States involving many symposia and individual research projects took place in 1960–61. One aspect of the study analyzed the catalog listings in anthropology for 66 institutions, selected because they offered a major and a degree in anthropology. An earlier survey that omitted junior colleges had dipped into no fewer than 600 catalogs to discover that at least one course in anthropology was being given in 305 universities and colleges during the period 1948–50 (Vogelin 1950). By 1960 the number had greatly increased, but resources were not available for a detailed study. Of the 66 institutions surveyed, 37 had independent departments or programs of anthropology, 29 had combined departments (21 Sociology and Anthropology, 3 Anthropology and Sociology,

1 Anthropology and Geography, 1 Economics, Sociology, and Anthropology, and 1 History, Anthropology, and Sociology), and two had anthropology courses in the context of other departments. Forty-seven of these institutions offered a general introductory course in anthropology (Lasker, Pohorecky, and Klein 1963:8–10, 12, 15).

A casual leafing through catalogs gives the impression of a fair degree of diversity in the way introductory anthropology is handled. The schools that offer such courses sometimes (but not very often) try to do the whole thing in one semester. David Mandelbaum (1963:57), an experienced teacher, says flatly: "The introduction to anthropology cannot adequately be taught in less than an academic year . . . A three semester sequence . . . offers considerable advantage." At best such a course sequence requires tremendous labor of selection, cutting, and editing on the part of the instructor; condensed to a single semester, most anthropologists wonder if what remains has any value. On the other hand, there are ever-mounting demands on the student's time. How many nonmajors, even with the best motivation, will be able to accommodate a three-semester sequence? The other side of the problem is a Parkinsonian law telling us that the volume of trivia increases with the length of a course. Definition of the trivial will, of course, be hotly debated. The professor is sure that his students must know about *Australopithecus* and *Homo erectus*. What about *Zinjanthropus* and *Atlanthropus*? Shall the line be drawn at *Dryopithecus*, or shall it include *Ramapithecus, Sivapithecus, Kenyapithecus, Hylopithecus, Ankarapithecus, Griphopithecus,* and *Udabnopithecus* as well? Obviously the answer depends in part on the instructor's philosophy of teaching and learning and his concept of anthropology.

While diversity of specialized interests among anthropology teachers means that the forest will decompose into trees at different points, it is possible to specify (1) certain overall themes that can unify the introductory anthropology course no matter on what scale it is given and (2) certain more specific themes capable of nesting under the major themes while increasing the coherence of smaller segments of the course.

Two of the most overarching themes have already been mentioned, and others implied. The unity and diversity of man, physically and culturally, is an obvious cornerstone, as is evolution, again both physical and cultural. With these notions as a grid, various theoretical problems or approaches can be introduced. Does man make himself, or is he culturally as well as physically the helpless product of forces beyond his control? Are there laws of physical and cultural development? What interplay of biological and cultural factors accounts for male/female relationships as they have existed in the past and in the present? What light does anthropology throw on other major concerns of our time, such as the originating and perpetuating conditions of proliferating human population, pollution and environmental exhaustion, colonialism, imperialism, and exploitation, racism, sexual discrimination, and war? What are the prospects for the future?

Cora Du Bois advises that the essentials of an introductory course comprise the following: some knowledge of human paleontology and prehistory, a grasp of the concepts of human evolution and culture, and a sense of the grand sweep of human history. Equally important is a grasp of cultural relativism and the comparative variation of cultures, plus a feeling for culture systems as wholes, and for their structure and functioning (1963:28). Mandelbaum agrees with this but offers a pointed warning:

> The emphasis should be more on man than on anthropology, more on concepts than on factual tabulation, more on selected examples than on a complete representation of the disciplines, more on asking relevant questions and discovering pertinent answers than on listing technical terms. [1963: 52]

Students getting any less have every right to complain.

In recent years there has been a mounting demand among students in general for greater voice in the determination of the curriculum. Certainly, I can see considerable benefit from increasing student involvement in critical educational decisions. Yet, I would be less than candid if I did not admit that mine has long since become a professor's view. The major decision making with regard to the content of a general anthropology course seems to me an inescapable responsibility of the instructor on at least two grounds. First, it is the instructor who has been there, over the subject matter, and therefore is in the best position to make discriminations. This doesn't mean, of course, that students should not be consulted, urged to make suggestions, and encouraged to ask the kinds of questions that help direct the course as it unfolds. Such questions and suggestions can be solicited throughout the course and, combined with an opportunity for the students to criticize the course after they have completed it, offer excellent basis for anticipating the needs and requests of the next semester's students. Of course, the second reason for placing major decision-making power in the hands of the instructor (or committee of instructors) has to do with the strengths and weaknesses of the teacher's own training. This is a complex problem to which I will return after touching on a matter that affects the organization and teaching of introductory anthropology courses—the textbooks.

Students are unlikely ever to see many of the textbooks they are not using in any particular course; reading the one that is assigned may be traumatic enough. If students of anthropology did try a systematic comparison of texts, they might come up with a few surprises. For instance, despite the propensity of the instructor to introduce formidable controversy into everything he teaches—the age of man is one million, or two or three, or more; *Homo habilis* is/is not an australopithecine; pottery did/did not come to the Americas from Asia; law is/is not a cultural universal; and so on—most of the textbooks seem to be in agreement, particularly if published at about the same time. They also tend to be bland although seemingly assertive, often amusing the instructor who realizes that it is a consequence of the widespread tendency of textbook writers to average out differences in opinion wherever possible.

The available texts also display relatively low concern for some of the most relevant issues of the day as far as academic anthropology is concerned. Without going beyond the theoretical mandate of the discipline, it is possible for a textbook to raise with some degree of detail and specification certain of the problems that the present generation of students consider most pressing and significant; yet this is almost never done. Curiously, many anthropology texts, particularly those that identify themselves as introductory to cultural (or social) anthropology, have little or nothing to say about racism. Few have any words at all about sexual discrimination. Urban problems, particularly those of the inner city, are almost invariably left to advanced courses even for preliminary treatment, along with such subjects as colonialism and imperialism. Indeed, the notion that societies may be based on other than capitalistic economic systems seems not a proper one for consideration in introductory anthropology courses, except for treatment of primitive economics. Indeed, in introductory courses, the use of primitive culture material seems at least as often a technique of evasion of significant problems as a means of getting at problems. It is possible here merely to state programmatically that introductory courses can be constructed to include some discussion of such matters, although detailed treatment can continue to be reserved for the more advanced courses.

Textbooks for introductory anthropology courses tend to be of two kinds: those that make a real effort to present equivalently serious materials on the four fields, and those that neglect three of the fields to present the fourth. Particularly in the case of introductions to cultural (or social) anthropology, there are two differing editorial modes. One ignores physical anthropology, linguistics, and archeology altogether; the other makes a stab at offering a résumé, a few pages, rarely more than a chapter, to most of the contingent subdisciplines. Frequently linguistics is excepted from this, particularly where a certain theoretical view is held, usually in covert fashion, favoring the analysis of culture as a system of rules. Given such an approach, linguistic materials will be not merely included but emphasized.

The writing of a textbook is much like the teaching of a course, and is subject to similar problems. Although some current texts are the result of collaborative efforts, most are the work of a single anthropologist, perhaps two. Accordingly, the presentation is highly synthetic, particularly in the areas beyond the expertise of the writer or writers. In response, the instructor who chooses such a book often feels he must supplement it, and at that point he may have recourse to one of the many available "readers." What these volumes lack in coherence and smooth transition from subject to subject they often make up in the professional treatment accorded individual topics. Works of this sort make the actual creative production of the discipline part of every student's experience; although some of the articles are detailed beyond the interest and comprehension of the beginning student, he learns what goes into different parts of the discipline and can better appreciate what his textbook is trying to do. It is incumbent upon the instructor, however, to tell his students what he expects of them, perhaps by taking a sample of several readings and analyzing them.

Many instructors detest the notion of using a textbook, even when it can be extended by other readings. Before World War II, there were so few people studying anthropology in most institutions that the instructor could turn his students into the library without hesitation. Now, of course, even with the most assiduous use of the library reserve, it is usually possible to maintain adequate library resources only for advanced and research courses. Furthermore, and this may come as a surprise to some, I have found that the main pressures toward the selection of a single pivotal text come from the students. The motives are straightforward: however rambling the lecturer, the text is always there to hold and summarize the main ideas that any reasonable student can expect to find on the exams.

Now who are these instructors that pay little attention to their own texts when lecturing and, what's worse, when preparing their tests? The answer depends very much, to be sure, on where the course is given—in a major state university, in a private college, or points between. In some universities, as we all know, the individual student may never have the dubious pleasure of seeing his instructor in person; he may even have had to fight to get an unobstructed view of the television. If the course is given by an academic television star, it is likely that the role will go to a tenured member of the staff, probably a full professor, one who has been associated for years with the introductory course. For better or worse, I have never been involved in that kind of presentation. The things that I have heard about it make me somewhat suspicious about its efficacy, but I cannot be sure that what I have heard is correct or that my reaction is not biased in favor of the familiar and comfortable—a live class. I understand that the television preparation, because it emphasizes the formal and makes each individual presentation seem somehow larger than life, tends to become frozen; the same lecture is often given year after year, sometimes even via video tape. Some instructors, however, treat a live class the same way, even if they can't do it kinescopically. Furthermore, the lift in the formality of the medium can improve the level of presentation by increasing the amount of preparation, since some lecturers after a few years of experience lose whatever fear they may have had of facing the audience and proceed to lecture more and more off the cuff, with deteriorating results.

A little less remote is the professor seen across a great lecture room. Speaking into a microphone, he has fractionally more contact with his audience than has the television lecturer. Both are likely to be associated with a structure of recitation sections manned by teaching assistants. We brush by the many labor problems of the teaching assistants (number of hours of teaching per week, rate of pay, tuition costs and exemptions, choice of sections, and the like) to proceed to questions about their utility in such a course. From my limited experience as a teaching assistant many years ago, and from the point of view of a course instructor who has had the services of teaching assistants, I can say a number of good things. First, while better and worse systems exist for handling smaller discussion groups feeding into a large lecture course, the crucial element is the caliber and personality of the teaching assistants themselves. But there are institutional features that will attract good people and enhance their efforts, and none is more important than maintaining a reasonable load without mind-killing repetitions. Second, the institution must insure the interest of the teaching assistants by having regular means for them to play active roles in determining the nature and unfolding of the course and, where they wish, taking responsibility for some of the major lectures. For the graduate student nothing teaches so well as the responsibility of teaching. Beyond upgrading his control of the material, the teaching assistant may also gain from his teaching if his efforts are constructively criticized by the main instructor, by his peers, and also by the student audience. The value of such criticism is great. Almost nothing in the formal training of anthropologists equips them for teaching. The assumptions are implicit in the similarity of training from institution to institution: given the theoretical basis and enough data, seasoned by the field trip on which the thesis will be based, the graduate student will come to teaching in a "natural" way. Thus most people "trained" for teaching in this way will, often quite unconsciously, tend to emulate the instructors who most impressed them. Rigorous development of a teaching assistant program can be useful as a means of professionalizing the teaching of the discipline. It would be unrealistic to leave it at this, however, because any drive to tighten control over the teaching assistant runs counter to the prevailing ethic of teaching. In the social sciences and anthropology in particular, it is usually assumed that no one presumes on the privacy of the relationship between the instructor (or teaching assistant) and his class. (The story may be apocryphal, but it was told at Columbia when Dwight D. Eisenhower was president of the university that the General decided in the friendliest way to "drop in" on a few classes, thereby showing his interest in the educational process. When he entered such a class the instructor, who was talking, immediately stopped and left. It is said that the class stared at the president expectantly for a few moments until, ruddy-faced, Mr. Eisenhower quietly left, never to try it again.)

Students often request the most famous professors for the introductory course. Particularly when an institution includes both undergraduate and graduate courses, there is a feeling that the undergraduate classes are invidiously shunned by those who have already made their reputations and are taught by junior members who lack the power to have it otherwise. Despite that notion, there are some good reasons why those able to will avoid the general course. To begin with, it is a lot of work, even when much of it is delegated to teaching assistants or other assistants, such as readers for the exams. Assuming the integrity of the professor, there are even more compelling reasons for its avoidance. As already indicated, no one comes out of giving the introductory general anthropology course a recognized master of all the fields. Anthropology can no longer boast its "renaissance scholars," those who seemed as much at home in archeology as in physical anthropology, in linguistics as in cultural anthropology. Furthermore, the incoming students are often much better equipped than in the past. If, for example, part of the course is devoted to a survey of human genetics, some of the students are right there with the latest in biochemical theory, not to mention mathematical statistics. Being human, the (wise) professor may prefer to retreat within the defense perimeter of his specialty rather than expose himself to areas in which his knowledge is thin.

Yet to do so is to miss the beauty of the general introductory course. I think that the important thing is to catch the spirit of the fusion of the hard and the natural sciences with the social sciences and the humanities. There are problems in the teaching of introductory general anthropology, and one of them seems to be gaining a confident understanding with the class about the nature of the topic. Unfortunately, what should produce a tolerant attitude in both can lead to anxiety and hostility instead. To avoid this, the instructor in an introductory anthropology course must keep reasonable standards with regard to the students' control of the materials he is teaching. This is best done by avoiding the creation of an examination system which awards top grades for mastery of a strange vocabulary or even for the ability to retain specific information likely to be useful in a professional career in anthropology. The object of a good introductory course, even for those who will go on in the discipline, is not the same as for the more specialized course. All power to the larger theory! Let the details illustrate the larger points. To that end, the student who demonstrates partial control of the data, but can use what he knows to illuminate the theories he has learned, should be entitled to the maximum rewarding grade.

A final word on the teachers of introductory anthropology. I have learned that the better teachers of these courses are among those about to receive their doctorates, or who have just gotten them. These are people who are likely to regard teaching with a fresh eye and who should be able to project their own excitement. More heretically, among the best teachers of general introductory anthropology are some individuals who failed to get their doctor's degrees and probably never will complete them. Many want to specialize in something that no anthropology department recognizes as a major—general anthropology! Two main reasons for finding excellence in these teachers are their ability to keep their eyes on the main objective, the big messages of such a course, and their ability to confront the course with genuine and self-renewing enthusiasm. Even an old full professor who can display these two virtues might be encouraged to give the course.

THE UNDERGRADUATE MINOR

anthropology is . . . less subject matter
than a bond between subject matters
—Eric R. Wolf

My first reaction as author of this chapter is one of disbelief. Who would possibly want to read it? If no one reads it, then there is no reason to write it. On to the next chapter! Mind you, no one besides myself was responsible for putting it into the original outline; perhaps no one would object if it quietly dropped out. Yet, there is something to say—namely, that students in increasing numbers are electing to take courses beyond the general introduction, without going so far as to become majors. Such students need advice—something that may be novel enough to be useful, something that is not quite available in the catalog of the institution they happen to be attending. (What competition! Who reads the catalogs, except to get the numbers of the courses required or to be audited?)

The first problem applies to the nonanthropologist as he looks over the curriculum and tries to decide what features of anthropology may be relevant and interesting. However unlikely, the response is, sometimes, everything! (Of course, the Orwellian formula applies here: everything *is* germane, but some things are more germane than others. It is pleasant to contemplate the dilemma of the child in the well-stocked candy store, but the fact is inescapable that the child's appetite is not much more extensive than his budget, and his priorities are very low.)

For the student who has not made up his mind, advice about taking anthropology courses beyond the introduction can only be dada. (But one does not have to be an anthropologist to realize that the pressures on college freshmen and sophomores to make final career choices tells a great deal about our culture. Of course, most cultures have few or no career choices for their youth, and many of those that do, require that the choices be made even earlier than the ages between seventeen and twenty-one. The matter can be complex and serious. I have no intention of pursuing it further here; the larger sociocultural problem that it represents is seriously entangled in the more minor one that we face—advising about curricular options.) In many institutions the courses in anthropology are severely limited in number and content.

Choice may be so limited as to be meaningless. On the other hand, there is a growing number of institutions with proliferating course offerings in anthropology on the undergraduate level, not to mention the many universities that permit qualified undergraduates to take courses in the more extensive graduate list. It is also possible for students to increase their range of courses by attending summer sessions in colleges other than their own.

The greatest demand for anthropology courses among nonmajors usually comes from majors in the social sciences, particularly sociology. These students should consider four broad categories of courses: anthropological theory, anthropological methods, ethnography, and a residual category of miscellaneous courses of divergent content. Looking at these in turn, let us delay the question of priority.

All majors in sociology would profit from taking a systematic course in the history of anthropological theory. To be sure, some of the major figures are treated in both courses but the anthropological theory course will present them in a different light. The history of anthropology is also an excellent complement to the general introductory course, which I presume the student has already taken. The history course shows the interests comprising anthropology as they change through time, sometimes producing merely faddish results, while at other times following and developing deep and permanent currents. As already suggested in Chapter 2, the history of anthropology has its grim, distressing passages; approaching it without undue presentist apologetics or criticism, one can sort out the better ideas from the trash and see the beautiful dreams, even among failures. A decent model of self-critical but constructive historical analysis is surely a good thing to bring across disciplinary lines. Especially is this the case when the intellectual histories of even more remotely related fields show that they have gone through similar crises. For example, evolutionary and anti-evolutionary thrusts, and concern for grand theory versus concentration on small-scale problems, have tended to recur cyclically in the social sciences at large. There is also the problem of the association of the rise of anthropology and the florescence of European and American capitalism and imperialism. The question is applicable far beyond the realm of anthropology, and the student of history of anthropology could well apply the lessons learned there to the study of his own proper discipline.

It is less certain whether a sociology major would get enough out of a theory course dealing with concepts of culture to warrant adding it to a busy schedule. Although anthropologists are not always happy with the perfunctory way in which the culture concept may be handled in sociology courses, the combination of what is given in such courses plus what is readily available in paperback editions probably covers the ground as well as can be hoped. An exception would be the case of sociology majors who are intent on specializing in theory. Similarly, there are students outside both anthropology and sociology who stand to gain a great deal in the possible altering and broadening of perspectives as a consequence of taking the theory of culture course. I am thinking specifically of philosophy majors, who will get firsthand benefits from viewing close up some of the major epistemological assumptions and postulates of a discipline that straddles the hard and soft sciences. I think exposure to this course could be of great value also to students of psychology, both those who intend to specialize in human personality and intelligence, and those who will concentrate on animals other than man. The argument about the definition of culture, and its presence or absence in nonhominid populations, can perhaps stimulate psychologists to take fresh views of subjects they thought already squeezed dry.

More likely to be of permanent value to the developing sociologist is a course on social organization. Once again it can be noted that a portion of the subject matter of such a course can be expected to be included in some of the most basic sociology courses. Cross-cultural data on family structure and functioning, for example, is often included in introductory sociology courses, more specialized courses on marriage and the family, and in treatments of small groups. There is even a certain amount of treatment given such classical anthropological subjects as kinship systematics and terminology. Rarely, however, does one encounter the sociologist who deals with such materials as an anthropologist does.

Because the general course in social organization is usually taught at a level intermediate between the introductory courses and more advanced work, it has special value for the sociology student who wants a more detailed view of anthropology than he received in the introductory course. By the time he is done with it, however, even if he expects to minor in anthropology, he probably has few credits left to squander. If he takes the advice I will shortly elaborate on, namely to get some good ethnography, he will not have opportunity to take such usually enticing courses as those in economic anthropology, frequently called by titles such as "primitive economics," or "the economics of tribal society." As a matter of fact, under the older titles, few students not majoring in anthropology found any particular allure in the topics conjured up by such references. More recently, in response to events and pressures on campus and off, some course titles have been changed and perhaps even the courses themselves. One direction of change is an attempt to tie the institutional analysis of quite simple economies into problems of third-world economics, costs and results of colonialism, the economics of imperialism, or problems of economic evolution and the competition between economic systems. Another tack explores, from an anthropological viewpoint, the relations between economic institutions and other aspects of culture; this is now often done in the broadest possible ecological contexts, utilizing such concepts as "carrying capacity," and the terms of functionalist input-output theory. To my knowledge, such courses have never been very popular among students specializing in economics. Yet, it would be more sensible for economics students to take such courses during their upper undergraduate years rather than during their graduate study. I say this mainly because it seems that the more advanced such students become, the less latitude they have for either taking a maverick course or bucking the intellectual establishment in their major departments. There is certainly room for other attitudes toward simple economic systems or culturally diverse developing economic systems than patronization or neglect. Unfortunately, the incoming economics student will discover only the beginnings of a reasonably professional body of work, measured by the technical standards of disciplinary economics. To some extent he will be disappointed to find the work at a relatively low level, lacking quantified data and tools of rigorous analysis. Hopefully, the latter will constitute a challenge and lead to a better mix of anthropology and economics in the future.

Actually, the present outlook of academic and professional economists is none too secure. The rumblings of discontent with the kinds of analyses they favor are to be heard not merely outside their profession and in radical circles, but within the academy itself. Economist Sumner M. Rosen, for instance, notes, among other criticisms of his professional forebears and colleagues:

> Most of the other major issues of our time, some of them newly emerging and others familiar from the past, have not attracted the attention of many economists. The crises which this society and others are likely to face in future decades involve . . . perhaps most important of all—the long term relationship between "haves" and "have-nots," both within the society and in the world at large. On most of these, the economists have little to say, or when they speak, nothing of real significance or intellectual distinction. [1968:79]

I do not mean to suggest that taking an undergraduate course in economic anthropology will lead to a new birth of economic theory more in step with the real problems of our time. Nonetheless, it does present one possible way for future economists to break from what C. Wright Mills called "this abstracted empiricism," which, as Robert Engler says, "is divorced from any sense of social urgency and thus from sensitivity to the desperate needs of people" (1968:197). The economic anthropology course, if it does nothing else, raises the problem of assuming the applicability of essentially European concepts of scarcity and value to any and all cultures and societies, and that is a very good problem for fledgling economists to confront.

There are similar benefits for majors in government or political science who take a course in political anthropology. Unlike the situation in economics, however, there has been for some time a considerable degree of interest among political scientists in the cross-cultural data of the anthropologists. Indeed, it has become much more common for graduate students of political science to undertake field work in pursuit of their advanced degrees. This enhances to the greatest extent possible the importance of would-be political scientists undertaking anthropological work. An excellent plan is to get the political perspective of anthropology as an undergraduate, leaving more detailed work in method or in the conduct of field research for the graduate years, when it can be tied tightly to a specific emerging project in a particular locale. While still an undergraduate, however, the government major would probably find it of considerable use to take a course in culture and personality. This course appeals to a variety of nonanthropology majors and is discussed separately below.

Students who intend to major in history sometimes see a romantic appeal in an anthropology minor, but there are practical advantages as well. Within the disciplinary confines of history, particularly in recent years, there has been a mounting controversy about what history is. Mavericks like Staughton Lynd and Martin Duberman insist that conventional history writing is part and parcel of the propaganda apparatus of metropolitan cultures, playing a decisive role in the maintenance of oppressive systems. The question of the nature of "historical truth," however, is by no means a new one, though the range of discussion has widened in recent years. One part of the argument has concerned the sources of historical data, with contrasting evaluations being made of written and oral materials. There is, of course, an "oral history," and to some extent interview materials have been accepted in various professional circles in the discipline of history. Anthropologists have long relied on methods of oral history, and some historians look with favor on the application of the methods developed in anthropology to various tasks faced by historians.

There is a variety of courses likely to be of particular interest and advantage to the history major. Courses or seminars in ethnohistory or culture history are obviously attractive, as are area courses covering cultures implicated in the specialist designs of the student. Yet there is also great value in taking work in areas that may not lie directly athwart those designs. Just as the anthropology major profits greatly from obtaining as deep as possible a knowledge of conventional history, so the historian can gain fresh insight and perhaps even methodological stimulation from exposure to anthropology.

Returning to the sociology major interested in supplementing his program with a good sample of anthropology courses, I would urge him to take a course in anthropological field method if it is available but would counsel against taking anything in quantification or mathematical anthropology unless special conditions prevail. With regard to the field-work course, I may be making trouble. At some colleges such courses are primarily for the majors. A good field-work course requires a fairly intimate relationship between instructor and student and fairly close supervision as well. As a result, the class is usually kept to a small number and outsiders may be rejected. However, it frequently happens that sociology majors are given preference for whatever vacancies may be open when, indeed, special provisions are not made to recruit them into such a course. In any event, the well-run course in field methods usually requires some actual independent performance on the part of the student. One way of running such a course is described in the next chapter, which applies to the undergraduate major in anthropology. A last point concerns a particular use that can be made of this type of course by nonmajors. As I suggested earlier, one of the crucial personality factors that separates most anthropologists from other social scientists is the ability to sustain close personal relations in the pursuit of basic information. In the undergraduate field course a student has an opportunity to discover if he has what it takes to make a fieldworker. But a few warnings must immediately be given. It may come as a surprise, but I think that field-work courses given in our own cities expose students to some of the toughest problems of gaining entry and establishing rapport that exist anywhere in the world—and things are getting worse all over. Members of minority groups almost without exception are increasingly apprehensive. They don't want to be treated as objects of study, if for no other reason than that it violates their privacy for no visible return. A few years ago people tended to treat college students with formal respect, in accord with the conventional definition of the college student's social class status; today, however, that status has undergone great change, partly because it has become much more accessible, partly because the stereotypes with which the status is associated have shifted in the light of student happenings of recent and continuing vintage. At any rate, the student who wishes to study any group in his own society may have a considerably harder time "getting in" than one who travels abroad to achieve the same thing. More about these problems in the next chapter; here let me conclude by saying that the student who strikes it rich in access and rapport might well reconsider his future and wonder if cultural anthropology is not more his field than he thought.

Let me explain my earlier rejection, seemingly out of hand, of a course in mathematical anthropology or even statistical methods for anthropologists. Any college or university that sports a course in quantitative methods specially designed for anthropologists probably has similar courses for other social scientists, and sociologists in particular. There is no reason, then, for any but anthropology majors to take the special course occasionally found in anthropology departments. One exception occurs to me—the student who is primarily concerned with comparative methodology of the sciences including the social sciences, perhaps someone being trained in the philosophy of science, would profit by making a close observation of small differences in the approaches to quantification in the various fields. As for exposure to courses in mathematical anthropology, I can see real dangers in taking such courses without considerable previous work in nonmathematical anthropology. I will merely state and not argue the point here; I do believe that potentially extravagant social costs may be rendered as a bill after dehumanization of the subject matter of anthropology. There is no easier way of dehumanizing our lovely subject than by replacing the people who are the only known carriers of culture by formulas. While the formulas may be more easily inserted into the computer, the results may lead to further bending, stapling, and mutilating of human beings in the name of science, national security, or, probably, under joint auspices. Once again I deny that the intent is to divert science from its manifest destiny. It seems reasonable, however, to gain the assurance that the scholar has some ascendancy over the machine at least to the extent that he has more extensive knowledge of and rapport with the humans whose behavior is being computerized.[1]

If sociologists or any other social science majors not in anthropology want to go beyond the introductory course, I would urge them most strongly to take a course in ethnography. The kind of course I

[1] The reader who takes these remarks as an indication that the author leans to gothic fantasy spiced with a touch of science fiction should consider the evidence that the Advanced Research Projects Agency (ARPA, an agency of the United States Department of Defense) in 1967 had a number of so-called anthropologists on various projects in northern Thailand. When queried about this, one professional anthropologist stated that only two of the people so identified were "professionally trained anthropologists," the others were "recent A.B.'s in Physics or Public Administration, or are graduates of training programs in Systems Analysis. . . ." The anthropologist making the remark went on to wonder why systems analysis should be of any value in studies of the culture and society of northern Thailand. It has been suggested, however, that computer simulation and game simulation of political behavior in peasant villages is an important aspect of counterinsurgent work. Pacification statistics in Vietnam are compiled by computers. (See The Student Mobilizer 3:4 [2 April 1970]: 26–27.)

have in mind does not exist in all institutions, even those with fairly extensive anthropology offerings. The course—or seminar, since it is sometimes given that way with great success—would be one that deals with a single integral culture, trying to convey and project its main components. There are not too many cultures for which such an approach is possible. Theoretically it can be handled by an instructor with reasonably deep research experience in a culture, but few anthropologists who spend most of their time teaching have the kind of exposure to another culture that enables them to slip easily into the informant role. The alternative is to take a culture exhaustively described in the writing of one or more ethnographers, such as that of Tikopia or the Trobriands. Ideally, the students immerse themselves in the materials, understanding that the only way to achieve the desired effect is to read just about everything available on the subject. The idea, of course, is to try to acquire, albeit artificially and incompletely, the feel of another culture. When done well, the impression of such learning can last indefinitely, supplying its bearer with an added perspective against which to try the traps of viewpoint that assail everyone. This is of particular importance for the sociologist, who must constantly attempt to maintain a more or less objective eye, yet finds difficulty doing so amid an unrelieved stream of data, impressions, and personal involvements in the culture and society he is analyzing.

I realize that the actual courses to which the student may have access probably differ from the foregoing for practical reasons, if for no other. The likeliest ethnographic courses to be found are those that treat a culture area or set of culture areas, or deal with the culture and society of a great nation state such as China. It is sometimes difficult enough to find a course on the American Indian, not to speak of a course on one specific American Indian culture. As for the common "area course," it is to be hoped that the reading required for such a course includes at least one book-length monograph on a specific society and culture. If not, the serious student might well do such reading on his own, perhaps settling on the culture and the book after discussing the matter with his instructor.

Certain other courses are often available which merit the consideration of the nonmajor. Of broad interest, and usually well subscribed in consequence, is the course on psychological anthropology. Although a considerable degree of variation may be found as the result of varying "schools" in which the instructors of the course were trained, the student may expect to find certain material covered in any course given under this title. There is likely to be a critical analysis and evaluation of the concepts of culture and personality, and a logical sorting out of their possible relations. Something must be said about notions of modal or basic personality and cultural character, as well as the construct of national character. All of this will probably be transmitted in the context of a critical review of the methods by which the data were assembled and analyzed. Such a course can achieve significant results, not merely by tearing down specific invalid stereotypes, but by providing the student with a knowledge of proper methodological considerations which should enable him to survive what one commentator has already called "the nonsense explosion."

Sociologists in particular will also profit from taking whatever work they may find available in the anthropology department in the field of demography. There are now probably fewer than half a dozen anthropology departments offering such work, but the mounting demands for ecologically oriented courses may produce change within a few years. At any rate, two kinds of courses in anthropological demography will be of great interest, especially to sociology majors. The first of these deals with population size and processes in the prehistoric, preliterate, or predevelopment world. Through the skillful use of various kinds of data, plus ample speculation, some fascinating problems emerge in the critical points in population growth in past times, each associated with what we would now call an ecological crisis. The other type of demographic course takes a much shorter range look at its subject and inquires into the relations between family size and other aspects of culture, fertility and diet, and many other variables that govern on the lowest effective unit the dynamics of population growth. It is in courses such as this that cross-cultural attitudes toward the use of abortion or contraceptive devices are studied and compared; the advantage of having dealt with such material is considerable for those who expect to go on into specialized studies dealing with the population problems of our own society. There is also much here that will interest and be of value to the premedical student.

Speaking of the premed student, I must pause to express regret that in most institutions his program is so rigorously set out that he has little opportunity to take a variety of courses that would be of considerable advantage. Such would seem to be the case with the sort of course just mentioned, in which cross-cultural data are introduced concerning childbirth practices and early postnatal care, as well as problems of sterility and techniques for achieving abortion or contraception in the absence of modern medical and chemical technology. In broader terms, "medical anthropology can be used to investigate the process of human biological and cultural adaptation," as one medical anthropologist (Alland 1970:179) puts it. His concern is very much with problems of feedback—how somatic disease patterns arise in the interaction of organisms and environment, how therapeutic regimes cross biological and psychological boundaries, how ideas of health, disease, and cure span areas far beyond the merely "medical," involving social structure, religion, and other parts of culture. Oddly enough, the educational processes that most medical specialists pass through have little or no content such as this. Those who manage to get something of it on the undergraduate level will never regret it.

Misgivings were strong when I started this chapter. It does not seem reasonable to me that this message will be seen by those for whom it is intended. Why should premedical students read a book on the study of anthropology? Why should students who are more or less set on entering a career in one of the hard sciences? Yet the latter can also derive enjoyment and sometimes career-sharpening insights from taking certain courses in anthropology.

We have already said enough about the role of biology in anthropology to make clear the uses of certain anthropology courses to biology majors. For the most part, these courses will fall within physical anthropology, but some work in archeology as well as demography and medical anthropology would also be of considerable interest. The clearest advantages of familiarizing biologists with the anthropological view of essentially the same subject matter is put in the previously cited words of one anthropologist—that anthropology's main concern is with *human* biology rather than general biology, with *human* behavior rather than generalized animal behavior (Mandelbaum 1963:52). A physical anthropologist puts it this way: "Physical anthropology's one claim to a place in the sun is its ability to interpret biological variability in its cultural setting" (Hulse 1963:70).

The appeal that anthropology may have for geologists is on quite another basis. A geologist may become involved in anthropological problems with little intent to do so, particularly if his specialty is in Cenozoic geology or glaciology. Any suggestion such a geologist may make about dating the strata he encounters is likely to be of very great concern to the archeologists working in the area. Indeed, to some extent there is a certain degree of circularity involved, as geologists sometimes cite paleontologists as authorities for dating pronouncements, while the latter, in turn, may have recourse to archeologists who got their bearings from geologists in the first place. In any case, it is obvious that a reasonable feeling for the information and methods in the adjacent fields can be very useful.

When we consider what courses in anthropology can be of value to students pursuing major interests not already mentioned—mathematics, literature, physics, graphic and plastic arts, chemistry, hotel management, engineering, architecture (the mind boggles at the list)—we come around again to the question of anthropology in the program of general education. One anthropologist, who has made a special study of educational institutions and processes, sums it up this way.

> *Anthropology as the "study of man," . . . is admittedly a*
> *prime potential contributor to a good general education.*
> *While no claim is made here that anthropology should neces-*
> *sarily become the skeleton or the core of a complete "liberal*
> *arts" education at the secondary school or college level, it*
> *seems clear that no other existing discipline provides an in-*
> *tegration, however loose, of so much that is important con-*
> *cerning man and his manifold behaviors.   [Spindler 1955:6]*

Although anthropology has its share of hucksters and academic empire builders, it is not necessary to make claims for the discipline such as those used to sell religion, political parties, or detergents. Anthropology is not a panacea nor even a remedy for specific ills, whether of individuals or of societies. It is a developing field of knowledge that cuts across traditionally discrete academic spaces. In skilled hands it may be set to many socially constructive and intellectually rewarding purposes. In short, it may be studied for fun or profit. How can it not be part of the American Dream—and Education—Machine?

UNDERGRADUATE RESEARCH

Anthropological fieldworkers . . . have been defined as "otherwise intelligent and literate persons who do not accept the germ theory of disease."
—Elman R. Service

In usual circumstances, particularly when instruction is given to very large classes, the student in introductory anthropology has no opportunity to perform any research task whatsoever. Indeed, some instructors believe there is no place for research in an introductory course, even if given under ideal conditions. The argument, basically, is that the student lacks preparation for meaningful research and may be frustrated and demoralized if set to research tasks too early. On the other side, however, is the fact that some instructors have success at using research tasks as a medium of instruction, although admitting that it is very costly in time and effort, not only for the instructor but for the students who carry it out. There are also potentially harmful side effects, the previously mentioned frustration being only one such danger. More significantly, the main fear of initiating field research among inadequately prepared fledgling anthropologists reflects some concern for the population among whom they will carry out the research. This fear remains when advanced undergraduate majors are involved; indeed, it continues to exist beyond the terminal stages of graduate work.

Research is the deep study of some carefully delimited subject for the purpose of better understanding. In the case of a newly discovered object or phenomenon, the goal may be primarily descriptive and taxonomic. The subject is described in exhaustive detail and its place in the universe, its relationships and affinities, are established and confirmed. In physical anthropology, let us say particularly in human paleontology, a prime objective is to recover more and more fossil remains of early hominids and other extinct primates, to describe the precise finds quantitatively and qualitatively, and to use this data as far as possible to reconstruct what the creature probably looked like in life, to determine its line of descent and probable relationship, if any, to more recent and perhaps even living species, to establish as far as possible its habitat and how it fit into that habitat—in other words, how it lived.

Research is a continual activity and a restless, unsatisfied one. Theoretically, everything that is "known" is open to question; as research goes on, it can topple ideas that just moments before seemed to be solid and permanent parts of knowledge. Sometimes this occurs because discoveries slowly require restructuring of belief. Thus, the original finds of the australopithecines did not seriously trouble the concepts of human phylogeny then held, because those australopithecine fossils seemed very late, more recent than the *Homo erectus* materials recovered from Java (and, at the time, called *Pithecanthropus erectus*). When further discoveries were made, and when physical-chemical dating techniques indicated a far greater antiquity for the australopithecines than scientists had previously been willing to grant, it became absolutely necessary to revise the existing view of human evolution. Failure to do so would have drowned the entire field in ridiculous anomalies. (Fear of anomaly does not by any means work immediately to purge a scientific field of error. For quite some time it was fashionable procedure among human paleontologists to locate every single actually retrieved fossil to one side or the other, but definitely off man's actual family tree. Franz Weidenreich, a physical anthropologist who became famous for his work on the *Homo erectus* of Chouk'outien [formerly known as *Sinanthropus pekinensis*], denounced the practice, exclaiming contemptuously that it left man totally without ancestors.)

The excitement of discovering evidence of our ancient ancestors is usually reserved for a handful of highly skilled professionals, although the actual incidents of discovery are often serendipitous, involving people who do not realize what they have come upon. Be that as it may, discoveries of this type are not reasonable expectations in the line of student research, even under the most favorable conditions. It is not even possible, within the realm of anthropology, for the research-minded student to do a deep piece of ethnographic description or analysis, except under special conditions. What then can such students do in the way of research? What sorts of projects are feasible, given the evident restrictions on students' time, mobility, access to possibilities of original data collection, and the current demands for relevance? This chapter will attempt to offer some practical answers to these questions, always with specific reference to the circumstances and objectives of undergraduate students. The research problems of graduate students are addressed in Chapter 10.

The basic goal of science is explanation and prediction. The means of achieving this goal devolve ultimately into two kinds of functions. One is the collection of relevant phenomena; the second is the constructing, testing, and application of theory, which acts as the instrument whereby understanding of the phenomena is achieved and explanation and prediction take place. As philosophers of science point out, from Charles S. Peirce to Ernest Nagel, the link between observable materials (the data, the real world, what do you call it?) and theory is a domain of somewhat diverse composition comprising definitions and rules of procedure. Not wishing to bog down in a lengthy epistemological side trip, I will make our point of departure the two major constructs originally posed: data and theory. (For a better understanding of the intermediate realm of rules and definitions, with special reference to problems faced in anthropology, see Pelto 1970:Chapter 3.)

Without reliable descriptive data, scientific notions are insubstantial and without merit (although such notions may be appreciated as aesthetic creations). Indeed, without basis in some kind of empirical material such constructs are more easily subsumed and understood under the rubric of theology or of myth and legend, or perhaps nowadays, of political ideology. As for the truth of the data that have been collected, several problems are involved. Indeed, it is precisely in this realm that the noise level rises when compared with conditions in the natural sciences. As many commentators have pointed out, much information in the realm of natural science is the product of techniques of observation, measurement, and recording applied to regular and recurrent phenomena. While some phenomena in the realm of natural science are essentially ephemeral and nonrepetitive, and some phenomena in the realm of social science are regular and recurrent, the balance is such that the social sciences suffer by contrast. It is worth keeping in mind, however, that some critical subjects of natural science methodology are ephemeral and nonrepetitive at least insofar as dealing with them is concerned. For example, the transition from nonlife to life in the history of our planet is an event that was terminated long ago. Present attempts to reproduce similar situations under laboratory conditions are closer to simulations than actual re-creations. Even in this instance we can see that the laboratory simulation of a historic event in the area of natural science may come closer to actuality than most possibilities available to the social scientist. Consider, for example, the problem of simulating any great situation of cultural emergence, such as the appearance and development of culture itself, or the appearance and spread of domestication and agriculture, or the rise of the state. The only models of such situations that we can readily conceive are symbolic. Even the most plausible of real-life replications among these, the simulation of an emergence of culture situation among one or another contemporary nonhuman primate population, is bound to be much further from the mark than contemporary laboratory simulations attempting to synthesize simple living matter. For one thing, with reference to the latter, the simple basic chemicals involved can be more or less safely assumed to be identical to their counterparts existing billions of years ago, and the same thing can be said of the energy required to make the transitions. But the primates that made the transition to cultural behavior are gone beyond recall, as is the environment in which the transition occurred. Beyond recall, that is, of a physical nature, it is through the use of symbols that we attempt to replicate that species and that environment.

The concern displayed in the previous paragraph for careful rational control and evaluation of identities, analogues, and methods of comparison will be rejected by some students. This will be in line with what sociologist Robert Nisbet (1970:1) calls "the astonishing reversal of belief in the scientific, that is, the objective, the detached, the dispassionate character of the social sciences." I will get back to a discussion of this point of view and its implications later in this chapter, and again in Chapter 10. It seems important here simply to indicate awareness of the existence of this very troublesome theme. Even if we place it to one side, a variety of questions remains about the conduct of scientific, objective research, and some of these questions are very important to any consideration of research in anthropology on the undergraduate level. Let us examine three (setting aside a fourth, the question of political threats to objectivity): (1) the problem of establishing what is now usually referred to as *intersubjectivity*, (2) the problem of abstracting data from a usually undivided continuum, and (3) the problem of sources of information and sampling.

Intersubjectivity raises major problems in a realm that we promised to leave aside—that of definitions and operational rules for handling data comprising the linkage between data and theory. It is necessary, however, to say just a few things about this realm, because it will affect the student researcher's view of his specific project while simultaneously offering some students a reasonable goal as they carry out a piece of research. In short, research can be constructed to illuminate, for the person or persons who carry it out, the problems involved in the question of intersubjectivity and the nature of some solutions. Intersubjectivity relates to the problem of solipsism, the belief that knowledge arises in and reflects the individual ego. In its most extreme form, as presented for example in Mark Twain's somber tale *The Mysterious Stranger,* the "real world" dwindles to a projection of a single mind. In broader terms, however, solipsism stimulates questions about the transfer of information from one person to another. How can we be sure that red means the same thing to different people who use the word; perhaps in their own mind's eye they see different portions of the color spectrum when they use or hear the term *red*? The scientific answer to this riddle cuts the Gordian knot by *assuming* the independent existence of the outside world and goes on to specify as closely as possible the operations that are carried out in observing and recording that reality, so that others may use similar tools and techniques to see the reality in the same way.

Few anthropologists are concerned with these problems in the form that I have chosen, which is more to the liking of a philosopher of science. Anthropologists are concerned, however, with the question of *operationalizing* their research. This means that the operations performed in the course of research are specified as closely as possible so that any other comparable situation may be handled in a way that approaches total replication of the previous episode. But, as Pertti J. Pelto reminds us:

> *Operationalizing research procedures is not carried out simply for the edification and information of other scientists, however. The scientist tries for better and better research operations in order to generate more accurate observations, hence more effective theory building and testing. Specification of observations enhances his control of extraneous variables, increases the precision of basic measurements (or other types of observations), and provides the framework of information which permits the researcher to retrace his steps mentally in order to understand both predicted and unpredicted results.* [1970:49]

Apart from the substance of research, it is possible for an undergraduate class in anthropological research to focus on problems of operationalism and intersubjectivity. What is required is for two or more students to take a common research problem and collaborate in seminar fashion in discussions and criticisms of method while carrying out the actual research separately. For example, two or more students agree to focus on the religious services of a particular religious community and carry out independent (participant-) observation while repairing at regular intervals to a common seminar at which they discuss the methods they are employing. After an appropriate interval for accumulation of reasonable bodies of data, substantive comparisons are made, looking for deviations in descriptions and analysis. The focus of such a research course obviously remains on methodology and not on the substantive problems of the religious group being examined.

In my experience, one of the most difficult things faced by students undertaking their first anthropological research is abstracting data from an undivided stream of activity and impressions. The problem is much less acute in physical anthropology, archeology, and linguistics. Each of these fields works with phenomena that are more finite and, in a sense, more discontinuous than those faced in ethno-

graphic studies. In physical anthropology some data come in dissoci-
ated packets, fossil bones and teeth, or fragments of the same, being
conspicuous examples. Where phenomena are more continuous, as in
the case of living specimens, arbitrary points are selected for measurement or as the basis of comparison, with absolute assurance that the
points or organs or features concerned will be found in every specimen
unless special reasons prevail. Archeology, too, enjoys a fairly high
incidence of data discontinuity; indeed, most archeologists find troublesome the lacunae in their data, which are caused by differential preservation of various things through time. Often they speak of their envy
of the ethnographers who deal with the behavioral stream in all its
undivided glory. I think that is the point of archeologist Alfred Spaulding's remark, that

> it is archeologists who keep asserting that the present can be
> understood only through the past. . . . It seems that a discus-
> sion of the place of archeology within anthropology might
> better begin by reversing the dictum and asserting that the
> past can be understood only through the present. All studies
> of the . . . [archeologists] are successful insofar as there is a
> good stock of knowledge to apply to their relics and insofar
> as they are diligent in seeking out and applying this knowl-
> edge.   [1968:37]

Yet the matter is not left at that point by all concerned. Archeologists
receive a marked boost from at least one ethnographer, Bobby Jo
Williams, who contrasts his ethnographically derived data on the settlement pattern of the hunting and gathering Birhor of Bihar, India, with
the kinds of residential data usually recovered by archeologists:

> the archeologist has at his disposal data which in some ways
> are a more direct reflection of the culture of a people than
> are those of the ethnographer. I suggest this because the
> ethnographer returns with data which are largely weighted in
> the direction of verbal behavior only; retrospective historical
> accounts, informants' descriptions, explanations, and ration-
> alizations concerning their way of life. Some of this verbal
> material is after-the-fact discussion of ecologically influenced
> cultural regularity and may obscure as well as reveal certain
> relationships.   [1968:161]

The reasons so many ethnographers return with a preponderance
of material of verbally weighted behavior are not difficult to determine.
First, let me say with a straight face that the culture of anthropology
favors such an approach. To the extent that field work is taught, so is
this emphasis. But there is reason to believe that such an emphasis

would be regularly rediscovered if it were not taught. For one thing, it is a means of cutting through that undivided behavioral continuum that we have been speaking of. For another, there is the ethnographer's fear of not grasping the meaning of the activity he is so painstakingly studying. This is how the problem was put by Edward Sapir:

> Let anyone . . . try the experiment of making a painstaking report of the actions of a group of natives engaged in some form of activity, say religious, to which he has not the cultural key. If he is a skillful writer, he may succeed in giving a picturesque account of what he sees and hears, but the chance of his being able to give a relation of what happens in terms that would be intelligible and acceptable to the natives themselves are practically nil. He will be guilty of all manner of distortion. His emphasis will be constantly askew. He will find interesting what the natives take for granted . . . and he will utterly fail to observe the crucial turning points in the course of action that give formal significance to the whole in the minds of those who do possess the key to its understanding.   [1963:546–47]

The position expressed in Sapir's statement is of considerable significance in a current theoretical controversy about ethnographic field work. Sapir is calling for what we now speak of as an emic approach to the collection of field data. The emic approach derives from and depends upon "contrasts and discriminations significant, meaningful, real, accurate, or in some other fashion regarded as appropriate by the actors themselves" (Harris 1968:571). It contrasts with the etic approach, which depends "upon phenomenal distinctions judged appropriate by the community of scientific observers. Etic statements cannot be falsified if they do not conform to the actor's notion of what is significant, real, meaningful, or appropriate" (ibid.: 575). While conflict between emic and etic approaches is sometimes adduced, Harris has steadfastly asserted that the two approaches are complementary, each being applicable to different ranges of data. Problems occur, however, when researchers fail to distinguish between the approaches or confuse the data they return.

Here, then, is another focus that an undergraduate course in fieldwork research can be structured around. A common phenomenon can be tackled by two students, or two teams of students. One side approaches the subject etically (for instructions, see Harris 1964); the other side works emically. Conferences reveal the strengths and weaknesses of the two approaches, appropriateness and inappropriateness, and prepare students for an informed choice of methods at later stages of their careers.

We began this section by noting the problem of abstracting from a complex continuum. This is a crucial problem for any researcher, and there is no single sure solution. One thing seems apparent from the anthropological work done thus far: the problem orientations of one particular historical period are usually not those of other periods. Another fact is at least equally clear: there is no such entity as a theoretically unbiased work. Even those ethnographies that purport to be unvarnished collections of whole cultures are forced, by the physical impossibility of transcribing the entire content of even the simplest culture known, to adopt some more or less arbitrary procedures of abstraction. As we have seen, the most common one occurs as a product of the social organization of field research—the ethnographer turns to a small, selected range of informants and attempts to derive from their verbal responses a model of the culture which is being studied.

Other ethnographers attempt to break the tyranny of the undivided behavioral continuum by taking a "problem" into the culture to be studied. This is usually phrased as a hypothesis and, as such, frequently relates to a specific cultural rubric or the interaction between two or more delimited rubrics. An example of the former would be an investigation into the caloric productivity of swiddenage (swiddenage is the use of cleared or recleared land for agriculture, previously used lands being permitted to return to forest growth). The hypothesis might be phrased in a variety of ways; one possibility is to predict the time when secondary forest will be recleared, i.e., after five years, ten years, twelve years, and so on. A number of variables operate to make more or less regular the decision to clear a patch of secondary forest (for example, population pressure on arable land resources, the fertility of burned-over forest land at different stages of regeneration of the forest cover, the progressive difficulty of cutting down trees as they age and thicken, or the difficulty of moving a house or a whole village). Hypotheses may be of even more complex nature when additional variables are taken into consideration, such as the relation between cultivation cycles and religious and ceremonial cycles, or the requirements of peace and war, or the economics of ownership and distribution. In any case, such problem-oriented research furnishes built-in means of breaking an otherwise undivided behavioral continuum into manageable segments. Unfortunately, the divisions made to satisfy such problem orientations may be of little interest or value to other problem-oriented approaches. While this is one means of keeping the specter of technological unemployment from ethnography, it also interferes with the synthesis of a total approach to the subject culture. This is a particular difficulty with regard to many cultures on the verge of extinction as they are overrun by modern industrial civilization, not to mention those that have already disappeared.

Once again our consideration of problems inherent in ethno-graphic field work has outrun the probabilities of involvement of the undergraduate anthropological field researcher. But the big question is there, quite clearly. How is the undergraduate to realize and begin to train for confrontation with such problems in the context of those that he can attack closer to home? Before turning to this particular ques-tion, let us note that one accomplishment is to command the techniques of accurate procedure that must apply to any competently handled research.

Unfortunately, students may sometimes display marked repug-nance and hostility to the focusing of the field-work class on research methodology. Unless the subject is properly introduced, and unless proper reinforcements are provided along the way, the purpose of such focusing becomes obscured and the charge of intellectual sterility or irrelevance is raised. The danger is a very simple but terribly real one — the tendency to confuse the goals of the methodological course with those of the field or even the discipline at large. The entire subject falls under the heading of what C. Wright Mills called "abstracted empiri-cism," the seizure upon one stage in the process of scientific work, upon the gathering of concrete data, to the exclusion of other tasks (cf. Mills, 1961:50–75). Political scientist Robert Engler glosses the concept of abstracted empiricism in this manner:

> This "abstracted empiricism" . . . is divorced from any deep sense of social urgency and thus from sensitivity to the des-perate needs of people. . . . Some [sociologists] have become staff members and researchers for the modern welfare bu-reaucracies, liberal and reformist in origins and now con-servative and often antihuman in function. Their clinical approach, sometimes a defense against the unanticipated and relentless grimness of what they experience, when combined with a deeply built-in class bias, helps to set them almost hopelessly apart from their clients. . . .
>
> . . . Meanwhile, sociologists continue to teach the skills and grace necessary for successful living in a bureaucratic world. Or they theorize on an abstract level divorced from all reality. Few questions are asked about the alternatives to the social disciplines now operative in our industrial econ-omy. [1968:197–98]

As portrayed by Engler, the consequence is bound to be of concern to a sensitive student:

> Professors are experts who teach techniques, whether in economics, sociology, politics, or the behavioral sciences. Research is elevated as the ultimate goal. Amply footnoted

> *platitudes elucidate the obvious. Isolated events are magni-*
> *fied out of all proportion to their value. . . . Measuring the*
> *measurable rather than asking fundamental questions of*
> *content, value, and alternative, becomes the road to a vigor-*
> *ous ordering of evidence.* [*Ibid.:193–94*]

Before taking up this indictment, at least one more thing must be added to it. Earlier I referred to the witty criticisms that have been leveled against anthropological researchers by writers such as Vine Deloria, Jr. There is not only the matter of American Indians who object to being made the subject of studies and investigations, which have no payoff as far as they are personally concerned. There is also the matter of being treated like a subject of scrutiny, which is becoming a cause for resentment among more and more previously accessible people. Some of these attitudes have already fed back to students, increasing their reluctance to try out field work that requires approaching people of exotic sociocultural background.

If we return now to the first criticism, pertaining to "abstracted empiricism," a number of positive things can be said. The research stance per se is both politically and morally neutral. Not that it does not have consequences, but in and of itself it is amoral and apolitical, much like the automobile, or the intellectual procedures that have brought so much technical and scientific advance. Admitting that any of these things can be employed for antisocial purposes, for destructive ends, is not to deny that they can also be used to create what most people would consider extraordinary benefits. The potential benefits of scientific research applied to social ends are various; none is more important, however, than the matching of ends to means in the planning of the economy, a state that has yet to be achieved anywhere on earth but a goal that is pursued in a number of social systems. Regardless of the social system in which research is pursued, research can have salubrious payoffs only if conducted in as objective a fashion as possible. I would offer as supporting evidence the social disaster in the People's Republic of China known as the Great Leap Forward. Although there is no place here to document my case, I think there is evidence to show that one of the prime reasons for the campaign's failure to increase both agricultural and industrial production by considerable margins was the absence of reliable information of the most basic sort concerning such things as the demographic statistics of China, the distribution of labor force and consumer needs, and an appreciation of levels of skill and attitudinal orientations of the masses of Chinese peasants and workers. In place of real information, I believe, the government was fed what lower echelons believed the bosses wanted to hear—not very different from the position of more than one President of the United States regarding entrapment in the Indochinese war. The concept of research as the handmaiden of particular political regimes is not restricted to any particular regime. Everyone does it; everyone pays the penalties. Although strongly phrased, another remark of Nisbet, the previously quoted sociologist (1970:2), may be quite appropriate. Considering "the revolt against objectivity" in social science research, he concludes that those who pursue it have "a rendezvous with suicide." Unfortunately, Professor Nisbet finds the main locus of the negation of objectivity in the American left. I agree that the malady is sometimes displayed there in a fairly advanced form, but it also appears elsewhere, conspicuously on the right, and is much more widely distributed than he seems to know.

Against this background, let us return to the problem of undergraduate research in anthropology. I long ago relinquished the notion that one can convince everyone of the advisability of any particular course of action or the validity of any particular interpretation. As a result, I say to undergraduate students of anthropology that it is worthwhile to learn how to carry out more or less objective sociocultural research. Furthermore, I think enough has been said already to justify the notion that courses in which methodology and technique are taught do not have to be simultaneously avant-garde with respect to subject matter. In fact, there is basis for contending that subjects of current controversy might better be rejected for a methodological course on the ground that pursuit of controversial matters might distort and complicate the prime intention of the course, which is to concentrate on method and technique and not upon a vital substantive issue. After all, the test, whether political, moral, or merely scientific, is not whether one or more students come out "properly" on some current issue of our time, but whether these students are properly prepared to supply the information, the theory, or the testing that their mature work will require. This may be construed as the worst kind of mechanical professionalism—precisely the thing that so many students are currently protesting, and the sort of activity that Robert S. Lynd characterized so contemptuously: "Research without an actively selected point of view becomes the ditty bag of an idiot, filled with bits of pebbles, straws, feathers, and other random hoardings" (Lynd 1939:183). Let me speak to the paradox.

I cannot agree with the assumption that one course, the research course, has to bear the main weight of achieving relevance, or that all courses have to be unified behind a single purpose and philosophy. Where the latter course has been attempted, as in the People's Republic of China, great difficulties have resulted. At the same time, the unification of the formal learning process behind single-minded support of Mao Tsetung Thought has been an instrument of the destruction of the intellectuals. It is not difficult for me to repudiate such tyranny. As for burdening the course devoted to teaching the essentials of research method with a heavy moral and political freight, such a procedure strikes me as inefficient at best, and all too likely to be destructive of scientific method. There is a wider curriculum, after all, and the student is expected to synthesize his own view of the goals of professional and personal life.

Admittedly, this is a simplistic statement of a profound and critical matter. I am aware, and have tried to reflect, that much of the structure of all education, including higher education in the United States, is part of a vast process of indoctrination and more or less subtle coercion. Within the spectrum of real educational procedures are some that approach more closely than others the state of intellectual inquiry and expression that I would designate, given my liberal bourgeois bias, as "free." In my order of priorities, such kinds of inquiry and expression are valued very highly, but not entirely for themselves. I believe that the achievement of most of the socially relevant goals, not the least those declared in the socialist camp, depends to a much greater extent than usually realized upon the preservation and expansion of free intellectual inquiry and expression. Conversely, I believe that contraction of these freedoms will be found to be causally linked with increased repression in other areas and with a deepening failure of attempts to solve the social problems that concern us all.

Let us now take up specific questions concerning research in anthropology at the undergraduate level. Before offering a brief overview of some of the possibilities in physical anthropology, archeology, and linguistics, there is one obvious but important point to mention. Research can comprise the pursuit of new data, the attempt to criticize or reorder one or more theoretical statements, or a combination of both. The gathering of data is often thought of in terms of field trips and field work. It is a romantic notion, as well as a sound scientific practice, but it falls far short of exhausting the category of original research. It is quite possible to do extensive original research at home, as Robert and Helen Lynd so brilliantly showed in their study and restudy of Muncie, Indiana (1929; 1937). The introduction to the first of those volumes, *Middletown: A Study in Contemporary American Culture,* was contributed by Clark Wissler, then curator of anthropology at the American Museum of Natural History and renowned for his scholarship on American Indians; he placed works like *Middletown* securely in the mainstream of ethnography. Actually, the Lynds' work, excellent as it is, was not the first to apply community study method to a modern city. Neither was it the last. We now have a fairly extensive literature pertaining to the United States as well as to the rest of the urban industrial world and comprising similar applications of both social survey and community study techniques.[1]

Original data do not have to be limited to materials brought back from field observations and interviews; they can also comprise documentary materials. In most cases such written sources of data are what are called *primary sources,* referring to original documents of record of various kinds: deeds to land, legal papers and transcripts, communiques, original letters, ledgers, surveyors' maps, and eyewitness accounts. Most of the documentary material that students, undergraduates in particular, come into association with, are *secondary sources,* which is to say syntheses based upon some previous culling of primary materials. Indeed, most of the books read in colleges and universities are even more remote from original data than this and could be called tertiary, quaternary, or even beyond. It is precisely because most of the material available to students is so remote from primary sources that the matter is worth bringing up. Students frequently submit as "research" papers that simply repeat the most available synopses from the most available books on the subject they are pursuing. Subsequently, such students are hurt and outraged when the instructor returns the paper with a low grade. Students sometimes take the position that a paper deserves the optimum grade if it does not contain factual errors. Further, it is felt that such errors are unlikely if the paper was based on many seemingly highly regarded books. Viewed that way, the main point of a research paper is missed or distorted. It is possible to conduct research on the basis of written materials alone, but the job requires some penetration in depth as well as broad coverage of the synthetic works on the subject. Thus, the student begins to perform research functions when he follows an author's work (or a small portion of that work) to its sources as revealed in the author's footnotes and bibliography. At the same time, the student should be looking for the critical reviews that were published about the book, or, if it is an article he is examining, he must try to find out if it struck some response which would usually appear in a later issue of the same journal, or might be revealed in one or another bibliographical index (see Chapter 7).

Many undergraduate anthropology majors of my acquaintance over the years have arrived at that status somewhat fed up with writing conventional papers based on data they get out of other people's books. They want to try something original, getting data that did not exist as such until they put it down. I will turn to the problems that this creates in cultural anthropology in just a moment, after a brief consideration of

[1] *Very briefly, the social survey technique is distinguished by its reliance on questionnaires and similar censuslike protocols, whereas the community study is much closer to the usual anthropological study-in-depth of a place and its population.*

the state of affairs in physical anthropology, archeology, and linguistics.

Physical anthropology presents an interesting case. I originally attempted to begin this paragraph by saying that because physical anthropology is taught, at least in part, through the use of laboratory sessions, it has not been much given to requiring individual student research. Rereading that statement several times, I finally realized that I disagreed with it so completely that it had to go. The fact is that physical anthropology is rarely taught to undergraduates in terms of laboratory sessions. Indeed, there are not too many schools in the United States where a real concentration of courses in physical anthropology is given even on the graduate level; hence there are pitifully few where undergraduates attracted to the subject can pursue it. Even where physical anthropology is taught at some depth on the graduate level, laboratory facilities tend to be in short supply. While it is true that matching funds from government grants have helped some departments create or enlarge such facilities, they still are scarce enough so that laboratory courses in physical anthropology remain relatively rare. This is unfortunate, because a number of highly interesting problems are best developed through laboratory work. For example, physical anthropologist J. S. Weiner of the London School of Hygiene and Tropical Medicine set out a list of exercises comprising fifteen sessions for an undergraduate course in physical anthropology given at Oxford in the Department of Anatomy. The sessions fell into five main categories under the general heading "Methods of Studying Morphological and Constitutional Variation in Man": evolutionary variation, age and sex determination, body form and composition, integumentary features, and statistical treatment of biometric data (Weiner 1958).

It really doesn't require great laboratory facilities to carry out simpler forms of somatic research. I am not referring to serological studies or refined problems of anatomical structure. I am referring to comparative measurements, growth studies, and the like. Such work can be undertaken on modest scope, using an accurate set of scales, tape measures, rulers, calipers, and similar tools. Samples can be obtained at school or outside. For those interested in problems that are relevant, comparative measurement studies can be undertaken involving members of different ethnic groups, different socioeconomic classes, different subcultures. In some instances diachronic contrasts are afforded by data found in published articles, in university medical offices, in departments of health; even where such contrasts are not currently available, the student may be happy to know that he has deposited raw data that can be used for similar purposes twenty-five or one hundred years later.

The students in archeology are much more fortunate in having a number of good opportunities for supervised research. Some schools have regular courses in archeological field work, often with Saturday or weekend sessions at an actual site somewhere in the locality or within reasonable automobile distance. Should such opportunities be lacking, there are a number of summer schools that specialize in providing a directed field archeology course, usually at a rich site that has been yielding data for years. Such on-the-site courses are not open to everyone; usually they are looking for serious students who have adequate preparation. Worse, they may be discriminatory, refusing qualified women (Carroll 1970).

There is no substitute for the opportunity to engage in dirt archeology. Many of the things that have to be learned are best acquired by actual experience: seeing how the site is detected, following the test trenching operations, participating in the fine work of artifact removal, identifying the geological strata in which the finds are made, gridding and mapping, determining if the specimen is suitable for radiocarbon or other physical-chemical dating, and the multitudinous other details that must be painstakingly handled. In the absence of such opportunities, there still are things to do. The fact is, of course, that field work takes up only a small part of even the most active archeologist's time. Apart from teaching (if he is at a university), the major activity usually entails assembling, cleaning, identifying, dating, classifying, labeling, and perhaps reconstructing the objects already retrieved. Find an archeologist and usually you will find someone who needs help carrying out precisely these tasks. Of course, he won't let just anyone get his hands on his precious artifacts, but someone majoring in anthropology who wants to learn what goes on in different fields and branches is likely to be made welcome. (I presented myself to Clark Wissler at the American Museum of Natural History in 1940 and he passed me along to an old archeologist, Nels Nelson. Dr. Nelson had me repairing old pottery from the Southwest before I knew it. I wasn't paid for it, but I still remember with warmth and pride the Saturdays I put in there.)

One last concern regarding archeological research. It is difficult to see how it fits into the concept of relevance as we have discussed it so far. I refer explicitly to the archeological research that can be participated in by undergraduates in the United States. The sites available to them will yield, at best, postcontact evidence of the Atlantic civilization, and precontact evidence of Indian occupation. Since we already know that everything in sight "belonged" to the Indians before the advent on the continent of the Europeans, and since we know how miserably unfair were those relations between Indians and Europeans, little if anything can be added to the story by archeology. Yet, elsewhere in the world archeology has played a political as well as educational role. In China, for example, archeology has played a great role in reinforcing the Chinese belief in the value and glory of their own culture and civilization. What is more, national pride swelled with discoveries of ancient pre-sapiens hominids, such as the *Homo erectus* of Chouk'outien. The present government has enlarged on the previous government's efforts with respect to old sinanthropus; there is now a museum and monument dedicated to "Peking Man" at Chouk'outien. Archeology in China is directed not only at reclaiming those parts of Chinese history that preceded written records but also at enriching knowledge of fully historic periods. The effort is national, and the data recovered are considered the property of all Chinese. At various times during the past twenty or so years, the government has pressured the academic archeologists to involve ordinary citizens—peasants, for the most part—in their digs and interpretations. It may be that revolutionary enthusiasm ruined some sites; in any event the policy does seem to have been abandoned, although it might have flared again in the Cultural Revolution. It does give us pause, however, and we might well ponder strategies for creating broader popular interest in the lively subject of archeology, albeit not at the expense of destroying actual sites merely to involve a united front.

If a relevant archeology seems an unlikely development on the undergraduate front, projects in linguistic research at all levels are rich in possibilities of relevance. Before addressing that subject, however, let it be noted that on the one hand linguists have perhaps the easiest access to field work, while on the other they have probably the most precise and formally stated methods of procedure in capturing living data. It follows from the latter point that the student should be reasonably well drilled in those formal techniques before he sets out into the field, even if the "field" is a social club to which he himself belongs, and the problem is the detection of linguistic peculiarities among its members.

Anthropological linguist Dell Hymes has summarized the "prime questions" forming linguistic research: "How to collect verbal data accurately? How to organize it usefully? How to find out meanings?" (1963:291). Hymes' discussion of these three disarmingly simple propositions makes it clear that fully professional results are unlikely except from very extensively trained individuals, but smaller and quite original contributions certainly lie at hand for people at earlier stages of training. Thus the accurate taking of texts and some of the simpler analytical steps can probably be done quite well. As Hymes says:

> The anthropologist should know that for his field work
> needs, success in the gathering stage may suffice, and so he
> need not be inhibited into linguistic inactivity by uncertain-
> ties which properly pertain to collation. That is, if he dis-

*covers that /p/ and /b/ contrast initially in such forms as
/pil/:/bil/, but there is not a contrast among labial stops after
initial /s/- in a form such as /spil/, then he can make an adequate record. He need not decide definitively whether the
second unit in /spil/ is to be interpreted as /p/, /b/, an archi-
phoneme /P/, or part of the intersection of a voicing-irrele-
vant sequence /SP/ and a voiceless component.   [Ibid.:292]*

The student who understands what Hymes is saying in that paragraph
can, I presume, do some effective linguistic field work; others should
consider getting more training before they try.

Students who demand that their own research be relevant in the
terms already indicated, and who wish to carry out that research in the
context of linguistics, can easily find problems and projects to interest
them. Here, just to start things off, are a few interrelated suggestions,
such as a project in sociolinguistics, perhaps concentrating on linguistic
differences developing along class, ethnic, or other subcultural lines
within a single society. Some examples are furnished by the analysis of
the languages that grow in ghettos, ethnic enclaves, even in industries
and professions. Likely to be of greatest interest at present is the question of communications gaps that separate teachers and pupils in ghetto
schools and that are based in dialectical differences between the two
parties and in the certainty of some teachers that they are speaking *correctly* while the child is speaking *incorrectly*. Seemingly easy, however,
research on such a topic can be exceptionally difficult, not merely from
the point of view of technical linguistics, but in terms of the sociological
mise-en-scène and, what is more, of the difficulty of obtaining access to
the situation itself.

Difficulties of access and rapport apply eminently to the field
researches of cultural anthropology. Before turning to that subject,
however, a few words about nonfield research in undergraduate anthropology are in order. First and most obvious is the fact that beyond the
introductory course, instructors usually place heavy reliance upon having the students write papers, although there is considerable erosion of
this in places where mass enrollments continue into the intermediate
and advanced courses. There are institutions so pressed in terms of
faculty–student ratios that the writing of papers is confined, with only
occasional exceptions, to honors courses and senior seminars with restricted registration. In any event, except for unusual circumstances, I
assume that the anthropology major has some opportunity along the
road to write at least one "research paper."[2]

2 *Students seriously intending to go on to graduate school must create
opportunities to write papers even if none are presented by instructors.
It is absolutely essential to do a reasonable number of papers in order*

Speaking for myself, one of the discouragements associated with receiving student papers has to do with the commonly encountered tendency to take on the broadest and most horrendous problems in the context of a relatively brief essay. While I have never been handed a ten-page paper called "The Motive Force of Cultural Evolution from the Lower Paleolithic to the First Nuclear Explosion," I will not be surprised when I am. (Certainly not after this is in print!) I think most instructors would probably react like me to such a topic—with dread, fully anticipating a rehash of the most commonplace ideas. It is not really the rehash that is the focus of objection; it is the loss of hope of detecting anything fresh, anything representing the input of the individual writing the paper, that deadens. Consider, as an alternative, the careful reading of a couple of ethnographic monographs followed by a critical contrast of some aspects presented by these works. For example, if the authors worked at very different times, say thirty or fifty or more years apart, the essay might well turn on differences in approach having to do with the different periods represented by the authors, plus some observations on the effects of the passage of time on the subject culture. Focusing the paper this way gives the student a much greater opportunity to contribute fresh insights and give more of his own than in the more conventional approach—the paper that takes two or three monographs, whether from the same or different culture areas, and shows how different life is in these different societies. Sometimes the paper concentrates on a specific cultural topic, the family, religion, leadership and decision making, and so on. (You can guess for what courses such papers are submitted.) There is no question that the compilation of such papers is an exercise with certain heuristic value, but they run the pedagogical risk of boring the student, as well as the instructor, to death. In any case they present practically no creative possibilities, although it is a useful means of fixing a certain amount of ethnographic information in the mind.

The reader who concludes from the foregoing that anthropology instructors are hostile to big ideas is missing the point. It is very difficult to write meaningful essays about large, panoramic subjects, but if the

---

to get practice and to obtain criticism, thereby preparing oneself for the more rigorous essay-writing demands of graduate school. What is more, many graduate schools request submission of one or more of the applicant's undergraduate papers to give some idea of the caliber of work already achieved by the applicant. If papers are not requested on the undergraduate level, the serious anthropology major should approach instructors and request that they read and criticize a paper to be written for the course they have in common. Unfortunately, such a request may occasionally be rejected, but the likelihood is probably greater that it will fall on a sympathetic ear.

student has good reason to select such a subject, most instructors are probably ready to see what can be done with it. I write this with my mind on the question of relevance. A student may wish, for example, to discuss the problem of the evolution of culture in the face of colonialism or in the context of modern imperialism. Fine. But he should beware of turning in a paper that paraphrases Fanon or Ché or Lenin and remains simply another version of the old rehash already criticized. Just as many instructors may display an arrogant attitude toward students, assuming their knowledge and interests to be limited where they are not, so students commit similar offenses against their professors, assuming that they are totally unaware of the real political world around them. This does not deny the real existence of either; there are naïve students and hopelessly disengaged professors, but the a priori assumption that one is talking to either of these is, at the least, a tactical blunder. Thus, the student who would like to write a paper placing some particular culture in modern economic and political perspective is welcome to try it. He should be aware that his paper will be no better than the data it musters, that sloganeering will be more likely to turn the reader off than on. There is another alternative, however, and it falls within the reach of those willing to put out to achieve it. Take a particular ethnographic monograph pertaining to an area for which additional sources of data are available, and contrast the local view presented in the ethnography with larger-scale political and economic data derived from other sources. For example, take some ethnography relating to West Africa in the 1930's and dig up the political and economic data of the same area, preferably relating to the time of study. (Extrapolations are easier but infinitely more dangerous.) Contrast the pictures offered by the two sets of data and comment on the awareness or lack of it displayed by the ethnographer. Such a study is more likely to find a receptive professorial audience than one of the more cut-and-dried topics mentioned above.

There is really quite a lot that can be done by the serious undergraduate student in the way of nonfield research, provided that he has access to fairly extensive library resources. At a minimum, it is possible to bring into juxtaposition the works of historians, literary figures, politicians, political scientists, journalists, and anthropologists. What happens after this depends on the material and on the interests of the analyst. Do the field anthropologists display currents of racism manifest in the others? Does one group seem more objective in its treatment than the others? What is the nature of the "objectivity"? How have different commentators influenced each other? How have all the commentators been influenced by the same factors, however unconsciously? Where library resources are more extensive, it may be possible to get closer to the archival level, or find access to original newspaper accounts, perhaps through microfilm.

Most anthropology majors, no matter how successful at writing papers based on library materials, chafe to do a piece of field work. In several anthropological cultures there is great pressure to do so; the United States is one of these. There is a *mystique* which surrounds field work, but it should not be allowed to obscure two facts. First, there have been and are now some anthropologists of considerable or even great ability who never did real field work. The list includes such names as Edward Tylor, Émile Durkheim, Marcel Mauss, and Ruth Benedict. Second, many anthropologists who have gone on to do significant field work did not do so until after they completed their doctorates. Still, the feeling is widespread that field work *makes* the anthropologist. There are several reasons for this.

Just a few days before writing this, I was visited by a young anthropologist who was returning to France after more than a year of field work in the Solomon Islands. An Italian who gravitated into anthropology after some time as a radical journalist, he was happy to be returning to Nanterre, where he would be writing up his field materials as his dissertation. At lunch with some Columbia anthropologists, he expressed chagrin over aspects of his field experience and confronted the table with a hostile question: Why should anthropologists do field work?

Although his question was a complex one, involving many levels of response, it soon became clear that a major point of irritation was the widespread anthropological attitude toward field work which regards it as a kind of rite of passage, a favorite anthropological topic. Rites of passage, of course, have in common certain features. They mark major status transitions, none more important than that between childhood or adolescence and adulthood. They usually involve the humiliation, inconvenience, and physical discomfort of the one making the transition. They can be sadistic and painful; sometimes a portion of those attempting to make the transition die, although that is rare. The young anthropologist returning from the Solomons displayed a remarkable bitterness, questioning the belief in the efficacy of field work as the indicator that a student has become an anthropologist. Like most of those who have gone through initiation and regard a younger initiate, we who faced him around the table felt menaced by his accusatory question. We were united by our own participation in field work and saw it as, among other things, a social value. For that moment we had fallen into the young colleague's trap. Then we set about to give better reasons for maintaining insistence on field work.

It wasn't difficult. Without in any way detracting from the crisis rite, initiatory, significance of field work, we were able to marshal quite a few arguments for continuing to value it among anthropologists. Perhaps the most important benefit derived from field work in an exotic locale is the sense of perspective it develops in the fieldworker. At first, this is manifested in the ability to look at the host culture more objectively than he regards his own. Incidentally, it should be clear that objectivity in looking at a culture is not the same as criticism of it. Some otherwise clear-thinking people confuse the two. In particular, they assume that anyone who can criticize his own society must be objective about it; only the conformers, those who passively accept their society's rules and stipulations, are deemed lacking in objectivity. Put this way, the question probably needs little further glossing, for it is apparent that criticism may lack objectivity too. In any event, the objectivity produced by participation in field work is that of unfamiliarity. The trouble about working in the culture in which one grew up is that almost everything is taken for granted. Even those who are the most active rebels against their own society accept with little or no question most of its content. Their rebellion is selective, building on a mass of traditional elements in their own culture to change that culture. One of the best illustrations of this is available in a consideration of the relationship between the culture of Communist China and the culture of the preceding Nationalist regime and, even more, between both of those and the preceding Ch'ing and Ming imperial dynasties. In brief, all have incredibly more elements in common than are usually recognized. Even the political culture of the People's Republic of China is close to that of the imperial regime. Were a Chinese to be transferred by time machine, let us say between 1600 (late Ming) and 1970, he would find quite a bit to marvel at, somewhat less to adjust and adapt to, but no doubt would be still deep in a Chinese culture based firmly on the same understandings and assumptions he had known before.

A field trip in an alien culture can produce results greater than this imagined trip in a time machine. Even the simplest assumptions of the fieldworker about what he sees and what he must do to conform to his host's expectations of proper behavior may be in error. So much may this be the case that the expression for the dislocation brought by such exposure is *culture shock*. One of the great benefits of this kind of shock to the anthropologist is that it makes him sentiently aware of culture, alert to the minutest variations and to subtle links between newly experienced institutions and freshly observed behavior. What is more, anthropologists frequently joke about the culture shock they experience when they return to their own society after a field trip abroad. It is really not a joke at all, but a continuation of the same process of detachedly viewing culture.

Of course it is not possible to give the undergraduate an experience equivalent to sending him to interior New Guinea, placing him in a Chinese commune, or having him live with the warlike Yanomamö of the Amazon. On the other hand, one can find subcultural situations within the United States that are capable of presenting the range of difference associated with a fair degree of shock. Expose a middle-class adult to the full force of East Village acid rock civilization and you will have someone stoned out of his mind. The problems are somewhat different with the younger generation. In certain youth circles there is unusual ability to tolerate cultural differences, shown not only by slum dwelling and relative contempt for material things but by the frequency with which one encounters "hippie" types from Atlantic cultures in such places as Calcutta and Benares. Most members of the same generation, however, are far less willing to take the risks and make the sacrifices that go with living in poverty and rags in remote places. For better or worse, it is from the latter population that the great majority of those who will present themselves for an undergraduate field course in anthropology will come.

Many schools large enough to include courses in anthropological field work will be located in cities containing more or less extensive ethnic sections, black enclaves in particular. White students eager to do relevant work and instructors eager to get as close as possible to a culture-shock situation are likely to converge on the notion of working in the ghetto, or in an equivalent area. This is a wonderful idea—but! The conditional arises from the existence of numerous grave difficulties. Perhaps the most serious has to do with the responsiveness of the people of black neighborhoods to such studies. As indicated earlier in this book, the time has long passed when the status of student, like some potent cachet, could procure entrance and the cooperation of the community. This is not to suggest that such communities must be written off as focuses of student work, but it does require the realization that the students who are sent in, whether white or black, must be mature and fairly well trained. Furthermore, there may be problems about the nature of the work being done and the uses to which it will be put. To be avoided at all costs is the situation in which this or any other community is given the notion that it is being scrutinized because it is different and therefore freakish. Very few people react kindly to any hint that they are being studied "like animals in the zoo." Most students are equally horrified at such a suggestion and are convinced that it never applies to them, with their advanced and liberated ideas, but always to the next guy. Beware of being that "next guy," unknown to yourself, but very obvious to those among whom you are working.

Another difficulty likely to confront any student who attempts to learn about field work in the context of a project in a black neighborhood is the virtual impossibility of separating the research from deeply held personal views, and this applies to students whatever their racial backgrounds. I am not referring to deeply held racist views, or to the sometimes equally deeply held view that one is absolutely devoid of such notions. I am referring to the total ambience of views of the situation of the ghettos in American life and society. The student is extremely unlikely to be neutral in his views about such pressing problems. Of course we are glad if the student is involved and interested. But to carry out research in the face of such involvement is a tough job, and it should not be complicated by being combined with the task of learning about field technique at the same time. Let it be the first line of inquiry *after* the field course, if you will. (Of course, there are always exceptions. No rule applies to all, but the recognition of an exception should follow the closest scrutiny.)

The undergraduate field-work course can be fun. To provide an informal atmosphere for class discussion of individual projects, I have sometimes had the opportunity of using an off-campus apartment for class meetings. One semester I used my daughter's apartment and she occasionally came back from her own classes to find us still in session. She commented on the combination of ease and intensity that marked the conversation. Much of this grew out of the fact that each student made a personal selection of topic, arising out of a personal concept of relevance and commitment. Over the past several years undergraduate students have undertaken a variety of projects in my field-work courses. These projects can be classified in various ways: some are primarily oriented toward data collection through observation; others rely much more heavily on interviews, or at least on conversation. A sample of the topics undertaken may help other students formulate their own projects.

There are any number of repetitive scenes and institutional situations presenting opportunities for acute and accurate observation and recording and for analysis on various levels of complexity. Students have found nursery schools or kindergartens made to order for research. There are many possible focuses. Principal attention may be given, for example, to interactions between teacher and pupils, with special sensitivity toward the inculcation of approved cultural attitudes in the children, or the reprobation of culturally disapproved behavior. Another possibility is to concentrate on subtleties of student-teacher interactions involving differences of class, social race or ethnicity, even with regard to three- and four-year-olds. The focus might be on interactions among the children themselves, considering the teacher as part of the background. A particularly engrossing item in this respect is the formation of culturally approved sexual attitudes and stereotypes in the very young. Yet another possibility is to focus on one particular child in the context of the larger group.

It is usually more difficult for would-be researchers to gain access to elementary schools or high schools. Students in my research class have been ingenious and fortunate enough to be able to accomplish this. In one specific instance a black anthropology student was able to get permission to observe one of the classes in a higher grade at a Harlem public school. He also had access to the staff, but special conditions operated here, since he was active in the community and was recognized before beginning his work. Another student managed to wangle permission to observe two contrasting classes in a parochial high school for girls. Classrooms, of course, are only one setting in which school ethnography can be done. There are also lunchrooms and schoolyards. In any case, it is strongly underlined that some consultation with school authorities should be undertaken before research is begun.

The question of obtaining permission for carrying out ethnographic research is a worrisome one. Ethical considerations immediately obtrude, particularly where matters of confidence exist. The issues that every student intending field research should consider are treated to some extent in Chapter 13. There are, however, some situations less involved from this point of view. A public playground can be approached directly; so can most religious services of routine nature in church or synagogue. Weddings and funerals present a less certain case. Sometimes it is possible for a stranger to be present as an observer without communicating with the principal participants. Indeed in some funeral situations an attempt to ask permission to attend precipitates awkwardness and anxiety, where quiet entrance into the company goes unnoticed. Since such situations do involve cultural conceptions of privacy, however, it is advisable to discuss the matter with your instructor before arriving at a decision.

The point about all these opportunities, whether it involves observing dispassionately the last rites as conducted by one or another religion (or comparing two or more religions or sects with reference to such things as marital or funeral rites), or making a painstaking ethnographic study of a very small plant or industry (one student in a class of mine turned in a superb illustrated ethnography of a small, six-man factory; another suffered through a study of a small supermarket), is that the student gets so close to the subject that it seems to him that he has never really looked at it before. At that moment it is almost as if he were in some remote part of the world. Not all students achieve such a moment of breakthrough, and the feeling it conveys is hard to transmit in words. Those who experience it are likely to want to go with cultural anthropology to the bitter end.

There is an endless variety of possibilities stressing observation and description—everything from the close analysis of the work patterns of sanitation men loading garbage trucks to the regular and recurrent interactions of a group of *bocce* players on New York's Lower East Side. There is also a rich set of possibilities involving the use of the interview. Some of these overlap with projects already mentioned. The old *bocce* players may be a problem unless one speaks their Sicilian language, but even here most of the players can, if they take kindly to you, tell you about the rules of the game and how they play it, why, with whom, and why the world is falling to pieces as well.

A special part of ethnography shares its goals with other arts and disciplines and relies heavily on interviewing. This is the obtaining of life histories. The variety of subjects is overwhelming. Almost everyone is a candidate. True, most people do not have the kinds of lives that make them likely subjects for an exhaustive oral history project, but each can be a mirror of extensive portions of his society and culture if properly encouraged. The tastes and interests of the fledgling ethnographer can play a paramount role in the selection of a proper informant. Does the interviewer want to throw light on the role of labor unions in a sample life history? There are many places where old workers can be found, and many of them are eager to spend some time with a young person reminiscing about things past. The possibilities here are truly rich, limited only by the skill and imagination of the researcher and his fortune in linking up with an articulate informant. Speak to old people; they are great repositories who are usually neglected and eager to make contact. [One problem for me in this area, however, is that once such contact is made, it presents considerable moral problems. To drop the informant like a squeezed-out piece of fruit has obvious consequences.]

As mentioned before, one of the possible focuses of a student field-work course is on the contrasting utilities and values of the emic versus the etic approach (see above, p. 110). A team of students can pursue one of these research strategies and compare and contrast their results with those obtained by another team using the other strategy. The team that uses the emic approach will, of necessity, be doing a great deal of interviewing in the attempt to get "inside the heads" of the culture carriers they are studying.

Even within the confines of a familiar cultural scene, students come to field-work courses with high expectations and a degree of excitement they do not usually show when approaching other more prosaic courses. This enthusiasm should not be frittered away but built upon, and provided that students and instructors maintain contact and communication, there is a good chance of doing so. Yet despite initial good spirits, some students become rapidly discouraged. They quickly discover that such a field course can be more demanding of time than almost anything else they have experienced at college. In the face of their lively enthusiasm, they may discover that the world resists them, that it is hard to begin conversations with strangers. Some are shocked to discover that their presence as observer in poolrooms or school-yards is undesired; in other words, the role of ethnographer is not always easily accepted. Some, as indicated before, will learn that this role is simply not for them. This can be a tremendously important lesson; learned early, it can save a student years of toil and heartache. Conversely, some students once bitten by the bug of anthropological research will never want to leave it.

Although I know by experience how some students can display total dependence on the instructor of a field-work course, draining the instructor of his patience and his own enthusiasm about the course, I am also aware of how rewarding and interesting such a course can be. It is advisable for the instructor to be available to the students rather more than less in conjunction with such a course. I have found that a combination of sessions that bring together the whole class, and individual conferences, works best. At times, the student needs the encouragement and criticism of the whole group, and mainly of his peers; at other times he needs quiet reassurance and recollection of the goals of the course, and this is often best imparted by the instructor. Finally, I think that the instructor who spots someone who is going through hell to accomplish the work, obviously hates it, and is fighting it, should get that student either to drop the class or to convert his project into one that will redirect him into the library. Everybody doesn't have to be a fieldworker. Indeed, many professional anthropologists believe that, in the final analysis, courses such as this may help people find their subject and may even give them some professional tools to work with, but that they cannot produce fine fieldworkers from any kind of material. Fieldworkers are born, not made, no matter how much we may wish it otherwise.

7

LIBRARIES AND BOOKS

Dickens is said to have amused himself
with a shelf of dummy books, suitably titled
in gold lettering on the back, such as might be
found in any gentleman's library.

—A. A. Milne

Because of their association with field work and empirical research, anthropologists are sometimes thought to be among the least literary of academics. Where the image of the historian is of a scholar poring over volumes old and new, the popular picture of the anthropologist conjures up somebody looking rather like Margaret Mead and asking remarkably intimate questions of the most exotic people. Anyone who has dipped into Mead's books, however, knows that she is a voracious reader. The anthropological profession is a wordy one; much of each professional lifetime is devoted to reading. It was always this way. Nineteenth-century anthropologists tended to be much more at home in libraries than they were in the field. This remains true, even for the most seasoned fieldworkers. Like Marx haunting the library in the British Museum, anthropologists are creatures of the bookshelves. How else can we obtain the comparative data that are the lifeblood of our science?

Of all the aspects of culture that seem keyed to logarithmic rates of change, few develop faster than publication. It is well known that the rate of increase of titles of new serial journals is so great as to create a crisis of information retrieval, and this is without consideration of the increasing number of books published each year. While growth curves are most remarkable in medical sciences and in some physical sciences, anthropology has made a modest contribution of its own. Half a century ago it would have been possible for a very energetic and assiduous scholar to keep up with all published works in anthropology, including all its component fields. It was probably in the 1940's that it became impossible to do so, even with full time devoted to the project. Since then it has become physically impossible to keep up in one subdiscipline alone. The most burgeoning of all, of course, is cultural anthropology, with a total annual output now in the thousands of titles per year, including books and articles. How does anyone deal with such vastness, even after a rapid-reading course?

The answer given this question depends upon the purpose with which the literature is approached. Concern about a specific research topic is very different from the wish to know the latest thought in a closely defined portion of the discipline. An attempt to assess trends in the selection of research topics throughout the discipline will require different scanning and stimulate different selection of reading from that arising in pursuit of a particular question through its anthropological phases into adjacent areas of learning. These are only some of the multiple possibilities. Yet certain steps of general utility can be suggested.

Many undergraduate anthropology courses of my experience, and most graduate courses, begin with the distribution of reading lists and bibliographies. It is to these that first efforts should be directed. So obvious is this point that there may be embarrassment in raising it, yet experience indicates that some students fail to utilize such lists until they are well into their graduate careers. Undergraduates and beginning graduate students sometimes take patronizing attitudes toward such handouts from the professor and seem deliberately to avoid any item appearing in such bibliographies when they write term papers. This is to be deplored as a form of myopia; another form of the same malady applies to papers written on the basis of information derived solely from items on the professor's list.

Where no bibliographies are dispensed in a course, or in the event that the ones distributed are inadequate for the purposes of the reader, there are rich alternatives. Even where fairly exhaustive lists are given out in class, the diligent student and scholar will want to get into these additional bibiliographical sources as soon as he has made an adequate sampling of the lists received. One of the first places to turn in dealing with any specific problem is to a recent work on the subject—not for its content alone but for its bibliographical resources as well. Such a work might be a complete book, or an article in a journal. In either case, the steps performed amount to those undertaken at the outset of most jobs of bibliography compilation. One source leads to another and soon the problem becomes one of selecting the good from the bad rather than simple accumulation of titles.

Another approach, usually worthy of concurrent use, depends on the scanning of prepared bibliographical materials. There is so much of this available, and the field expands so rapidly, that what I say about it here merely scratches the surface. I mention only the most available materials and those which I frequently consult myself. Incidentally, most reference librarians in universities are well informed about bibliographic sources and services and will respond quite favorably to requests for aid.

Perhaps as a hangover from earliest research efforts in high school, students seem to head almost reflexively to the *Readers' Guide to Periodical Literature* when pursuing a topic. Although this guide has its uses, and though it does index such journals of opinion as *New Republic* and *The Nation*, it is relatively wasteful as a resource for social scientists and particularly so for anthropologists. Much more likely to have information of value is the *Social Sciences and Humanities Index*, which has been issued since 1907 (when it was the *International Index to Periodicals*). The advantage of using this index is its timeliness. Published commercially, it appears quarterly and keeps reasonably up to date. It is cumulative, its annual numbers are very convenient, and its topical headings and geographical itemization are useful for the anthropologist. The main disadvantage, however, is the narrowness of the segment of the literature that it processes. In terms of anthropological coverage, it handles only the most obvious sources and will not lead the reader to more obscure nuggets.

Fortunately, there are extensive resources in which to seek these nuggets. Perhaps the best is the *International Bibliography of Social and Cultural Anthropology* (first volume published in 1955 by UNESCO; since 1960 published by Aldine in Chicago and Stevens in London). The slow appearance of this annual, which makes it run at least two years behind current titles, is an annoying hindrance, but its breadth of coverage, including a wide variety of languages, makes it invaluable. Before using this bibliography, the student should read over its plan of classification, which offers useful insights into the organization of subdisciplinary and problem interests. These insights can be deepened by comparing the present roll of subjects with the original one. It is also advisable to look into the bibliographies published by UNESCO in adjacent fields. Depending upon your interests, these are *International Bibliography of Sociology*, *International Bibliography of Economics*, and *International Bibliography of Political Science*.

Also of great utility are various abstracting services. However, the brief synopses of the works listed, even though often contributed by their authors, are merely guides to content. Serious use of such references requires citation of the original if it can be located. Although a new publication, *Anthropological Abstracts*, is on the way, I have yet to see an issue. Perhaps of most general use to anthropologists, then, is *Sociological Abstracts*, first published in 1952. Of greatest interest to specialists in physical anthropology will be *Biological Abstracts*, which is associated with a computerized annual bibliography that is staggering in its breadth of subjects and sources culled. Also of considerable use to physical anthropologists is the compendious annual bibliography published in Washington by the Public Health Service of the U.S. Department of Health, Education, and Welfare. It is called *Cumulated Index Medicus*. The emphasis on specific diseases, diagnostics, and therapies should not distract the anthropologist from the wider possibilities presented by this bibliography, which also indexes works on biological sciences, psychiatry and psychology, the social sciences, and even the humanities. In the last category, stress is placed on the history of medicine, medicine and religion, medicine and ethics, medicine in literature and in wit and humor. Having mentioned psychiatry and psychology, let us note that perhaps the best way of digging into the vast literature of those fields is through selective use of *Psychological Abstracts*.

The field of bibliography is truly enormous and is growing at a tremendous rate. The service that is performed by competent bibliographers cannot be exaggerated. Some idea of what is involved may be gathered from the realization that the names of the periodicals whose articles are indexed in the previously mentioned *International Bibliography of Social and Cultural Anthropology* take up some forty-five pages of small type. This represents a high degree of selectivity! A publication of some years ago, *Documentation in the Social Sciences: World List of Social Science Periodicals* (Paris, UNESCO, 1966) was over four hundred pages in length. That being the case, a scholar can be grateful for anything that will enable him to scan titles at a rapid rate, so that he may draw off those that seem useful in pursuit of a particular problem or in the effort to see what trends exist in defining research problems and interests.

One of the convenient ways of accomplishing the latter is to regularly follow the "publications received" section of such journals as the *American Anthropologist,* but this will not give the reader any feeling for periodical literature. *Current Anthropology* supplies this in its regular summary, by title, of the contents of the important anthropological journals, a service performed many years earlier by such journals as *Anthropos* and *l'Anthropologie,* which also abstracted some of the articles or books listed. There are also other ways of trying to keep up with developments in anthropology in general or in specific fields. A fine service is performed by the contributors to the *Biennial Review of Anthropology,* which has been published under the editorship of Bernard J. Siegal since 1959 (Stanford University Press). The previously mentioned *Current Anthropology* is also notable in this regard, for it has a policy of featuring state-of-the-art treatments of sectors of the field, or of selected problems. There are also the annual overviews that appear in the yearbooks of various encyclopedias, such as the *Britannica* and the *Americana*. Unfortunately, these are of such superficiality as to be better left to the nonprofessional public for which they seem to be written.

There are many more general bibliographies than we have space to list, much less comment upon. Some of these, like the *Anthropological Index to Current Periodicals in the Library of the Royal Anthropological Institute,* developed out of the efforts of particular institutions; others, like *The ABS Guide to Recent Publications in the Social and Behavioral Sciences,* were issued for more closely specified purposes, in this case to respond to the cross-disciplinary needs of the readers of the *American Behavioral Scientist.*

Even more common than general bibliographies are those that apply to sectors of a discipline. In anthropology, probably the commonest means of categorizing whole bibliographies is in terms of area. The advanced student will quickly learn about the monumental bibliographical works in his own area of specialization, like the *Bibliotheca Sinica* of Henri Cordier in mine. Rather than go into detail, let me merely suggest that the student who is beginning an area and doesn't know where to turn might well try the following: for someone interested in Latin America, the *Handbook of Latin American Studies,* published since 1935 for the Hispanic Foundation, in the Library of Congress. For the Indian cultures of South America the best bibliographic source is also a great ethnographic treasury: Julian H. Steward (ed.), *Handbook of South American Indians,* 7 vols. (Washington, D.C.: U.S. Government Printing Office, 1946–59). Students interested in the New World have very extensive resources; in addition to those already mentioned, there is the *Handbook of Middle America* and a very comprehensive bibliography for the Caribbean, Lambros Comitas, *Carribbeana 1900–1965, A Topical Bibliography* (Seattle: University of Washington Press, 1968). There are many bibliographic leads to North American Indians, and the advanced student will certainly want to consult bibliographies that have been prepared by almost every state in the Union dealing with its own history. For general purposes, however, the likeliest place to turn is to George P. Murdock's *Ethnographic Bibliography of North America,* 3d ed. (New Haven HRAF, 1960); it may be worthwhile for the student with deeper interests to consult in addition Frederick W. Hodge's classic *Handbook of American Indians,* Bureau of American Ethnology Bulletin no. 30, part 2 (Washington, D.C., 1910).

Turning to the Old World, I must note first that the poorest area in anthropological bibliography is Europe; resources are scattered and tend to be located under country rubrics. The florescence of interest in European ethnography and community study will probably lead to more concerted bibliographic treatment, but this is still in the future. Things are a little better with regard to archeology; the entire eastern hemisphere is the subject of the bibliographies published sporadically by the Council for Old World Archeology (COWA). These are individually devoted to major regions.

Africa is relatively well treated in bibliography; there are many resources, although here, as elsewhere, there is an unfortunate tendency for well-launched bibliographical series to disappear quietly after a few useful editions. At any rate, the student will probably want to begin by checking the series published since 1958 by the International African Institute and the running bibliography available in its journal, *Africa*. Also of considerable use are such things as Liselotte Hofmann, *United States and Canadian Publications on Africa* (Stanford: Hoover Institute. First published in 1962), and SCOLMA (Standing Committee on Library Materials on Africa), *United Kingdom Publications and Theses on Africa.*

While great scholarly bibliographies pertain to the ancient Near East and also to individual countries of the region in more recent times, there are few bibliographies that pertain to the anthropology of the region in general that are at the same time reasonably current. Probably the best place for a student to start is with the excellent work of Henry Field, *Bibliography on Southwestern Asia,* 4 vols. (Coral Gables: University of Miami Press, 1953–57). The rest of Asia is treated in what can only be called a great richness of sources. There are so many that only a few can be mentioned here, either for their general utility and availability, or because they represent areas of current concern or a new fashion in bibliographic resources. To take the last first, consider G. William Skinner's remarkable compilation of some 30,000 titles in Chinese, Japanese, English, and various European languages, all relating to Chinese society since 1644. Although the items are so numerous, the bibliography is highly selective; more than an equal number of titles were screened but not included. What is more, through the use of computers, the bibliography is coded in such a way that the user can determine important things about the contents of each item before looking into the original. Unfortunately, the cost of compiling such a bibliography in labor and money is such that there are grave doubts that there will be any successor for many years.

The China field seems to attract energetic and talented bibliographers, perhaps because the culture itself has long been outstanding in the fields of bibliography and the writing of encyclopedias. In any case, one further example of the critically annotated bibliography is furnished by Charles O. Hucker in his *China: A Critical Bibliography* (Tucson: University of Arizona, 1962). This work attempts to rate items in a category in terms of probable usefulness. From one or a few sentences giving the scope of the item, the reader can make an intelligent choice of things to seek out in the stacks.

Although the area is well covered by detailed and specialized bibliographies, the place to which any student of Asia exclusive of its western portions should turn is the *Bibliography of Asian Studies,* published as an annual issue of the *Journal of Asian Studies* (formerly the *Far Eastern Quarterly*). Because this bibliography only recently was extended to include areas beyond China, Japan, and Korea, some supplementation is needed. This is furnished by readily available sources such as Robert J. Kerner, *Northeastern Asia: A Selected Bibliography*, 2 vols. (1939; reprint ed., New York: Burt Franklin, 1968); John Embree and Lillian O. Dotson, *Bibliography of the Peoples and Cultures of Mainland Southeast Asia* (New Haven: Yale University Press, 1950); and M. L. P. Patterson and R. B. Inden, *South Asia: An Introductory Bibliography* (Chicago: University of Chicago Press, 1962). As for the Pacific, a good place to begin is in the bibliography attached to Douglas L. Oliver's *The Pacific Islands,* rev. ed. (Garden City: Doubleday, 1961), pp. 427–42.

At the risk of offending some readers, I must add a few words about the idea of working with a bibliography. I realize that it isn't everyone's style, that many fine anthropologists place their energies in other directions. But deep down I cannot understand how anyone would seek an academic career if he didn't feel some excitement in this activity which may seem so deadly dull. The excitement lies in various situations. In the discovery of new publications, maybe with fresh views and materials. In encountering an old article, long overlooked, but brilliant and worthy of recall. In coming across a newcomer, rich in talent and ideas and worth getting to know, even if only at the distance of print. (It is perhaps in entertaining the notion that poring over long lists of names and titles might produce an exciting moment that the student born for such research discovers that he is different from someone who sees only drudgery here, who suffers this labor for other rewards, or who perhaps is not willing to suffer it at all.)

There are now a number of other, essentially nonbibliographical, aids available to beginning and intermediate students of anthropology, which seek to present a background in a hurry. The devices I am thinking of include everything from plastic information sheets of the "Anthropology-at-a-glance" type to the encyclopedia yearbook articles already discussed. Most anthropologists of my acquaintance have a strong antipathy to most things of that kind. The feeling is that anthropology, whatever else it may be, is not a discipline devoted to a corpus of small bits of deathless information. Yet the pressures that encourage teachers of anthropology to prepare thought-inhibiting examinations, particularly those of objective type that force students to memorize long lists of new words, also encourage students to look for easy ways out. It is necessary, too, to note that all published aids are not of the same kind. Some are valid as well as useful, such as the *Atlas for Anthropology*, 2d ed., by Robert F. Spencer and Elden Johnson (Dubuque: William C. Brown, 1968).

Quite apart from the articles appearing in their annuals or yearbooks, encyclopedias can be exceptionally useful adjuncts to any scholar, regardless of the level of his preparation. Obviously, the more detailed the reader's knowledge, the less likely is he to discover something new in the encyclopedia's treatment (and the more likely to find things to which exception can be taken); but no one's expertise is so great that he cannot learn a great deal from selective encyclopedia reading. On the other hand, because most encyclopedia articles are terribly compressed, they rarely have the sort of information worthy of citation in student papers. Better to use the encyclopedia for a bird's-eye view, proceeding from the understanding gained there to a more thorough understanding based upon consultation of sources closer to the data.

The number of general encyclopedias published in the English language since the beginning of the eighteenth century is so large that a fair-sized volume is needed merely to list them. There is such a volume: S. Padraig Walsh, *Anglo-American General Encyclopedias* (New York: Bowker, 1968). Actually, the anthropology student is likely to derive greater benefit from consulting a specialized encyclopedia. One of the most valuable for anyone with ethnological interests is the *Encyclopedia of Religion and Ethics,* often referred to as Hastings' Encyclopedia for its editor, James Hastings (13 vols., New York: Scribner's, 1913–27). What may not be apparent from its name is the remarkable ethnographic coverage of diverse societies and cultures in this encyclopedia. It is said that this work is being updated and reissued. This brings to mind the *International Encyclopedia of the Social Sciences,* 17 vols. (New York: Macmillan & Free Press, 1968). Actually, this work should not be considered either a revision or a reissue of the older *Encyclopaedia of the Social Sciences* (New York: Macmillan, 1930–35), since it is almost completely rewritten, with only a few articles from the older work appearing in the new one. Although receiving mixed notices, as is almost inevitable for a work of this size, the *International Encyclopedia of the Social Sciences* will remain for some years a prime place to which middle-level students can go for orientation. I say that without invidious intent; the encyclopedia will be used by scholars at all levels, but in terms of the present book there is particular utility in this encyclopedia for students who may find themselves in courses in which the instructor assumes too much and mentions concepts or fields of learning about which the student knows too little. A situation like that is precisely made for the *International Encyclopedia of the Social Sciences.*

There are too many specialized encyclopedias to permit even a listing of their names. I shall mention just a few that have been useful to me in order to indicate the wide range of availabilities and perhaps stimulate the reader's imagination to go on an encyclopedia quest. To begin with, there are the encyclopedias of some of the major religions, such as the *Encyclopedia of Islam,* the *Catholic Encyclopedia,* and the *Jewish Encyclopedia.* These are invaluable for information about individuals, doctrines, or events relating to these religions which are often not found in other encyclopedias. They also throw light on alternate world views, when treating subjects that do occur elsewhere.

Anthropologists often deal with art and music. Particularly those whose background is limited will find succor in the *Encyclopedia of World Art,* 15 vols. (New York: McGraw-Hill, 1959–68) and *Grove's Dictionary of Music and Musicians,* 5th ed., 10 vols. (London: Macmillan, 1954–61). For someone floundering with a problem of identifying an item having to do with the classical Mediterranean civilizations there is *Paulys Real-Encyclopädie der classischen Altertumswissenschaft* (46 vols. in 2 series and supplements, 1890–1965). At the other end of the temporal spectrum is the *McGraw-Hill Encyclopedia of Science and Technology,* 15 vols. (New York: McGraw-Hill, 1960). There is also an *Encyclopedia of Cybernetics* (New York: Barnes and Noble, 1968), which is translated from a German original. Actually, it reads more like a chatty dictionary, and has many words and concepts of interest to modern systems-oriented anthropologists.

Rather than continue in this vein, I will conclude with a few remarks about dictionaries. Probably more than other social scientists, anthropologists are much amused at attempts to interfere consciously in the linguistic process, whether by Charles de Gaulle and the French Academy, trying to keep French pure and without Americanisms, or by the pundits who vainly decried the third edition of *Webster's New International Dictionary of the English Language* (Springfield: Merriam, 1961). For the general purposes of the social scientist, I would say this is the best dictionary to use, although verbal developments occur so fast that many neologisms in the social sciences are not to be found there. For other purposes, other dictionaries should be consulted. For example, I find that the most useful etymological dictionary is the *Oxford Unabridged* (13 vols., 1933) particularly because it attempts to give early samples of usage, dating the entry of the word into the language.

Just as special encyclopedias are too numerous to mention in detail, so there is a proliferation of specialized dictionaries. There is a *Dictionary of Anthropology,* compiled by Charles Winick (New York: Philosophical Library, 1956), that has suffered general neglect, perhaps because of a widespread aversion of anthropologists to standardization of their own concepts and language. Careers have been made by attacking simple definitional conceptions of "tribe," "clan," "state," and the like. Nevertheless, the student who may be floundering in his instructor's vocabulary may be grateful to Winick for some basic assistance. More recent, and overlapping the lexical coverage of the previous dictionary while supplying a larger number of related concepts from sociology and related disciplines, is George A. and Achilles G. Theodorson, *A Modern Dictionary of Sociology* (New York: Crowell, 1969).

As a final item I offer the *Dictionary Catalog of the National Agricultural Library* (1862–1965), which is much more bibliography than dictionary. In seventy-three massive volumes this source scans the literature of the world relating to agriculture. Thus, one can look up particular cultigens and find works devoted not merely to their cultivation or botanical characteristics, but to their history and distribution as well. Used with imagination, such a source supplies bountiful crops of titles relating to agricultural history, rural sociology, and other topics of great concern to anthropologists.

Sooner or later, the collection of bibliographic data must pause and the reading of books and articles commence. When the reading is done for specific research purposes, the main problems, apart from finding the titles for which one is searching, probably have to do with determining the reliability of the materials being read. Clearly, there are no absolutes here, but there is often the widest divergence in statements about the same thing. How can the student, especially one just beginning his training, make evaluations? Two methods may be suggested at the outset; the individual will go on from these to evolve his own. First, particularly useful with respect to materials that have been available for at least a couple of years, is to look for follow-ups, other works that take up the substance of the original and work it through critically to the same or divergent conclusions. Second, and much easier, is to avail oneself of the services of the *Book Review Digest* (first published in 1905) and of the *Book Review Index* (first published in 1965), particularly the latter. Of course, in all of this there are problems of academic establishments against the maverick thinkers, but there will always be the nub of the problem that will require individual and independent judgment. That's what all this is about.

As the final topic in this chapter, let us consider the nagging headache of the basic reading list. I am not referring to compilations relating to specific courses—instructors may play with that one themselves. What I have in mind are the more ambitious lists that are sometimes given to undergraduate majors who face comprehensive examinations or to graduate students as they begin their residence. Some departments have such lists now; many have had them from time to time. It is likely that many such lists are related by descent from one or a few common ancestors, although including novel titles of their own. Such lists try to accomplish a variety of tasks; I shall mention four. First, there is the desire to have students read certain classic works, which, it is thought, comprise a common heritage of the discipline. Second, there is the wish that each student be familiar with at least a few of the important works from each major division of anthropology. Third, a high value is placed upon having students steeped in ethnography, with certain monographs being rated particularly high for their comprehensiveness, clarity of observation and expression, intensity, or strategic coverage of some problem. Fourth, there are certain treatments of theory with which every professional anthropologist should be familiar.

Consideration of these four points alone, against the backdrop of what is available in a well-stocked anthropology collection, will lead to the conclusion that the list either will be very, very long, or it will be short at the cost of a great deal of arbitrary cutting. If too long, the list becomes self-defeating, and may even become counterproductive as students are thrown into despair that they cannot master such a list and still maintain their regular studies. If the list is short, many of the individual choices loom larger than they should. There is something of a middle way, consisting of lists which bracket several titles together as representatives of a genre, a problem, an approach, a point of view, allowing the reader to choose his own but knowing what constitutes a set.

The problem of basic reading lists is complicated by specialization. Quite apart from the weight of reading that a specialist must do in his evolving and continuing field of interest, there is always a larger bibliography which differs according to special interest. While it might be a good idea for all archeologists, linguists, and even physical anthropologists to have some firsthand acquaintance with Charles Darwin, Karl Marx, and Sigmund Freud, there is likely to be much less enthusiasm for equally universal reading of, say, Max Weber, or Nicholai Vavilov, or Leonard Bloomfield. To continue with this problem is, I think, to return to our earlier discussions of general education and the conflict between generalization and specialization in undergraduate education. Most anthropologists I know liked the general areas of their undergraduate learning. It was there that they got a major portion of their foundations in reading. I would say that it is too late to look for this in graduate training, but I know a number of exceptions. Hope blooms eternal; no star is lost.

part two

GOING ON WITH ANTHROPOLOGY

MAJORING IN ANTHROPOLOGY

> ma'jor . . . 5. *Educ., U.S.* Designating
> a principal subject of study, chosen by
> a student for a degree, in which he is
> required to take a certain number of
> courses or hours.
> —*Webster's New Collegiate Dictionary*

> Major students should proceed from the
> introductory courses, to concepts,
> regional, and methods courses, to the
> integrative course at the senior level;
> those who qualify can study in the
> specialized and honors courses.
> —David G. Mandelbaum

> But as each department has extended its
> major program, it has increased the
> number of points required, in some cases
> so enormously . . . as to take up almost
> the entire time of the student, leaving
> no room for electives outside the
> specialization and its related field.
> Daniel Bell

The short passages quoted above form a collage pocket history of the concept of the major in American undergraduate college education. Another chapter might be tacked on. I might take it from the Cox Commission Report, *Crisis at Columbia,* and the text would begin like this: "But the simple fact is that a constantly growing proportion of the best students does not look forward to careers molded along the established lines of professional or business success" (Cox Commission 1968:22). Indeed, according to a study made by Stanley Raffel, a graduate student in sociology, about half of recent freshman classes at Columbia College expected to take up the academic profession, but by the time they finish the college only about a sixth continue to hold such ambitions. The Cox report (p. 22) indicates Mr. Raffel's belief that the college environ-

ment apparently turns students away from academic careers. I don't
know if any studies exist that purport to show how this phenomenon,
if widespread, is attached to the major system. Obviously, from the
ground we have already covered, the major system cannot be blamed
solely or even mainly for the apparently widespread student discontent
with the state of affairs in academia today. But there can be little question that disquiet about the major system is a symptom of the general
condition.

As likely as it may seem to current generations of college students
that the major system is as old as the idea of university itself, the truth
is otherwise. The background of the system is to be found in the development of departmental specialization in Europe, particularly in Germany. Here, in one sweeping paragraph, is the synopsis:

> Two distinct and far-reaching steps have given the present
> college its form. The first, the so-called free elective system
> introduced by the authoritative figure of [Harvard] President
> [Charles W.] Eliot in the seventies and eighties, opened finally
> to American students the floods of specialized knowledge
> then streaming from European universities but offered before
> then only to Americans who studied abroad. This, the first
> long step away from the restricted curriculum of earlier times,
> was entirely necessary, even inevitable. But the exuberance of
> freedom to which it led raised difficulties. If students could
> study anything that they chose within the now greatly ex-
> panded curriculum, what assurance was there of coherence
> and intellectual discipline in their work? This discipline might
> exist, but there might be simply a careless, indiscriminate
> tasting. Moved by such considerations, faculties as time went
> on increasingly hedged the student's freedom by requiring
> him to take a portion of his work, varying in different col-
> leges, in more or less closely related subjects. He was, to be
> sure, likewise required to take work outside these subjects,
> but as the scope and importance of the main field grew, these
> other requirements became more and more incidental. This,
> the so-called system of "concentrating" or "majoring," rep-
> resents the second step. It is the system now in force in the
> great majority of American colleges.   [Harvard 1945:37–38]

Although some student problems have to do with curriculum,
especially the quest for relevance (as we have already seen in Chapter 2),
departmental structure as a division of information has been given relatively little attention. The exceptions to the general conditions of de-
partmentalism are interesting but not very consequential: the "free uni-

versity" experiments in some instances attempted to organize curricula on the basis of revolutionary problems rather than the departmentalization of subject matter. Although the present crop of such experiments has not yet proved viable, the future is still uncertain. Nonetheless, no serious threat to the departmental structure of knowledge is yet discernible. Another exception is comprised of scattered student demands for unrestricted privileges in selecting courses freely and with a minimum of prerequisites. This is sometimes coupled with demands for the elimination of course grades. For those who view the formal educational system as a process whereby successive generations of youth are prepared to fill positions in society, the notion of completely free choice of courses and elimination of grading is almost incomprehensible and is probably as much suggestive of anarchy as any of the more physical events that have taken place around universities in recent times.

Indeed, the antiformalist, antigrades student activists are, in a curious way, struggling against history and the evolution of culture. It has been student demand, as much as anything, that has produced the majoring system and spread it across the country. In fact, it is my impression that at most institutions where students have raised demands, the call has been more frequently for increased course offerings under the major system rather than the abolition of this system.

In a sense, the matter comes to a head in efforts to achieve courses of Black Studies in various schools. Frequently the demand is phrased in terms of a program of such studies; sometimes it is for a department, sometimes an institute or other administrative means of handling an organized curriculum. The point lies in that last concept: the centrality of an organized group of courses. It cannot be more than a short step from a Black Studies program and major to a list of required courses and approved sequences. What is more, it is easy to predict that given the continuation of circumstances current at this writing, Black Studies will flourish and tend to emphasize grading. The reason for this is simple: in an otherwise stable or contracting market for college- and university-level teachers, it is programs of Black Studies that are crying for trained personnel.

There is no question that one of the mainstays of the majoring system is its relationship to the economics of academic life. Several issues are involved. Close to the core is the dynamics of academic employment. Even when the supply of qualified professionals lags behind demand, the employer seeks high quality, although the criteria of quality may undergo some variation from establishment to establishment. In most situations one of the invariable criteria is a good record of grade achievement in graduate school. It is worth noting that this is a minimum and not a maximum requirement; the establishing of good performance on the record is followed by solicitation of personal references that are expected to make exceptionally fine distinctions among students in the same cohort.

It seems clear that one of the main reasons behind the "success" of the major system, gauged by its diffusion throughout the contemporary academic world, is the relation the system bears to the training and employment of successive generations of professionals. In anthropology, as in many other disciplines, it seems that the system is reinforced from different angles—students, anxious to achieve what are considered good positions, play roles supporting the system as actively as older members of the Establishment. Incidentally, and for whatever it is worth, the same system prevails in the so-called Socialist camp. The Soviet Union went through a moderate crisis of student-faculty relations in the early 1920's. Some of the student demands were very reminiscent of those we have already touched upon. After a brief period of experimentation, however, Soviet university education settled back into a mold not very different from what had been known in czarist days, with a status gap between professors and students much wider than anything known in the United States. It is also possible to state flatly that departmental and majoring systems are quite similar to those in the United States, although the rank system relating to the faculty is thoroughly European. Similarly, massive examination regimens are the rule, seemingly without exception. The notion of dropping the principle of competitive grading is virtually unthinkable in Soviet education (see Moos 1967:111–16).

Similar observations have been made on the postrevolutionary university system in Cuba. Dr. Marcel Roche, president of the Consejo Nacional de Investigaciones Científicas y Technológicas of Venezuela, received a fellowship from UNESCO that enabled him to visit institutions of higher learning and research in Cuba in 1970. According to Roche, José Miyar Barruecos, rector of the University of Havana, stated:

> . . . A government by majority vote in this business [the university] cannot be admitted. In the university there is a single criterion, which is the product of reality. The university is not exactly parliamentary. In the last instance the direction of the university depends on the direction of the Revolution . . . that is, on the Prime Minister . . . . [Roche 1970:346–47]

In all fairness, I should note that at the time of writing the sole society that seemed to be pursuing goals of academic organization anything remotely like those announced by the most radical of campus activists was Communist China. After a period of about four years, during which the universities of China were virtually inoperative, they reopened in 1970. Labor service was interdigitated with academic studies, and attention to mastery of Mao Tsetung Thought was emphasized. Strong bias favored the admission of soldiers, peasants, and workers to these programs, preferably those of impeccable proletarian or poor peasant origins. The system of grading was unclear; examinations seemed at least temporarily in disuse. Classroom discipline was uncertain, but films supplied by official government agencies showed students marching to classes in military formation. Politics to one side, it must be apparent that what is going on in China, like it or not, is the greatest sociocultural experiment the world has ever seen. It exceeds in size and scope the Soviet attempts to change a people's value system and society, and its fate, more crudely its success or failure, will have profound effects on all other social systems, including our own.

Switching back from the world-shaking Chinese revolution to the immediate problem of this chapter requires a leap that has its comic aspects; nonetheless, it is essential to maintain perspective and proportion. We can see our problem for what it is. The majoring system is a transient aspect of the social organization of higher education. At the present time, despite grumbling and rumbling, its time for replacement does not seem to have come. Indeed, with a little reform and patching here and there, it seems likely to ride out the century. How far into the future can we look? It is the operating reality of the structure of our higher education, so we might as well see what it has to offer for people wishing to become anthropologists.

The first thing to question is whether someone who wishes to end up in an anthropological career should major in anthropology on the undergraduate level. The pragmatic affirmative answer to this query is already given in the foregoing discussion, but let us take a look at the alternative.

A number of well-known anthropologists, past and present, entered the profession after building academic foundations having little or nothing to do with their fields of ultimate specialization. Many did so without even specializing in anthropology in graduate school; as for a major in anthropology on the undergraduate level, it existed in very few colleges until fairly recently. The backgrounds from which anthropologists have come are quite diverse. Some years ago there was something of a concentration, some of the individuals concerned having specialized in those aspects of anthropology that lie close to jurisprudence, but others, like Robert Redfield, moving rather apart from their disciplinary origins. Anthropologists, in short, have come from backgrounds in other social sciences and from the arts and humanities. Some have come from mathematics, the sciences, from engineering, dentistry, and medicine. One of the brightest anthropologists to receive a degree from Columbia in recent years came into the department with a degree in hotel management, a fugitive from a very successful hotel in the Berkshires. His thesis was on pigs, war, and ritual in a primitive society. (How far can one get from weddings, confirmation parties, and conspicuous consumption?)

Before the end of World War II, it is likely that most graduate students of anthropology went to school only part time, supporting themselves and earning tuition at least part of the period they were in residence. The period of residence itself was indefinite. Ten years was not considered a long interval between bachelor's and doctor's degrees, and cases taking twenty and thirty years were known in many departments. The big change came with the educational benefits provided for veterans. People who would never have considered higher degrees, certainly not doctorates, suddenly discovered not merely that they had a chance to obtain higher education, but that they could benefit economically from pursuing it.

Our prime concern in this chapter, the undergraduate major, was seriously affected by the developments just sketched. The bounty that began with the G.I. Bill of Rights quickly spread to the foundation world and then back to the government, as very large programs of various types of scholarship, fellowship, and research support were made available. Talking only about anthropology, there was a general leap forward in the amount of the funds available for student support, so much in fact, that at various large graduate schools the goal was 100 per cent of students on full support. The part-time student was a thing of the past, or so it was thought at the height of the program. The effects of this on student preparation in undergraduate years was remarkable. (Once more it is tempting, as an anthropologist, to dwell on the functional interconnections in a sociocultural system. Input at one locus sets in motion the most far-reaching changes, with few consequences being seen in advance.) However it was learned—and to a considerable extent it was simply a product of the increased availability of anthropology in the curriculum—applicants responded to a new concept of what it took to get into a prestigious graduate school. Transcripts of undergraduate records showed that there were undergraduate majors who had taken between thirty and sixty credits (up to twenty and more separate courses) in anthropology prior to "beginning" its specialized study in the graduate school. In some cases students had, while still undergraduates, taken as many or more graduate courses than were required for a master's degree. Some had passed portions of the higher degree examination requirement.

Consider certain things that flow from the condition just described. Some anthropologists are of the opinion that excellent members of the profession are developed on the basis of broad, nonanthropological backgrounds. But it is very hard to turn down someone who has already demonstrated competence for anthropology in favor of a brilliant student with no visible anthropological ability. It is particularly difficult to do so when the invitation to study in the department carries with it a fellowship that pays tuition and supplies some funds for a living. Even though many of these stipends have suffered such devaluation that some of their holders participate in the Federal Food Stamp Program, there continues to be great competition for them Accordingly, there may be one or two individuals on the committees that dispense such grants who would take risks on an applicant in the discipline, but committees as a whole are certain to vote, even more so over the long haul, for the "safest" candidates. As we have seen, the message early reached the undergraduate schools, so that *applicants* with little or no specialized background in anthropology have become rather scarce. (This, too, has been facilitated by an economic device, namely the application fee that is now routinely charged by most graduate schools.)

If I turn back now to the question raised at the outset of this section—whether someone who hopes to enter anthropology as a career should major in anthropology as an undergraduate—the answer is heavily determined by the conditions that exist. At least two things must be added. First, the present generation of students includes a large number who are contemptuous of formal restraints of various kinds. These students have also seen the reduction or elimination at a number of campuses of several different kinds of admission criteria on the college level, including College Entrance Board Examinations, minimum point averages in high school, or the inheritance of the school tie. There is reason to believe that efforts for broader and more egalitarian admissions to graduate school may also develop. Second, the foundation and government support of higher education is in bad trouble at this time. Many specific programs are being eliminated or reduced to skeleton proportions. Few universities have thought out ways of removing themselves from the jams in which they now find themselves. Most seem to be taking the ostrich stance, hoping that an upturn in the economy, with or without cessation of the Indochinese war, will see the return of heavy government funding. Recently, a portion of the academic community did everything in its power to obtain restoration of funds cut from "university study programs in the language, history and culture of countries that are outside Western Europe but nevertheless crucial to modern American diplomacy" (*The New York Times* 29 April 1970:15). The arguments that were presented are of some interest:

> The college presidents argued that the per-student costs for
> the study of Asian and Middle Eastern languages were con-
> siderably higher than the costs for more traditional academic

*disciplines, and that such courses were therefore "unpro-
ductive" for the universities undertaking them.*

*At the same time, the argument went, it is in the na-
tional interest to develop a trained corps of scholars in the
language, politics and geography of areas with which the
United States seems increasingly involved.* [Ibid.]

It should not come as a shock to readers to discover that universities
pursue cost-accounting techniques in determining problems of curriculum, nor is it necessarily evil to do so. The university has the problem of making choices in order to ensure that its resources, always
limited, best accomplish its stated goals. The problem, of course, is to
achieve this with minimal injury to the very goals being pursued. The
university cannot pretend to be an instrument for the pursuit of pure
learning if, at each financial crisis, it evokes the question of service.
There are times when learning and service are not compatible.

Recently, universities in the United States have been suffering a
serious financial crisis with potentially profound implications for students concerned about majoring in anthropology. For several years
prior to this crisis, as we have already indicated, emphasis mounted in
graduate departments on accepting as few students as possible not
covered by important grants. As also indicated, this tended to produce
increased specialization on the undergraduate level as students prepared themselves for higher and higher degrees of competition. Some
of my colleagues think that this trend will not be reversed, but I am
not so sure. Things may be changing. The tightening of funds and the
contraction in fellowship and scholarship support may see the return
of some of the older folkways governing admission to professional
careers. Those in the profession who decry what they consider to be
premature specialization may now have increased opportunity to admit
to their graduate departments more of those likely looking students
who have not yet concentrated efforts in anthropology.

As previously indicated, a prime determinant of the curriculum of
the undergraduate major in anthropology will certainly be the availability of courses at the student's college. But, again, this seeming
truism may be altered by the judicious use of summer study at other
universities. What can be accomplished by such means is once more a
function of the rules of the student's home department. Although there
is rarely any trouble obtaining credit for the summer session work
taken elsewhere, there are stated rules concerning the distribution of
courses within the major and without. A book such as this cannot with
its generalizations specify conditions at particular schools, hence concerned readers must fill in their own details by consulting catalogs and
other sources of reliable information, including their advisers.

Most schools providing an anthropology major request the majoring student to complete a minimum number of courses comprising a set number of required subjects and a balance of electives. The means of handling the latter are diverse. In some institutions choice is genuinely free; elsewhere various kinds of plans are found—one from column A and two from B, and so on—reminding one of the family dinner menus so popular in American Chinese restaurants (but virtually unknown in China). The required courses show some variation from one place to another, but in general they display a high level of consistency. The usual beginning is the introductory course, which we have already treated in some detail in Chapter 4. It is of some consequence, however, to determine if the introductory course is a one- or two-semester synthesis, or a three-course sequence. The one-semester overview is bound to be so fragmentary and superficial that the serious student will be compelled to take additional work in almost every topic in order to reach a level of adequate understanding. Curiously, the one-semester introduction to four-field anthropology has much to recommend it to those who already know that they wish to major in anthropology. Such a course is likely to have its main thrust placed upon four salient topics: man, the product of biological evolution; culture; cultural relativism; and the integration of anthropology. From such a course the major can proceed to take more detailed but still introductory courses in linguistics, in archeology, and in physical anthropology. (The absence of cultural anthropology from the list of second-tier courses in this scheme is not an oversight but proceeds from the difficulty of specifying the nature of such a course. I will return to that problem in a few moments.) The anthropology major who has completed this four-course regime and done the readings indicated in the courses should be very well prepared for the remainder of his undergraduate work and will be in a secure position to enter graduate school. Something like this could be found until recently at the University of California, Berkeley. It may still exist elsewhere, but if not totally absent, it is certainly rare.

Where there are full-fledged departments of anthropology, the most common arrangement of the introductory course is that which extends over the normal academic year, occupying two semesters or the equivalent. It is for use in this type of course that most texts and assembled readings are geared. What concerns me here is that such an introduction may be associated with more problems for the majoring student than either of the other arrangements mentioned. The very short course is unlikely to mislead any professionally oriented student; he will be well aware of the deficiencies in his preparation. The long series, which is comprised of a highly general introduction plus specific courses in linguistics, archeology, and physical anthropology, is not enough in itself to produce an anthropologist, but it does lay a very good basis, as we have seen. The most common sequence is likely to create difficulties, leaving the student much too weak in certain areas, but unevenly turned out in any case.

It would seem that to be consistent, I would have to argue that all departments should adopt the four-unit approach to introductory anthropology or, failing that, fall back upon the one-unit, highly general approach. Unfortunately, the matter is not that simple. The former requires a minimum staff that exceeds the resources of a large proportion of departments. It is not merely a matter of the number of staff members, but of resource skills. Proper instruction in a four-unit approach requires the participation of scholars competent in linguistics, in archeology, in physical and in general cultural anthropology. To be sure, institutions frequently make out with a missing spoke and give good courses. The absence of an archeologist is perhaps most easily tolerated, but in point of fact it is rarely the archeologist who is missing from the team. (This is not an Aesopian suggestion to cut down on the number of archeologists employed in departments of general anthropology! Rather, it is an attempt to deal candidly with a problem of staffing that is not often mentioned, much less given serious consideration. The fact is that many benefits are gained by having one or more people available to handle local archeology. This subject has remarkably wide and uniform appeal throughout the United States and is found most particularly in state university complexes, which are also among those universities having the greatest development of anthropology departments.)

Even more serious objections to solutions to the introductory anthropology course on other than a two-semester basis come from sectors of college organization and structure that have nothing to do with the content of anthropology as a discipline. In many schools introductory anthropology occupies a two-unit niche and that is that; any change can be effected only at the cost of considerable additional changes affecting many other departments. The considerations that are active here may be of considerable academic importance, belittled only by essentially anti-intellectual critics. On the other hand, the critical attacks on the treatment of such curricular problems are often given strength by the conduct of faculties that take an "economist" stance. (Régis Debray has an excellent definition of economism in this sense, which we may borrow and adapt: Economism is the zealous defense by departments of their own professors' subject-matter interests against encroachments by other departments.) We could go on to analyze the social structure of academia and the larger society into which it fits, thereby gaining a better understanding of why things are as they are, sometimes at great material and psychic cost to students and others. However interesting, this leads us away from our main topic, the question of majoring in anthropology and the way to approach it. Let me return again to that central topic.

One point that emerges from the foregoing is that the majoring student will make different selections of courses in subsequent terms depending upon the nature of the introduction he received. It is essential that students have access to professional counseling at this juncture, and I refer to professional anthropological counseling, not the general advice that may be obtained from someone in an adviser's office who may have no knowledge of, never having taken a course in, anthropology. The advice that is given will have to take into account the kind of introductory course already taken, plus a number of additional variables. While most undergraduate premajors tend to approach anthropology as a great and somewhat formless vista, totally uncertain of their place in the landscape, there are a fair number of exceptions. In my experience, most of those who have more fully formed views of their objectives look forward to specializing in cultural anthropology, with a substantial number interested in archeology. Linguistics and physical anthropology are less well represented. The conscientious adviser will try to make provision for this special interest where it exists, suggesting enough work in the specialty to nourish the interest and provide preliminary training, while making sure that the student is systematically introduced to other parts of the discipline. Not infrequently, a student in the course of the undergraduate major will shift and redefine his special interests, making much more highly informed career choices after selective exposure to parts of the discipline previously unknown to him, or rejected on flimsy grounds.

Prosaic as this information may be, I should like to stress it. The undergraduate major should use the variety of courses available to him to sample in some detail the various portions of the field. Such experimentation is less likely to be done in graduate school, although opportunities still exist at the higher level for shifting interests. One good reason for making the sampling as an undergraduate has to do with selection of a graduate school. Since many of those schools tend to be stronger in one part of the field than another, the student is well advised to be careful in making his selection. This is best accomplished when the student has more than an inchoate understanding of his own goals and furnishes one more positive reason for the viability of the undergraduate majoring system.

While less likely to be practical, some consideration should be given to areal interests even at the preprofessional level. The limitation is obviously going to arise in the first place from the restricted number of courses available. Beyond that, questions can arise about the desirability of premature concentration on a particular area or culture. Some of my colleagues would argue strongly that the most important thing is to master the general theory and broad data of anthropology, coming to a real focus in terms of an evolving sense of problem. Other colleagues point out that this is well and good, but some anthropology majors come into the discipline because they have already been inspired by a great interest in a certain culture or group of cultures. Some students have already had firsthand experience, perhaps in the Peace Corps or in Vista. Wanting to know more about East or West Africa, or China or Japan, or India, or Brazil, Latin America, Mexico, the Caribbean, or certain sectors of our own society, they make the rounds of various disciplines and then rush into anthropology where they feel they can learn about the area in the holistic way anthropologists keep boasting about. Advising such students is not always easy. Since comparison remains central to the anthropological viewpoint, the adviser may press for more work outside the main geographical area of interest than the student wishes to undertake.

Something of a similar problem exists on the graduate level. This enables me to make a general suggestion about such problems. The student who, as an undergraduate, concentrates in a quite one-sided manner upon a particular culture and goes on to further and even deeper one-sided study in graduate school is pursuing an intellectually dangerous course. Such a student is exposing himself to all the ills of narrowness and overspecialization and is likely, as far as anthropology is concerned, to end up lost in the contemplation of a tree, blind to the forest. Of course, there is nothing implicitly "wrong" about such an approach; indeed, it applies beautifully to some other cultures or to our own culture at some other time. On the other hand, such monolithic devotion is likely to impair the scholar's ability to make sense of the phenomena he most wishes to explain, since the perspective necessary to such understanding may be available only when comparison and the extension of the area under concern are carried out.[1]

If undue specialization through course work in one particular culture is to be avoided, there is a specific kind of preparation that is

---

[1] To give one good example: the understanding of most indigenous political systems in sub-Saharan Africa was for a long time completely distorted and obscured by the narrow views taken of the systems being described. Treated in terms of the phenomena observed at certain social levels and confined to relatively restricted areas, such massively important things as colonial rule, foreign district officers, and military forces or police, indeed the total disruption and realignment of indigenous political structure, were casually overlooked. As a result, the narrow studies gave little or no basis for understanding events in sub-Saharan Africa following upon the retreat of some, but not all, of the colonial regimes. Among the essential but missing elements were analyses of the local effects of colonialism and imperialism, and the nature of these systems at home, in the metropolitan countries.

very much to be encouraged. The student with highly developed interest in a particular culture should be urged to begin, as early as possible, to acquire proficiency in the language of that culture. Sometimes, of course, it is not possible to do so within the framework of even the most lavish curriculum. Eskimo, Sudanese, Hakka, Algonkian, Ge, most of the world's languages, are not taught in any college in America on a regular basis. But many other languages are, and some of these can be of the greatest utility to the future areal specialist: Indonesian, Mandarin Chinese, Japanese, Arabic, Swahili, even Spanish and Portuguese. Where the match between language and area study is very close, the indicated path is obvious and should be taken without delay. Where it is not, consultation with an anthropological linguist is in order; if one is not available on the campus, the student should write.[2]

One final mention of the language problem with respect to the undergraduate major must bring up the question of credit for the language work. Generally speaking, the actual learning of a specific language is not credited toward the specialization in anthropology. In other words, whatever credits are amassed in taking specific languages are not accepted in most departments as part of the anthropology concentration. This is in contrast to courses in linguistics, which are usually given such credit. Similar rules will be found to apply in most, perhaps all, graduate departments of anthropology.

Turning briefly to consider the content of courses taken by majors after the introduction, I find it is notable that other commentators have generally recommended a two-tiered approach involving an intermediate and an advanced level.[3] The intermediate level is richest in the variety of courses, says Cora Du Bois (1963:28); and David Mandelbaum agrees, specifying the variety of substantive contents at the middle level: concepts and comparisons; methods of obtaining and analyzing data and formulating and testing concepts and hypotheses; and regional ethnographic courses (1963:57–62). For Du Bois the third level differs from the second in quality rather than substance; in brief, intensity is maximized "rather than broad coverage" (1963:28). Differing from practice at the introductory and intermediate level, technical details are now emphasized. It is at this level that she sees training in relevant language(s) becoming important. I have already indicated my own view

[2] To find out where to write, look into recent issues of professional journals, or the current Guide to Departments of Anthropology.

[3] The skeptical anthropologist looking at our own culture is always amused to discover yet another "natural" tripartite arrangement, in this case the three tiers of introductory, intermediate, and advanced courses. Such culturally reinforced systems feel very natural, but each is an artifice.

that wherever possible such language acquisition should take place as early as possible.

Mandelbaum visualized the senior level of the undergraduate major as providing opportunities for integrating previous learning on one hand, and extending specialized skills on the other. In the latter he seems in agreement with Du Bois, but the former emphasis is his own. He sees the implementation of the integration in two courses, one dealing with theory and the other with the history of anthropological ideas. This is no place for a full-scale critique of Mandelbaum's ideas, but I cannot refrain from commenting that they seem to me visionary to say the least. It is not merely that Mandelbaum's vision is idealistic and impossibly sanguine, though that would be serious enough. Too many students exposed to anthropology are led to believe that at the end of the rainbow of study is the pot of gold containing synthesis and integration. Something far more limited appears instead. Even the minimal goal of integrating the divergent subfields of anthropology turns out to be beyond possibility after years of graduate work, much less at the end of an undergraduate curriculum. What is more to the point, the expectation of integration leads to two deplorable conditions. One of these is the student's conviction that the integrating impulse, indeed the synthesis itself, will be supplied by the teacher. I believe that to the extent any integration and synthesis occurs, it will be done mainly by the individual student to his own tastes and requirements. The second is much more insidious, presenting eclecticism as the standard approved mode of thought and analysis. This is to say that in much of American thought, and anthropological thought is no exception, the student is taught that there are many points of view of more or less equal validity. The balanced interest group theory of idealized bourgeois politics thus becomes the model of scientific inquiry. There is a confusion here. The scientific approach is, at its healthiest, an open one in many respects: information is supposed to be free and experiments and observations must be replicable; all ideas, no matter how heretical, must be given a hearing. The latter point, however, is frequently distorted in a variety of ways. Sometimes the distortion produces a claim that all ideas, tested or untested, accepted or rejected, must be accorded equal respect. That is nonsense, and its observance could destroy science. The converse is also encountered, and it is here that we meet eclecticism as the belief that there is some good in every viewpoint and that the best course is to cull the best of all available conflicting opinions. At its most banal and most dangerous extreme, this view tends to average out scientific differences. Does a certain fossil have a cranial capacity of 600 cc as one camp contends, or is it 800 as the opponents insist? The eclectic tends to solve such a problem by opting for the figure of 700 cc, but unlike political democracy, science does not work that way. In fact, those favoring the 600 cc figure may be absolutely right. Yet many major programs in anthropology conscientiously drill their students in eclectic approaches to the critical issues of the discipline. The student must beware.

Theoretical eclecticism can be dangerous, but disciplinary eclecticism may enrich an undergraduate major in some beautiful ways. Unfortunately, few undergraduates have made sufficient determinations about their career choices to pursue the options I am about to discuss. I am thinking, for example, about the determined archeologist-to-be. If there is sufficient certainty about the goal, such an individual can lay in specific kinds of course work that will save him great anguish as a graduate student. Courses in general geology and Pleistocene geology come immediately to mind, but there are others, such as in botany (for plant fossil identifications), biology (for faunal remains), or even physics, enabling him to deal more competently with the new methods of physical dating. If such course work is behind him when he enters graduate school, he can concentrate on developing his own specialty. On the other hand, this is likely to be accomplished at the expense of education in breadth. Does it profit the specialist to become an early expert at the cost of general appreciation of his culture? I doubt that there is any final answer; my own preference, to record it, is for general knowledge first and specialization later.

A final word about the undergraduate major, a chilling word but not a surprise. The undergraduate major in anthropology, in terms of providing entrée into a professional career realm, is like the safe deposit key held by a depositor. It requires at least two keys to open the box, the owner's and the bank's. The baccalaureate degree itself provides no admission to any profession involving anthropological skills, except in rare and special cases. All others must go on to get some other training and degree before presenting themselves for professional employment. There is no reason why anthropology majors must go on to become anthropology professionals. Indeed, it would be disastrous if all would attempt to do so, since even in the most expanding economy, the positions available at the end of training are fewer than the number of those entering upon training. Fortunately, the undergraduate major in anthropology has great potential value for many other career paths, although in many cases this value is comprehended dimly or not at all at present. I shall suggest only a few.

In terms of preprofessional training, anthropology might be an excellent focal point were it not for the realities of admission policy in the professional schools. Take the situation in medicine, where emphasis in undergraduate preparation continues to be placed on mathematics and the natural sciences despite changes in the conception of the medical professions which bring them closer to the orbit of the social sciences. Student activism in the medical schools may help to ease the admissions problem in the future. Also likely to help is the continued development of the subdiscipline of medical anthropology which can be added to such already well advanced fields as human evolution, human variation, and comparative primate anatomy, which fall within the usual purview of physical anthropology. It may be merely my own view, but it seems that our society can only profit by such redirection of the education of premed students. May a burgeoning of student interest in this area soon occur—it may provide us all with better doctors!

Even the would-be English major may gain invaluable new perspectives if he begins in anthropology and switches later to English or comparative literature. This can be the case, whether the student hopes to become a teacher of our language and literature or one of the newer varieties who specialize in socioanthropological analyses. The same advice can be given to aspirants to careers in many other professions—ranging from art to law, in diplomacy and even business.

Most departments of anthropology act with reasonable cheer to turn out such nonmajor majors. But the main thrust is and probably will continue to be directed at the production of candidates for the profession. We come to the next step in the process, graduate education, in the following chapter.

CHOOSING A GRADUATE SCHOOL

the function of education is to prevent the truly
creative intellect from getting out of hand
—Jules Henry

We know relatively little about the reasons why particular people elect to enter anthropology as a career. As psychologist Jack E. Rossman points out, there has been little study of anthropologists as such, and he set out to get some systematic data on the subject. Rossman sent out 410 "Strong Vocational Interest Blanks" and as many questionnaires to anthropologists employed in graduate departments; 179 (44 percent) replied. The results were scarcely surprising. The interests of anthropologists tended to be "most similar to those of psychiatrists and psychologists; mathematicians and chemists; musicians; and lawyers and author-journalists" (Rossman 1968:8). Least like the interests of anthropologists were "those of members of the skilled and semi-professional occupations (farmer, carpenter, forest service, etc.); most social service occupations . . . and businessmen" (ibid.). Anthropologists differed from sociologists and psychologists in having interests closer to those of architects, librarians, and writers; their interests were said to have less of an applied orientation. Another distribution of the same vocational interest inventory by Shirley Beran yielded the conclusion that anthropologists tended to be "antichurch" and "feminine," the latter rating being applied because of a predilection for "clean-handed" tasks, and interests in art, music, and literature (Newsletter of the American Anthropological Association 10:8 [1969]:7).

While anthropology hardly rates as a glamour profession except among a small coterie of romantics, it has its modest advantages in the bourgeois world and even some in the so-called socialist countries, China not presently included. (The lot of anthropologists and sociologists has been particularly hard in the People's Republic of China, harder even than that of other intellectuals. To begin with, their fields of competence have virtually been abolished.) For those who make it to professorial ranks (full professor, that is), salaries aren't bad and working conditions are usually good, which is to say that there is a reasonable amount of time for doing what one wishes. As professions go in middle-class American society, there is little or no reason for anyone interested in money as a marker of success to go into anthropology. On the other hand, from the vantage point of the lower class, and a large portion of the lower middle class, including members of ethnic groups struggling with problems of social and economic mobility, the wages generally received by anthropologists undoubtedly seem fairly good. Certainly this factor has operated in the past and may help to account for ethnic and subcultural distributions among the ranks of anthropologists.

Students are attracted to anthropology for a variety of reasons that have nothing to do with income. Some students, for example, come to anthropology with the conviction that it is a revolutionary discipline. They are thinking of the cultural anthropologist's ability to look objectively at any culture, including his own, spotting its warts and wens. However real and widespread this talent, the field of anthropology itself is simply a limp agent of its practitioners and, more important, of the social system within which it flourishes. As a discipline, anthropology is forever potentially neutral. The social system of fascism, under the Nazi government in Germany, could and did turn anthropology into an undertaking that repels and revolts all anthropologists I know. There is no theoretical reason why a racist and reactionary anthropology cannot exist. Some students seem to expect that whole fields can lean structurally in some political direction rather than another, that some fields can be pure by the nature of their subject matter. Alas! If there is any such field, it is certainly not anthropology. Discovery of this simple truth can be traumatic to some students and may mark the beginning of a process of disintegration, at least in their work. Dropout follows, although sometimes foolishly delayed by an attempt to pursue the subject somewhere else, transferring to another graduate school, basically the same as the department just fled.

I seem to have started this chapter talking about disappointments and dropouts before mentioning the positive aspects of graduate school, or at least indicating some of the more rational bases for selective choice of a graduate anthropology department. Yet the fact remains that during the academic year 1968–69 there were some 4150 graduate students of anthropology in the United States, while against this total enrollment about 160 doctorates were granted, and about 400 master's degrees, all in anthropology. It happens that the master's degree is usually not adequate to providing permanent employment in anthropology; therefore, most recipients of an anthropology M.A. (or the rare anthropology M.S.) go on to the doctorate. Indeed, there is an unfortunate use of masters' degrees in some graduate schools as a consolation prize and device of separation for candidates judged unable to complete the doctorate. It is known in the trade as the "terminal M.A.," but is not acknowledged as such in any catalog I've read. Even against this background, the level of degree production in anthropology seems to be somewhat out of phase with admissions, the latter being too much greater than the former. Part of the reason might lie in the accumulation of students in the limbo known as ABD—"all but the dissertation."

Until the last years of the 1950's, few universities had any restrictions on the time it might take a candidate to finish his doctorate. Nor was the ABD student, or even a student stranded at an earlier career stage, expected to maintain an active status in the department in which a degree was being sought. In practical terms, this meant that the student paid no fees during what might amount to one or two decades of imminence. This is no longer the rule, although exceptions can be found. It is now commonly required that the candidate proceed from entrance into graduate school to the doctorate in a restricted span of time, often no more than seven years. Failure to do so can lead to the unilateral termination of the candidacy by the university. There are, of course, extenuations and possibilities for extensions. Nevertheless, cases have occurred in which candidates have been cut off because their time ran out.

The reasons for the rules are diverse. There was a low level of dissatisfaction for many years with the situation in which candidates grew older but no closer to the successful completion of their degrees. Those that managed to come up with dissertations sometimes did so ten or fifteen years after the completion of their course work. They were perceptibly older—and so was the anthropological fact and theory that they controlled. Under such circumstances, departments awarding higher degrees came to wonder what it was they were certifying when such a degree was awarded.

It was not these conditions, however, that sparked the actual formulation of rules restricting the period allowed for completing the degree. If there is any portion of sociocultural life in which a relatively simple economic determinism operates, it must be the academic. The absence of time-restricting rules prior to the 1960's was a corollary of the fact that graduate education was expensive and usually undertaken part time. At a minimum, a large proportion of students counted on teaching when they passed the M.A. level. Writing the dissertation in the face of teaching duties and family responsibilities was for most a slow process. In the absence of alternatives, the university was structured to accommodate such slow progress.

Then came the 1950's, and the beginning of the fellowship boom that peaked in the following decade. Departments approached what many defined as their ideal state: 100 percent of graduate students on full support. Of course, the costs of running universities were mounting, but few seemed to worry about it. The remedy was too simple: increased dependence on subsidizing funds, and increased fees and tuition prices. For many in graduate school, the latter was simply another part of the former, since student fellowships not only included full tuition but often paid additional overhead charges. Now universities asked payment for maintaining candidacies when the student was totally away from the campus. When such a student returned, it was often to find that he could use the library only after paying a whopping fee, along with other assessments that might be levied.

As long as the fellowship level remained high, few criticisms were heard of this drift in university affairs. The group from which most complaints might be expected, the students, had already been screened, so that those in the on-going programs were precisely the ones that were covered by grants and not likely to question the system. Those who were the victims of the new policies were excluded from the status of complainant, having failed to negotiate the selection process. They were never admitted.

But, as we go through the 1970's, the picture has drastically changed. The supporting funds have undergone great reduction or, in some programs, have disappeared. Governmental priorities have changed and the universities have seen almost all forms of subsidy decline. The number of graduate students who are resuming older pathways to their degrees, stopping along the way to keep their families afloat, is increasing. Yet the universities are still holding to the policies that were geared to different economic conditions. Change must come soon, and I venture to predict that one specific item will be the loosening of present time-restricting regulations.

It is interesting to look at the real situation of candidates vis-à-vis granted doctorates in anthropology. If it can be assumed that half of the population of anthropology graduate students were doctoral candidates (probably an underestimate), the figure for academic 1968–69 was about 2100. The number of Ph.D.'s granted in that year was about 160.[1] If the statutory period of seven years is assumed as the time it takes to achieve the Ph.D., 300 degrees might have been expected; taking ten years as the period, there might have been 210 degrees. The indicated attrition rates, therefore, seem to be between 25 percent and almost 50 percent. On the other hand, if we compute the M.A. program as a three-year span, the number of M.A.'s granted should have been on the order of 700, whereas the recorded number was about 400. The figuring here is very rough but tends to confirm my impressionistic conclusion that the bulk of the dropouts disengage themselves from graduate

---

[1] This figure is based on analysis of the Guide to Departments of Anthropology 1969–70 (Woodbury 1969). The actual figure obtained was 151, but a crude adjustment was made on the basis of personal knowledge of lacunae in the reported data.

anthropology during the first year or two of study. There is another period of loss much later on, when the candidate fails to complete his dissertation.

The business of dropping out of graduate school deserves attention and emphasis because it is socially wasteful and potentially destructive of individual egos. Unlike undergraduate education, the object of graduate education is not and cannot be the "whole person." It is the place for specialized training; it does not have any commitment to the concept of general education.

The general education functions of anthropology courses or curricula are found at the undergraduate level and must be resisted at the graduate level. The reasons for this should be obvious, but mention of a few points may dispel confusion.

Perhaps most important is the need of graduate courses to be truly graduate—to free the participants from the necessity of constantly defining elementary terms and concepts and of assuming virtually no ethnographic background in the student. Unlike courses in mathematics, which have, at least in part, a kind of intrinsic logical sequence, there are few areas in anthropology that suggest natural orders of prerequisites. The problem is compounded by the fact that most of the courses are taught mainly in what the student recognizes as a variant of normal speech. Thus an undergraduate student sometimes enters graduate courses, especially "area" courses such as pertain to Africa, Latin America, or Asia, and discovers only in the fourth or fifth week of the course that it is not what he anticipated. If the instructor now attempts to bring the course more closely into alignment with the nonspecialist expectations, a disaster may occur, namely, the abrogation of responsibility to the graduate students.[2]

Coming now to the main topic of this chapter, let us consider the factors that will operate in the rational choice of a graduate school for the candidate pursuing an anthropological degree. Some of these factors, important to the individual making the choice, are difficult to discuss meaningfully. Thus, for many, the question is not where to go, but where to be accepted; I doubt if statistics can be found to illuminate the matter, but a sizable number of students waken to anthropological interests late in their undergraduate life and then scramble to enter graduate school with mediocre records. As I already indicated, the present complex, whereby admission to graduate school in anthropol-

[2] *For those who ask about the responsibility of instructing the undergraduates, I think the answer obvious: area courses should also be taught on undergraduate levels where they can be more readily combined with less specialized demands. Admittedly, this may create a problem for the advanced major, who might be better off in the graduate course.*

ogy is tied more or less directly to undergraduate performance in the discipline, is something relatively new. Before the mid-'forties, competition to enter a graduate department of anthropology was anything but keen; an independent income was much more likely to be a factor than was previous performance. As performance has increased at the undergraduate level, so have the expectations of the graduate schools. One consequence has been the increasingly national, not to say international, composition of graduate student bodies. As this situation has developed, and as the number of schools offering anthropology has greatly increased, another question that has emerged has related to the area of the country in which to locate. Indeed, an increasing number of students look abroad for graduate work.

A student ready to undertake graduate work is usually regarded as an adult not only by the legal system but even by parents. The question of the site of the graduate school, however important personally, is treated publicly as trivial. The student who has already been weaned from the parental home might move back into the natal area without complicating personal life to the detriment of professional studies. More seriously, students who have spent four years at a local college should give very high priority to any scheme that would take them physically away; that is, they should conscientiously seek to go to graduate school in some other part of the country. Experience tells that the main complications attending the selection of a graduate school site arise from the fact that so many graduate students are either married or in an advanced state of pairing. Often the earnings of the spouse play a part in the fiscal plans. To change locale may be to lose a lucrative job or to take a chance on finding equivalent employment. The question is a serious one, just as serious as that presented by either conjunction or conflict of interest between the partners to a relationship, perhaps a married couple, perhaps not. Both may be aspiring anthropologists; usually not. But frequently both are students and one has gotten the nod here and the other there. If you are in this dilemma, I sympathize with you, but I have no advice to give. It's tough.

Let me back out of that corner into another one. It should be easy to take a stand on the question of choosing a graduate school in terms of its eminence, but there are certain complications. The most obvious have to do with the definition of eminence. The usual criteria are fairly mundane: size of the faculty and size of the student body. Beyond such crude arithmetical indices, the criteria are increasingly difficult to objectify. Total departmental staff productivity is relatively easily assessed in terms of volumes or pages, but what about quality? How is that gauged? How does one compare an exquisitely detailed ethnographic monograph with a volume of essays that appeals to a wide public? How about rating departments in terms of the fresh ideas that have come from their members? Unfortunately, the test of novelty is age; while a department may warrant the designation "innovating," the innovations themselves may not be very good. Enjoying brief vogues, they may fail to achieve acceptance. It is only from the hindsight of another generation that reasonable evaluation becomes possible, and by that time the department will probably have changed considerably.

There are attempts to rank the graduate departments in many disciplines, including anthropology. These have usually been made by educational foundations, which have sponsored such studies in attempts to find an objective basis for making supportive awards or for evaluating programs already subsidized. The usual method for carrying out these studies is by questionnaires distributed to department heads, deans, and distinguished scholars. Most such studies are confidential, partly out of fear that their circulation might enhance existing trends, thereby continuing or even increasing imbalances, and partly out of recognition of the deficiencies of the studies themselves. In any case, they are vulnerable to criticism on many grounds.

Perhaps the most prestigious attempts to rank graduate programs in the United States are those conducted by the American Council on Education. Taking off from an independent and rather restricted study conducted for the University of Pennsylvania in 1957 (Keniston 1959), the Council mounted its own studies in 1964 (Cartter 1966) and 1969 (Roose and Andersen 1970). The last report, in particular, is presented in conditional language and shows acute awareness of the problems attending any rating game. Some of its findings are quite general. For example, considering the 29 disciplines common to its 1964 and 1969 studies, none showed any decrease in their frequency of inclusion in graduate school curricula. All increased, that is, were taught at the graduate level in more universities around the country. Astronomy experienced the greatest increase, jumping from 16 to 35 graduate programs, more than doubling previous availability and apparently reflecting gains as the result of new interest in space and space sciences. No other discipline was even close to this, but anthropology registered the second largest increase, approximately 75 percent (Roose and Andersen 1970:5, and Table 2, p. 6).

The ACE questionnaire inquired into the quality of graduate faculties, asking respondents to scale their appraisals between distinguished (1) and "not sufficient for doctoral training" (6); number 7 was reserved for "insufficient information [to respond]." The ACE questionnaire offered respondents no guidelines to what might constitute distinction or mere adequacy. One hundred seventy-six questionnaires were sent to anthropologists: 31 to chairmen of anthropology departments, 35 to "senior scholars," 21 to "junior scholars." This totals 87. Who the other 89 were is not indicated in the ACE report (ibid.: 30).

TABLE 1   ACE List of Leading Departments
("By Rated Quality of Graduate Faculty")

1969	University	1957	1964
1	University of Chicago	1	1
2	University of California (Berkeley)	4	2[1]
3	University of Michigan	7	4
4	University of Pennsylvania	6	5
5	Harvard	2	2[1]
6	Yale	5	6[1]
7[1]	University of California (Los Angeles)	8	6[1]
7[1]	Columbia	3	6[1]
9[1]	Cornell	9	9
9[1]	Stanford	14	10[1]
11	University of Illinois	—	—
12	University of Arizona	—	12[1]
13[1]	University of Pittsburgh	—	—
13[1]	University of Wisconsin	15	10[1]
15	Northwestern	10	15
16	University of Washington (Seattle)	11	12[1]

Source: Roose and Andersen 1970:56
[1] Shares this rank with one or more other departments

The ratings of departments of anthropology with respect to the estimations of respondents to this questionnaire of the American Council on Education appears in Table 1. The listing includes the 16 departments reported in the ACE survey to be rated "Distinguished" or "Strong."[3] The highest rank, which is to say the department most often rated #1 (distinguished), is indicated by the lowest number. The 1969 column refers to the most recent ACE study, the 1957 column pertains to the findings of the Keniston study, and the 1964 column to the earlier ACE study (i.e., Cartter 1966).

The ACE survey also asked for an assessment of the "effectiveness of the doctoral program." The specific instruction to questionnaire respondents was as follows:

Circle the number below the term that corresponds most closely to the way you would rate the institutions listed if

[3] An additional 10 departments were rated "Good." In alphabetical order these were Brandeis, Colorado, Indiana, Michigan State, Minnesota, New Mexico, North Carolina, Oregon, Texas, and Tulane.

> you were selecting a graduate school to work for a doctorate today. Take into account the accessibility of the faculty and its scholarly competence, the curricula, the instructional and research facilities, the quality of graduate students, and other factors that contribute to the effectiveness of the doctoral program. [Roose and Andersen 1970:111]

Five possibilities were provided: (1) extremely attractive, (2) attractive, (3) acceptable, (4) not attractive, (5) insufficient information. Six departments ranked in the highest category: Chicago, Harvard, Michigan, Pennsylvania, Berkeley, and Yale. In the second category were Cornell, Stanford, UCLA, Illinois, Arizona, and Columbia. Twenty departments were listed alphabetically in the third category (ibid.:57).

Released to the public in January 1971, the second ACE study stirred immediate reaction. Like its first report, the second ran into considerable negative criticism. The earlier report had been dismissed by one critic for nostalgia, hearsay, and bias, and by another as "a compendium of gossip" (ibid.: ix). Although the sponsors of the ACE report declared that one of their major objectives was "to protect the potential consumer of graduate education from inadequate programs," it would seem that this might better be achieved by stimulating departments and universities to raise quality, rather than by influencing the shopping habits of prospective degree candidates.

The ranking of departments by "quality" or "effectiveness" is so controversial, and so subject to invidious and divisive results, that I prefer to continue by treating departments in terms of their size. Even in this area there are confusions, since there is only a very general relationship among size of staff, number of graduate students, and number of degrees granted. Table 2 is much to the point. In terms of current levels of graduate student enrollment (1968–69 available as base date), Harvard ranked ninth with 90 graduate students, sharing this rank with the University of Illinois and the University of Washington. Illinois has supplied some 18 Ph.D.'s in anthropology to the current staffs of graduate departments in the United States; Washington has supplied 22. But Harvard has supplied 190. It is by far the prime university in the country from which present members of graduate departments of anthropology have come. Rated by the same criteria, the five leading departments are: Harvard, 190; Chicago, 152; Columbia, 140; University of California, Berkeley, 134; and Yale, 78. It should be noted that Yale doesn't even appear on Table 2. The reason is simple enough —Yale drastically cut the number of graduate students it admitted. In 1968–69, its total number of graduate students in residence was but 29. This is not the only department that has sought to reduce its student population; in most instances this is being done as one part of a larger

TABLE 2 Fifteen Largest Departments of Anthropology Determined by Current Graduate Student Enrollment. (All data relate to 1968–69.)

University	Graduate Students	Faculty		Representation on Faculty 15 Largest Dpts.[3]	
		full-time[1]	part-time[2]	no.	rank[5]
UCLA	165	30	7	6	
Arizona	161[7]	20	6	9	10
California (Berkeley)	155	34	9	41	3
Chicago	136	26	13	46	2
Columbia	136	26	7	34	4
N.Y.U.	113[8]	11	6	1	
Pennsylvania	97	13	15	13	5/6
Colorado	92	20	5	4	
Harvard	90	30[9]	19	65	1
Illinois	90	20	2	3	
Washington (Seattle)	90	21	8	2	
Wisconsin	88	16	9	4	
Pittsburgh	85	18	8	1	
Oregon	85	13	6	3	
Michigan	80	22	12	12	7/8

[1] The number given may be illusory due to variations in reporting among the different departments. Some indicate faculty members on leave, others do not. Some indicate visiting designations, others do not. The figure given here is the raw total of full-time staff as listed in the Guide for 1969–70.

[2] Part-time faculty computation suffers from the same problem noted above and is probably less reliable, as it includes anthropologists outside the reporting department. The category as used here includes anthropologists in university museums, medical schools, and other programs or divisions, as well as those listed as part-time by the responding department.

[3] This column attempts to show the number of faculty members of the fifteen largest departments who have their highest degrees from the university named in the left-hand column. Only full-time staff members have been considered. There is also a problem about "largest," since some departments distinguish full- from part-time students, others do not, and still others do not admit any but full-time students (see notes 6 and 7).

[4] The fifteen smaller departments (on the basis of graduate student enrollment) were selected by turning pages at random in the Guide. (The schools

program seeking to make sure that every entrant earns a degree and, moreover, does so in relatively few years—perhaps four or five, including field work. Once again, it must be noted that an almost inevitable consequence of such programs is the placing of greater and greater weight on the applicant's previous anthropological background. One further consequence has been the development of a Graduate Record

TABLE 2 (Continued)

Representation on Faculty 15 Smaller Dpts.[4]		Ph.D.'s in All Dpts. in U.S.		Degrees Granted		Graduate Students per Faculty Member[6]
no.	rank	no.	rank	M.A.	Ph.D.	
11	7/8	52	8/9	28	8	5
4		48	10	22	9	5–6
15	5	134	4	13	12	4
20	3	152	2	14	8	4
15	2	140	3	6	14	4
0		2		8	0	5
11	7/8	52	8/9	22	7	5
2		9		15	3	4–5
29	1	190	1	12	0	2–3
2		18		9	9	4–5
2		22		10	1	4
8	9	41		13	0	4–5
2		10		0	3	4
6		25		7	5	5
12	6	67	6	27	7	3

are University of California at Santa Barbara, Duke, Hunter College of the City University of New York, University of Kansas, University of Minnesota, University of Missouri, University of New Mexico, North Carolina, Purdue, Sacramento State College, Stanford, State University of New York at Binghamton, Temple, University of Texas, and Tulane.)

[5] Ranking was carried out only for the top ten.

[6] In computing ratios, part-time faculty was computed as half a unit each, as were part-time graduate students. Because of the imprecision of the data, figures are rounded to the nearest whole unit. Where the value was about halfway between two whole numbers, the designation indicates 1–2 (one to two students per faculty member), and so forth.

[7] This figure includes 50 part-time students as reported by the department in question.

[8] Of this total, 35 are "full-time" students, as reported by the department in question.

[9] This figure includes the staffs of both the Anthropology Department and the then Department of Social Relations.

Examination (GRE) Advanced Anthropology Test, a matter discussed in detail at the end of the chapter.

Let us consider the question of choosing a graduate school on the basis of its size. As Table 2 reflects, there is only a partial relationship between the sizes of staff and graduate student body. According to Nathalie Woodbury (1969:iii), the number of schools offering advanced

degrees in anthropology in the United States during the academic year
1969–70 was 119. Of this number, 9 represented newly organized and
activated departments, an increase of some 7.5 percent over the previous
year. The exact number of graduate students of anthropology in the
United States during that same period cannot be determined with any
accuracy from presently available materials. Most reliable are the data
collected by the American Anthropological Association and found in
its annually published Guide to Departments of Anthropology. However, it appears that some departments round their figures; others report all candidates for degrees as "in residence," although some are in
the field while others are teaching elsewhere and writing dissertations.
Still other departments, as we have already seen, include part-time with
full-time students, although many departments no longer accept any
but the latter. For what it is worth, then, analysis of recent Guides
indicates that there were about 4800 graduate students of anthropology
in the United States in 1969–70, up from approximately 4150 the previous year. There were about 270 graduate students of anthropology in
Canadian universities in 1969–70, up from about 225 the previous year.
Undergraduate majors and concentrators in anthropology in the United
States in 1969–70 exceeded 15,000, a remarkable increase since the
previous year's figures approximated 10,000.

In 1969–70, the total number of departments offering graduate
work in anthropology, having one or more graduate students in the
program, and reporting in the Guide came to 126, an increase from the
110 reporting in 1968–69. The total number of graduate students indicated in 1969–70 was 4829, compared with 4129 in the previous year.[4]
The distribution of students by size of departments is shown in Table 3.
Some interesting observations emerge from the table, although the
crude nature of the base data renders all statements approximations.
(The percentages that follow are rounded to the nearest whole figure.)
About 10 percent of anthropology graduate students in 1969–70 were
reported to be in very small departments, which is to say those with 19
or fewer such students. (The contrast with the preceding year, which
recorded 9 percent, is insignificant.) About 25 percent are in the very
large departments, those with 100 or more graduate students. This
compares with some 20 percent in the previous year, which may be
significant; in any case, the number of departments with 100 or more
graduate students increased from 6 to 10. On the other hand, about 58
percent of students were in departments with fewer than 60 graduate
students in 1969–70, up from 52 percent in the previous year.

[4] Discrepancies between these figures and those immediately preceding
are due to the rounding of the former. It must be emphasized that
orders of magnitude are likely to be accurate, but the same claim cannot be made for precision.

TABLE 3 Distribution of Graduate Students of Anthropology
(by size of department, 1968–69 and 1969–70)

Number of Students	Number of Departments		Total Number of Graduate Students	
	1968–69	1969–70	1968–69	1969–70
100+	6	10	850	1277
90–99	5	3	459	280
80–89	4	2	338	175
70–79	2	4	149	298
60–69	3	7	187	441
50–59	10	14	524	739
40–49	9	6	390	260
30–39	11	12	368	393
20–29	20	20	480	488
10–19	22	27	300	379
1–9	18	21	84	99
Totals	110	126	4129	4829

What does it mean to choose a department for its size? Table 4 shows the faculty–student ratio for fifteen selected departments whose graduate student enrollments (1968–69) ranged from 4 to 65. This may be compared with the equivalent data shown in Table 2.

Although again the data are imprecise and overlaps are evident, it appears that smaller departments have a more favorable (lower) proportion of graduate students to faculty. The average of the fifteen largest departments is just over four graduate students per faculty member, whereas among the fifteen selected smaller departments, the average is two to three. Such figures cannot, however, tell the full story. Not considered is the component of undergraduate majors. In some departments the burden of these majors is distributed throughout the staff, but elsewhere it is concentrated and made the responsibility of certain faculty members. Often the latter system is favored in larger departments. The separation of faculty members into graduate and undergraduate departmental sectors tends to produce invidious distinctions which can be a source of irritation to students and faculty alike. One excuse for the practice is based on the formality that examination for a degree may not be conducted by anyone who does not have the degree in question or its equivalent. However, many teachers holding doctorates are not involved in their department's doctoral program or participate only marginally. Usually the undergraduate load is heavier in terms of hours of lecture and preparation, examination grading and paper reading. Young faculty members pressed into heavy undergraduate loads consider it simply another form of exploitation and are not convinced that the differences are balanced by the senior faculty members' generally heavier load of theses, committee assignments, and

Table 4 Fifteen Selected Smaller Departments
(all data relate to 1968–69)

University	Faculty[1]		Students		Graduate Students per Faculty Member[2]	Degrees Granted	
	full-time	part-time	graduate	undergrad. majors		M.A.	Ph.D.
California (Santa Barbara)	18	1	40	500	2	2	0
Duke	8	2	12	NA[3]	1–2	NA	NA
Hunter[4]	18	1	NA	80	NA	5	—
Kansas	12	8	52	92	3	9	2
Minnesota	13	2	62	214	4–5	9	3
New Mexico	16	1	65	144	4	8	4
North Carolina	13	4	40	52	3	10	0
Purdue	5	1	4	12	1	0	0
Sacramento State[4]	18	0	50	275	3	10	—
Stanford	17	2	50	100	3	13	8
SUNY-Binghamton[5]	13	2	27	55	2	12	—
Temple[4]	18	2	25	60	1–2	3	—
Texas	27	3	58	144	2	1	3
Tulane	10	4	23	49	2	6	2
Wichita State[4]	7	2	15	74	2	5	—

[1] For explanation, see notes 1 and 2 to Table 2, p. 168.
[2] For explanation, see note 6 to Table 2, p. 168.
[3] Data not available.
[4] This department offers the M.A. but not the Ph.D.
[5] This department began its Ph.D. program too recently to have awarded a degree yet.

general administration. Although the problems implicit in these conflicts are very important in determining the morale of a department, hence may vitally affect the lives of the graduate students, the subject is raised here only to indicate how complex is the problem of ascertaining student–faculty ratios.

Before leaving the question of these ratios, let me make a few more points about the concepts of benefit which they usually stimulate. The vision of small classes and especially small seminars is, indeed, more likely to be realized where ratios are low. Yet, the student must go beyond appearances to determine reality. Thus, courses in the anthropology department may be more crowded than anticipated because they may be used for other purposes in the university, perhaps in conjunction with programs of international or area studies, or the like. On the other hand, favorable student–faculty ratios may not be associated with particularly close working relationships between faculty members and students, even in research stages of candidacy. For one thing, in anthropology, graduate research generally seems to have a tradition of considerable independence. Whereas some other disciplines, particularly in the natural sciences, favor the close association of degree candidate and professor, the former sometimes being the actual assistant of the latter, anthropologists tend to be lone wolves. Often this is specifically applicable to the critical problem of evolving the subject of the dissertation, and this may be a source of dismay to overly dependent students. But most departments insist that among the most fundamental things that graduate training seeks to accomplish are inculcation and development of a "sense of problem," and some ability to determine the workability of problem ideas.

Until recently the choice of graduate school was made by a good many applicants on the basis of competing fellowship offers. There are still a fair number of students fortunate to be wooed in this way, but there has been a contraction as various funding crises, to which reference has already been made, have forced universities to retrench. For those who receive competing offers, choices can be difficult. It is rarely if ever a matter of yielding to the attractions of the highest bidder. There are interuniversity agreements and foundation rules which attempt to make award offers uniform with respect to stipends. Some variation exists with regard to the duration of fellowship benefits, and students usually show obvious preference for those which assure the most years of grant, or include provision for subsidization of field work as well as residence and study.

The problems of choice faced by students being actively recruited are not very much different from those faced in general, with the possible exception of those pertaining to students being recruited in consideration of social race or ethnicity. In such cases, the factors that will be operative have little or nothing to do with academic questions; associated for the most part with campus and extracampus politics, the complications of such choices are of considerable fascination but must be forgone in this discussion.

Of interest to all graduate students, and a major basis for choice of department, is the question of academic employment. Sooner or later, if he does not drop out, the graduate student permits to rise to consciousness a serious interest in professional employment.[5]

When departments are seen in terms of their graduates, interesting patterns emerge. Let us begin this discussion by noting that the bachelor's degree in anthropology has little or no significance on the employment scene. The master's degree is more useful. It will gain its holder access to a number and variety of teaching positions, but bestows a questionable degree of job security. Most younger college teachers who hold only the M.A. are assumed by their institutional employers to be active doctoral candidates. Often a time limit is set within which appointees must complete the doctorate or resign their positions. It is very much to the point, however, to introduce two observations: (1) the staying power of the non-Ph.D. is in part dependent upon the individual's ability to play the local political games of academe; (2) these games are easiest to play successfully when the expansion of the educational apparatus is more rapid than the rate of increase of Ph.D.'s. Out of these considerations comes a message: *Tenure will be increasingly difficult to obtain without a Ph.D.*, as the rate of production of doctorates surpasses the rate of expansion of the academic employment of anthropologists.

Since the job-oriented graduate student is frequently as much concerned about *where* his employment will be found as about other aspects of the status, it is instructive to consider the origins of members of the 15 largest departments, of the 15 selected smaller departments, and of college-employed anthropologists in general. The overall picture is presented in Table 5, pertaining to 1968–69.

Quickly apparent is the remarkable consistency in the institutions furnishing anthropologists to the teaching staffs of American universities whether large or small. Harvard is in first place regardless of the level chosen—all institutions for which data are available, the fifteen

---

[5] *To be sure, some radical students struggle against the opinion advanced in Chapter 2 that performance of the role of academically employed anthropologist is incompatible with the role of revolutionary. The number of anthropology graduate students taking the "Haber road" (see page 38) is, to my knowledge, very small. Advanced students of seemingly quite radical orientation have been observed in numerous instances to display concern for the identical aspects of job placement that distinguish other candidates: location, course load, salary, and so forth.*

TABLE 5   Leading Departments by Placements of Graduates

University	Placement of Graduates in All Dpts.		Placement of Graduates in 15 Largest Dpts.		Placement of Graduates in 15 Selected Smaller Dpts.	
	no.	rank	no.	rank	no.	rank
Harvard	190	1	65	1	29	1
Chicago	152	2	46	2	21	3
Columbia	140	3	34	4	26	2
California (Berkeley)	134	4	41	3	15	5
Yale	78	5	12	7–8	16	4
Michigan	67	6	12	7–8	12	6
Cornell	56	7	13	5–6	7	10
Pennsylvania	52	8–9	13	5–6	11	7–8
UCLA	52	8–9	6	12	11	7–8
Arizona	48	10	9	10	4	13/14
Wisconsin	41	12	10	9	8	9

largest, or the fifteen selected smaller departments. Also among the universities that have placed their graduates widely and with regularity are Chicago, Columbia, University of California at Berkeley, and Yale. Indeed, the fifteen largest departments (in terms of graduate student enrollment) themselves had a total of 320 full-time faculty members of whom 186 (about 58 percent) had their highest degrees from one of four universities (Harvard, 65; Chicago, 46; University of California at Berkeley, 41; Columbia, 34). Two hundred sixty-one (about 81 percent) came from ten universities (in addition to the foregoing, Cornell, 13; Pennsylvania, 13; Michigan, 12; Yale, 12; Stanford, 10; Arizona, 9). In addition, some 27 (about 8 percent) of the faculty members of these fifteen largest departments had their highest degrees from a European university, mainly English (i.e., Cambridge, 8; Oxford, 8; London, 7). Added up, this means that a little more than 10 percent of the faculty members in the fifteen largest departments came from all the other smaller departments. Actually, of the 104 such departments, only 21 were represented in this last category.

Confronted by these statistics, many anthropologists will probably attribute a major part of the clustering to "inbreeding" (after noting, of course, that it is expectable that departments turning out the largest number of degree holders are more likely to place graduates than those turning out very few). There is no doubt that some of the skewing is associated with the practice of hiring one's own graduates, but the phenomenon is a spotty one. The most inbred department in the fifteen largest is Columbia, where more than half of the full-time faculty members have Columbia Ph.D.'s. Chicago is next with well over a third, followed by Harvard at about a third and Berkeley at about one fourth. On the other hand, the University of California at Los Angeles and three others of the top fifteen had not a single member of their faculties with a Ph.D. from their own departments. Nonetheless, a sharp contrast exists between the top fifteen, taken together, and the selected fifteen smaller departments. Ten of the latter had no inbred members, four had one such member each, and one seemingly atypical case (Sacramento State College) had six.

Conclusions about the degree of inbreeding must be qualified by information relating to the distribution of tenured and nontenured positions in a department. Obviously, it is one thing for a department to employ a good many of its own graduates temporarily, and quite another to have such graduates comprising a solid bloc of the permanent faculty. Indeed, it is precisely the latter that is the case in those departments with the heaviest inbreeding. Independent corroboration is supplied in John Sorenson's study of interdepartmental mobility of anthropologists (1970:4–5). Using the *Guides* as his source of data, Sorenson found a total of 2346 individuals listed as faculty members in all departments in the United States during the period 1962–69. (Of these, 1627 were holders of the Ph.D.) The number whose departmental affiliation changed at least once during this period was 978 (41.7 percent). At four of the largest schools (based in this case on size of staff), however, of some 76 faculty members present at the outset of the period no less than 62 were still around at its end. (Columbia was most sessile, with 100 percent.) In four smaller departments (Arizona State, North Carolina, Syracuse, and Wayne State) some 24 of 38 original faculty members lasted through the whole period. For all departments, total changes averaged about 3 per year per two departments, but about 20 percent of these shifts were clearly temporary and of the "visiting" kind.

Although the future may see a radical break with the growth rhythm of the past, Sorenson's analysis indicated a somewhat higher departmental growth rate in the creation of new staff positions among the largest departments as compared with smaller ones. Another study based on data relating to 1965–66 found that as of October 1965, there were 2117 anthropologists employed in the United States, exclusive of those employed by museums or by the state or federal governments (Public Health Service 1969). The same study asserted that as of October 1965, there were 682 unfilled positions calling for qualified anthropologists. The authors of the study predicted that an additional 1399 new positions would be opened by 1970–71, leading to an estimated total demand of 4198 in that year.

I must confess that I believe the previously cited study to be somewhat off the mark, but I must leave the question for others to decide. My own analysis of the *Guide to Departments of Anthropology 1970–71*, which contains data relating to 1969–70, indicates approximately 2000 full-time positions, exclusive of museums, which would add a little more than 200. Part-time positions might add yet another 500 slots, about 175 being in museums. Computation proves extraordinarily difficult, as many individuals appear two or even three times in different roles; in a sense, however, each of the roles can be defined as a job. On the other hand, some of the roles are not associated with salaries, or the salary is being paid to someone else, as in the case of one person filling the slot of another who is on leave. Even more confusing, some personnel identified as full-time in a museum are also listed as full-time in a departmental slot. Repetitions of this sort are sufficiently frequent to make me believe that overcounting might come close to balancing underreporting in the compilation of the *Guide*. What this means, however, is that the order of magnitude of academic jobs in anthropology has not increased at all in conformity with the Public Health Service prediction. This seems to be at odds with my own perception of developments in the anthropology job market between 1965 and 1970. Although the last year was notably one of declining rate of expansion, the earlier years seemed to be marking considerable annual increases. A competent study of the situation is evidently necessary.

This heavily statistical information about the structure of academic anthropology in the United States should help to illuminate certain problems of choice of graduate school. In turn, that act of selection exerts considerable influence on later aspects of a candidate's career. Yet, there are many other considerations that should enter into the choice of a graduate school. Many of these are thought, particularly by the candidates, to be of much greater importance than anything mentioned so far. I refer especially to the intellectual bases for distinguishing among departments.[6]

As we already are quite aware, anthropology is much more of a congeries of related disciplines than a single homogeneous field. Accordingly, it is very important for the entering graduate student to be aware, at the very least, of some tendency toward specialization; the

---

[6] *I cannot refrain from commenting on the dialectical contradiction that seems to be inherent in this situation. It is precisely the members of that generation which seems most attracted to a strategy of cultural materialism in its attempts to explain cultural phenomena who are most likely to deny the implications of such a strategy in analyzing their own relationships to their culture and to their chosen field. In short, at least verbally, they place ideological factors in command.*

minimum discrimination is that which applies to the four fields. A department of anthropology may be considered very strong, may have a large faculty and produce a lot of Ph.D.'s, but it may have nothing in the area of physical anthropology. In terms of the doctorate, physical anthropology is a rare specialty. That "relatively few" departments offer advanced courses in physical anthropology, much less are competent to train for the degree, was noted by Lasker (1963a:111); the situation has changed somewhat for the better in the interim. A student with professional interests in physical anthropology should obtain a copy of the current *Guide to Departments of Anthropology* and check out the Special Programs sections that are to be found under most university rubrics. A comparison of the suggestions found there with the staff listing should give some idea of the scope of the program in question. I recommend, however, that further inquiry be pursued, at least to the extent of consulting the catalog of the university in question. Finally, if a visit to the department is not possible, a letter should be written, either to the department chairman or to the faculty member most concerned with the specialization.

Similar advice applies to those interested in linguistics. While most departments have at least one linguistically oriented anthropologist on their staff, they may not be equipped to give the range and depth of training that should accompany the doctorate in the field. Indeed, in linguistics as in physical anthropology, it is possible to look for training outside of a regular department of anthropology. There are several outstanding scholars who have made excellent contributions to physical anthropology but received their training in medical schools or in departments of anatomy, of genetics and biology, or of paleontology (Lasker 1963a:111). I cannot say how widespread the attitude is among my colleagues in anthropology, but the segment of the profession I know seems united in expecting that a young contemporary physical anthropologist can and should have as deep a technical mastery of his field as can be gotten anywhere, but that it should be tempered by some exposure to the other portions of anthropology as well. In practical terms, this means that the most desired degree comes from an anthropology department, but much work is taken in other departments and even other divisions of the university. Students interested in pursuing an interdisciplinary program of the type alluded to must determine in advance that entering a particular department will facilitate such a program.

Returning to linguistics, it is obvious that the alternatives, found in various nonanthropological departments of linguistics, are far more concentrated. In general, the linguist considered for a position on an anthropology faculty must have some anthropological training, although exceptions can be found. Sometimes such linguists must participate in instruction in courses having ethnographic and ethnological rather than linguistic content. Sometimes it is a matter of responsibility for the entire introductory anthropology course, or an autonomous section of such a course. Even where the linguist is free to teach only linguistics, there is a fundamental problem of relations with his faculty colleagues and with the students, who will expect various kinds of assistance requiring a knowledge of and empathy with the anthropological content of the field. I would strongly recommend that the candidate interested in anthropological linguistics take his work primarily within a department of anthropology, albeit one with a fully developed program in linguistics.

When it comes to choosing a graduate school for advanced work in archeology or cultural anthropology, the question becomes one of defining ultimate interests rather nicely. To be sure, similar problems exist in physical anthropology: it can make a difference whether one wishes to specialize in human genetics, human evolution, or medical anthropology (and there are additional possibilities), but the scale of variation is somewhat less and the alternative choice of institutions is also more restricted. But programs in cultural anthropology are found in every graduate department, and opportunities for work in archeology are only slightly less extensive. Further examination of these departments quickly reveals a wide diversity of topical and areal interests. It can be a matter of matching the candidate's evaluation of his own interests against this palette of possibilities. Of course, there are reservations. The student who has covered enough ground to begin to make a reasonable assessment of his interests is the one who has already experienced a good deal of the discipline during his undergraduate major. Without such preparation, the choice of specialization may be based mainly on ignorance of the existence or the character of work in the other portions of the discipline. Furthermore, even advanced students can change their minds and replace older interests with new ones. Nothing I have said so far should be interpreted as implying that students must make early career choices and then rigidly stick to them.

It should be evident, however, that the student who is interested primarily in, let us say, psychological anthropology will be in various kinds of jeopardy if enrolled, for example, in a department oriented toward evolutionary studies, where little or no attention is paid culture and personality. Once again, the student bears the main responsibility for determining in advance the character of the department he wishes to enter. In the final analysis, the main disappointment will be his if he guesses wrong; transfers are sometimes difficult to arrange.

Some overtones in the last paragraph may be interpreted as supporting the view that most departments of anthropology are associated with or dominated by one or another articulated view regarding the theoretical disposition of anthropology. Students often exchange characterizations of departments which align them in one "school" or another. When the faculty hear such remarks, they usually react with displeasure. For one thing, given a vogue of theoretical eclecticism, individuals fear that too close association with one particular viewpoint will virtually stamp them as intellectual bigots. However poorly such an opinion describes individuals, I think it applies quite well to whole departments. If a department cannot display a range of theoretical opinion to its students, it may well prove unadaptive and could face the fate of other dinosaurs. Unfortunately, candidates who approach graduate school, even those with fairly extensive undergraduate majors, are not likely to know about, much less be able to evaluate properly, the theoretical positions dominating the departments to which they seek entrance. Departments in which there are outstanding personalities, anthropologists known for many books or for controversial ones, are likely to be viewed in terms of those particular personalities. To the student's surprise, upon arrival, the personality in question, while much in evidence, can scarcely be called dominant. Other points of view are discovered rampant. Surprising as it may seem, choice of department on theoretical grounds may be a waste of time, if not misleading.

One reason for making the previous assertion must be stated. I am a firm believer in the proposition that a major portion of graduate education is obtained from one's peers. To be sure, lectures and conversations with faculty members are one important source of information and stimulation, but reading—on a scale that rarely occurs in undergraduate work—is probably more important. Ideas come from all over and are worked through in argument, debate, and quieter talks with one's fellows. It may be that my favor for such a system is nostalgic, but it is also pragmatic. In any case, I wish the reader good access to a lively group of palaverists.

Before quitting the topic of choosing and entering a graduate department, let me return to a matter I brought up much earlier and then set aside. As I indicated, one consequence of the increasing emphasis on anthropological background in assessing applicants for admission to graduate departments has been the recent development of an Advanced Anthropology Test option on the Graduate Record Examination (GRE). Like the better-known College Board Examinations, the GREs are administered nationwide by the Educational Testing Service of Princeton, N.J. They have, however, achieved far less acceptance than the College Boards. Until the development of the special test in anthropology, those departments requiring applicants to submit GRE results tended to use the information, at best, in supplementary fashion, checking the applicant's verbal and quantitative scores but probably never using them as the prime reason for acceptance or rejection. Some departments may also have asked candidates to take the Advanced Sociology Test, but scores could not be given much weight. The obvious consequence, as anthropology grew as a postgraduate field of study, was the development of the Advanced Anthropology Test. By 1969–70, only a few departments of anthropology were requiring applicants to submit GRE Anthropology scores. In 1970 the American Anthropological Association announced that its Executive Board had considered a request that it endorse the use of the GRE Advanced Anthropology Test and had decided not to do so. The decision was influenced by unfavorable assessments presented by two of the members of the Educational Testing Service Committee that had prepared the third revision of the Anthropology Test.

Since the question of the use of an examination as a primary basis for selection is obviously one of prime importance to advanced degree candidates, let us go briefly into the matter. The chairman of the committee that developed the Advanced Anthropology Test was Professor Edward M. Bruner of the University of Illinois. In October 1967, Bruner reported to the Executive Committee of the American Anthropological Association on the general idea of an anthropology test. Although reservations were expressed, the feeling was quite positive, mainly because a "study conducted by the National Science Foundation of their fellowships indicated that the advanced test in the sciences was the best single predictor of ability to complete work for the PhD." (Bruner 1970:11). Concerned about "the high attrition rate in anthropology graduate schools," Bruner felt that the shortcomings of the objective test format were secondary. As he put it, "The key question is—*does it work?*" (*ibid.*:12, italics in original).

Pointing out that the main objective of the test was to qualify candidates for some kind of financial assistance as well as admission to a graduate department, two members of a 1969 committee charged with preparing the third revision of the anthropology test, Professor Ernestine Friedl of the City University of New York, and Professor Robbins Burling of the University of Michigan, took the opposite position. According to them, a large portion of the questions were forced by the nature of the test to be composed in such a trivial way that, "*we do not agree that his* [the candidate's] *knowledge of them has any predictive value for his success as a professional anthropologist*" (Friedl and Burling 1970:10. Italics in original). The critics went further, declaring the examination a danger:

> We believe the examination selects in favor of students who
> have taken a great deal of anthropology as undergraduates
> and who have covered all the conventional and traditional
> branches of the discipline. It selects for those who have spe-

cialized early in their college careers, and for the "fact sponge." On the other hand, we believe that it selects against some types of imaginative students who sample widely of varied disciplines and against the departments that prefer an unconventional program or are trying to innovate.   [Ibid.]

Although the attention of letter writers was soon to be drawn to the perhaps more explosive questions of ethical standards and interpretations for the profession (see Ch. 13), arguments and opinions, pro and con, continued to appear in the Newsletter, and at the time of writing no resolution of the debate appeared to be in sight. For myself, however, one of the most formidable points was raised by Friedl and Burling. In response to the argument that university or departmental admissions committees are aware of the limitations inherent in such tests, and may be presumed to temper judgments of exam performance in the light of previous exposure to the discipline, Friedl and Burling raise the specter of routinization, contending that committee interest flags and leaves the score on such a test the "objective" and easy way out.

There the matter lies. Requests for admission to graduate departments in anthropology may be expected to continue to rise, although slowing of the growth of new departments on all levels will probably bring a leveling off, if not a reduction, in graduate admissions. Economic recession or full-scale depression will obviously affect the trends. The National Science Foundation, however, has published a survey and prediction of considerable optimism; in Science and Engineering Doctorate Supply and Utilization, 1968–80 (National Science Foundation, NSF 69–37, Washington, D.C.: U.S. Government Printing Office, 1969) the present trends are projected into the future with the anticipation, however, that people with Ph.D.'s will much more commonly teach in institutions and at levels where the previous staff commonly held lower degrees.

What will the departments do? The trend among larger departments is already to reduce the number of admissions. Thus, graduate departments will become more and more elitist. Yet the ideological tide in contemporary academia runs counter to such elitism. It is only a matter of time until demands for changes in admission policies, now commonplace in undergraduate colleges, particularly those in larger urban settings, are directed at selected graduate departments. If such changes come, how will they affect the choice of a graduate school in anthropology? The question is a fair one, but its impact is still sufficiently remote for us to avoid it. Let us turn instead to a consideration of the graduate curriculum.

10

THE GRADUATE CURRICULUM

The students' minds must not be caged, nor for that matter those of their teachers.
—Mohandas Gandhi

Uncertainty marks the attitude of anthropologists toward the selection of their own professional young. Some aspects of this wavering can be seen in the clash over the use of the Advanced Anthropology Test in the Graduate Record Examination. As indicated earlier, the crux of the matter lies in the conflict between intensively prepared undergraduate candidates for admission to graduate school, and applicants of potential brilliance but little background. Anthropology, as a formal academic discipline, is too close to its origins to have forgotten that most of its most eminent practitioners received their education in other fields. The British social anthropologist Meyer Fortes, for example, muses about

> *Frazer's classical education, Radcliffe-Brown's schooling in the rigorous intellectual climate of Cambridge philosophy at the turn of the century. Malinowski's training as a physical scientist, Seligman's in medicine, and so on. In my own generation in British anthropology, Evans-Pritchard took his first degree in the Oxford School of History. Firth moved over from economics, Leach was an engineer and mathematician, and I drifted in from an arduous quinquennium of research in statistical and experimental psychology.* [1963:423]

So the roots of previous generations of anthropologists, in the United States and abroad, lie in many instances outside the discipline. This tradition helps to trigger a reaction very much like guilt when anthropologists take steps to raise the professional requirements of their candidates. Nothing shows the prevailing ambivalence more clearly than the present graduate curriculum in most departments, and its recent history.

In briefest compass, too many departments continue to insist that all entering graduate students submit to a synthetic introductory course, which, no matter how high its level in intention, actually succeeds in reversing the development of most students except those who have

183

come with little or no anthropology in their undergraduate preparation. It is, of course, one thing for the discipline to insist upon holding open channels of admission for outstanding candidates without proper formal backgrounds. It is quite another to exact payment for such a decision from the candidates who arrive with more than a modicum of training. But what else can flow from the system which exists so widely? As described by Fred Eggan:

> The common pattern of graduate instruction in most American institutions is to begin with a broad base in "general anthropology," and later to narrow one's interests to a single subfield or discipline and to specialize in that and closely related fields. [1963:411]

When many institutions couple that first broad-based anthropological year to an examination regime that determines the student's future, it can readily be seen why so many students, particularly those who have majored in anthropology on the undergraduate level, will be ripe for protest and revolution in their own discipline. One student remarked to me, in evident desperation, that he was sick to find himself, at an age when most of his contemporaries had assumed full adult responsibilities, to be stuck, still and seemingly forever, in reading the same books, hearing the same lectures and taking the same examinations. "Why," he demanded, "do they call this graduate school?"

We have already seen what justifications are given for the shape of the first graduate year, including the desire to certify the competence of the candidate to teach general anthropology. But honesty demands that the student be told the single most important reason: that is, to hold open the way for some unknown potential genius of anthropology who might otherwise be excluded were entrance requirements to be standardized and professionalized. The extraordinary thing is that much of this nonsense may be unnecessary. There are various possibilities.

Chief among them is placement, which can be achieved in various ways. A key problem is to ascertain the student's strengths and weaknesses. Placement tests have been one attempt to determine this, but such efforts have been awkward and not very practical. In addition, students resent and fear the examinations despite every effort made to put them at ease and guarantee that the only purpose to be served is placement. The method of placement that seems to work and wear best is the advisory interview with a member of the admitting department. In candid exchange, with the student's record before him, it is possible to thrash out the best options for the student's career. But this method has its own drawbacks. It is costly in faculty time and requires that faculty members be better informed about their department's requirements and procedures than is sometimes the case. On the student's side, candor is absolutely necessary. Permission to bypass one or another lower-level course is no prize to be won by manipulating an interview.

A placement system requires access to courses capable of making up reported deficiencies. What follows takes different forms at different institutions and different times; there is something of a cycle of fashion here. Sometimes the student is tested for overall general capacity and control of certain minimum bodies of anthropological information through a battery of examinations given specially at the end of the first year. Sometimes such examinations occur at the end of the second year. Occasionally, the lower-level courses are accompanied by normal examinations whose results are averaged to arrive at a determination of the student's capacity to continue toward a higher degree. Procedures at the schools I am familiar with invariably open consideration of the student's abilities to whatever additional evidence can be supplied. Thus, term papers are viewed in this light, and opinions are solicited from faculty members with whom the student has maintained closest working relations. Although it is difficult to convince students, such faculty consideration is much concerned with preventing the student from coming to harm by continuing to pursue a goal that seems incommensurate with interests or abilities.

Problems of the graduate anthropology curriculum have their loci in many factors other than the frequently uneven backgrounds of the students. To mention just two that have to do with the objectives of graduate education, there is the conflict between generalist and specialist training and between training for research and training for teaching. These two things are evidently related.

It might be thought that the problem of general versus specialized education would be resolved by the time one entered graduate school. That it is not reflects on the failure of the undergraduate curriculum in some instances, and on the diversity of aims among the members of the graduate anthropology faculty in others. The first point is obvious and needs no glossing. The second alludes to conflicts within individual faculty members, some of whom seem to be perpetually comparing themselves to the students to the disadvantage of the latter. Do the students know the minutiae of certain classical monographs? Do they respond to queries about great anthropological controversies of the past? Do they know lots of things outside the narrow limits of their specializations? I have no intention of downgrading the knowledge demanded by such queries but there is a real question about the priority such knowledge should receive. Without suggesting that older days can or should be brought back, it is instructive to note that if progression from a first generalized graduate year to a second specialized one and thence out into the field is most sensible,

> most of the anthropologists of the older generation had no
> such "logical" training. Students of Boas might be plunged
> into advanced statistical methods or Kwakiutl linguistics, or
> whatever Boas happened to be interested in at the moment,
> and were expected to pick up their knowledge of general
> anthropology on their own. When he felt they were "ready,"
> he sent them into the field with a problem. [Eggan 1963:
> 411–12]

Rather than being old-fashioned, it seems that Boas may have been avant-garde. He might, in this day of pleas for relevance, be very much in step if placed in proper perspective. Note that Boas, who dealt with perhaps half a dozen students at a time, would now be in a department with a hundred and twenty such students. Although it is true that not all would look to him for guidance (and what would that have provoked in Boas?), he would still have had many times the load he had previously known.

Turning from past to present, I note that most departments are currently using one of three major curriculum variants. Perhaps most widespread, particularly in large and moderately large departments, is the progression which begins with a general year and advances to specialization. Usually such a system incorporates two levels of examinations. At the simpler level, ideally taken after one year of residence, candidates are examined more in breadth than in depth, and a four-field approach is taken for granted. Success on this examination usually matriculates the candidates for the doctorate; that is, pronounces them qualified to take the remaining hurdles. Usually, it also qualifies a candidate for a master's degree, provided that an essay is submitted. (Some schools have abolished the master's essay, but its utility in deciding whether marginally passing students have the capacity to do doctoral work suggests that it will survive.) Given a free choice about the M.A., most Ph.D. candidates prefer not to divert their energies to writing the essay it requires, unless there is a special reason for it, such as offering it in conjunction with work in an institute or similar program which grants its own degree or certificate. (Thus, students in Columbia's East Asian or other institutes follow this procedure and receive in return a certificate in foreign language and area studies. This procedure adds at least a year and often two years to a student's graduate residence and can be a source of considerable anguish if not thought out in advance.)

A second possibility is presented by departments that mandate the M.A. Most that do this in anthropology are indeed limited to the granting of this degree. Since the M.A. does not usually provide security for its holder, those who seek careers in anthropology usually attempt to enter other departments to continue to work toward the doctorate. The reader who is in such a situation or who is thinking of entering one must be cautioned. Many anthropology departments, particularly the larger ones, are not enthusiastic about admitting candidates with M.A's. Although they have no rules against it, they prefer to save their graduate student slots for candidates who can be taken all the way through. There is also fear of admitting a candidate who has received the M.A. as a terminal degree,[1] since few if any institutions granting such a degree will admit the invidious distinction that goes with it. Such a fear should not apply to schools granting only the M.A. as higher degree, but it is easier to discriminate against a whole group than to make individually valid decisions, as any victim knows. Curiously, as scrutiny of various master's degree programs will show, the requirements associated with the previous scheme tend to be much reduced in the M.A. program. That is, the latter is less concerned with the preparation of the candidate in general anthropology and more with developing competence toward the turning out of the essay. It is worth the reader's keeping this in mind when he hears that the M.A. is a good basis for teaching in undergraduate programs, junior colleges, or the like—the very places where emphasis should be greatest on the ability to convey the general messages of anthropology.

The third of the major mazeways to an advanced degree in anthropology offers optimum individual freedom of choice of courses to the candidate. In consultation with an adviser, preferably one whose interests lie in the candidate's area of specialization, the student even in his first term selects what he wants to take, whether in his own department or outside. This he repeats until he has amassed the necessary credits or has endured the prescribed residence and is ready for his predoctoral examinations (often called "comprehensives"). Because such schemes are so free of restraints and compulsions, they are usually tied to extremely rigorous selection policies. Most of the students chosen to participate in them have already done a great deal of work in anthropology. If such students entered a department with placement procedures, it is likely that they would be sent directly into advanced courses, seminars, and research programs.

It should be clear by now that departments often manipulate students, coercing them to make certain curriculum choices rather than others, not by requiring one or more particular courses but by having it understood that the content of such and such course will positively be found on certain crucial examinations. Psychological warfare of this

---

[1] The euphemism "terminal M.A." does not usually refer, as might be thought, to a master's degree which is awarded as the normal conclusion of a program of studies calculated to lead to that degree. Rather, it usually implies that the M.A. in question was granted to a student who would have preferred to continue toward the doctorate, but who was found lacking for the highest degree although worthy of the lesser one.

type can force even the overqualified into courses they shouldn't take. Incidentally, key faculty members often do not consciously realize that such warfare exists; they simply haven't bothered to think their way through the implications of their departmental examination regimes and curricula. Such matters, too important to be left to a committee, are often determined by a small number of professors. True, in a large department many problems of curriculum must be delegated or nothing will ever get done. But the general philosophy and thrust of a structure of courses and examinations is the business of all. Indeed, it is essential that students join with the faculty in overseeing these affairs.

Now, what actually exists in the way of courses? Let me begin by saying that I am one of the inbred—I received my graduate training at Columbia and went immediately into teaching there. After some ten years, I began to develop an anxiety. I feared that anthropology did not really exist in the real world but was something that had been dreamed up at Columbia and was peculiar to it. To be sure, the evidence of such journals as the *American Anthropologist* and the *Journal of the Royal Anthropological Institute* indicated that the phenomenon was not only national but international. On the other hand, the only experience I'd ever had of another department had been at City College, where, before getting my degree, I had taught anthropology and sociology in the Sociology Department. To my relief, I finally enjoyed various visiting professorships elsewhere, at the University of Michigan, Yale, and National Taiwan University. Anthropology certainly existed apart from the university at which I had learned it, but the courses were pretty much the same. So much the same did it all appear, that any anthropologist would have concluded that it all undoubtedly did arise either from a single source or from very closely related ones. That being the case, the remarks that follow, although based mainly on my own experience and a selective sampling of university catalogs, probably apply to most of the graduate departments in the United States with the possible exception of the very smallest ones.

I should stress that while these remarks do pertain to most graduate departments in Canada, they do not pertain to most British universities and not to the large English departments such as at Cambridge and Oxford. The English system, although showing small signs of yielding, however reluctantly, to American influence, is committed to a quite different system, one in which the taking of courses is minimal, if not totally absent (Beattie 1963:442–43). Such work is relegated to undergraduate and "diploma" courses; once registered for a doctorate, the candidate is not expected to attend lectures.

There are many ways of classifying courses within a graduate department's curriculum. Rather than use the most general means of distinguishing them, which comprises the trinity of general, intermediate, and advanced, I prefer a somewhat more descriptive approach.

First there are survey courses of various types. Next comes a level at which cluster various different types of courses: the ethnographic detail courses, and those in subjects such as economic or political or psychological anthropology, or ethnomusicology, plus nuts and bolts methodology courses. Beyond this is a level of seminars, many having roots in the substance of courses lower down in this hierarchy. Finally, there is the extensive individual research that is carried out in consultation with one or more faculty members, which should reach fruition in the doctoral dissertation.

The survey level is itself striated. At the bottom is the course in introductory general anthropology intended for graduate students with background deficiencies. Usually this course goes through a cycle of praise and blame. As it is given, and as the level of preparation of most of the students rises, the level of the course itself is raised. As a consequence, the course loses all meaning for those for whom it was originally intended. The unprepared auditor flounders amidst an unfamiliar vocabulary and casual references to theoretical battles of which he has never heard. For all of this, the more sophisticated students find the course as a whole lacking in consistency and integration. Finally, the course is dropped. After a while, students agitate for its return. Wouldn't it be nice, they say, if there was one course which surveyed the whole discipline at a high level?

The general introductory course is only one of the survey courses; there are many others. As I already remarked, at the University of California, Berkeley, and at many other departments there is not a single integrated general course, but a sequence of relatively autonomous courses in the major subdisciplinary areas—physical, linguistics, and so forth. There are yet other levels to the survey course. Where else, for example, can we place such familiar archeology courses as Old World Prehistory, or New World Prehistory? What about the courses in general linguistics which span a full academic year and, of course, completely overlap whatever component of linguistics is offered in the general introduction to anthropology? As for physical anthropology, it offers well-attended courses on such survey topics as human evolution and human biology. Like certain other courses, these repeat at greater length and in greater detail much subject matter that has been reviewed in the general course. As for cultural anthropology, it presents most of its surveys in the guise of intermediate-level courses. We will get to those in a moment, but we can note the presence in some curricula of clear-cut survey courses in cultural anthropology, such as a "graduate introduction to cultural anthropology" taking two semesters, or a survey history of cultural anthropological theory.

The classical survey courses in cultural anthropology usually have familiar titles such as Social Organization, or Primitive Economics, Political Anthropology, or Social and Cultural Change. Skirting the deep analysis of most of the matters raised, although sometimes entering into surprising detail with regard to some subjects, such as the Australian "eight-class" system, or the Crow or Omaha kin terminological systems, such courses present encapsulated views of the subject matter in question and usually provide no opportunity for original work on the part of the student. Once again, it is a matter of learning a vocabulary and the history of a set of problems. Impatient students who do not know this vocabulary, or the history of selected problematic past ventures, might be set to do original work but at great personal cost. In short, they would have to retrace the history of the field, probably repeating a good many of its errors and false starts, before coming to realizations that can be achieved more economically by classroom work. It may come as a shock to some students, but I think it fair to say from my experience that many more dissertations are finally turned down because they are, unknown to their authors, already old-fashioned and behind the literature, than because they are vanguard trailblazers. Attention to appropriate courses at the level being discussed is one means of averting such a disaster, although it is by no means sufficient.

Another form taken by surveys in cultural anthropology is the high-level area course. This ranges from continent-wide treatments (Peoples and Cultures of Africa, Peoples and Cultures of Asia, and so on) to such "modest" courses as China. Pause a moment. When some "third-world" aggregation of students charges racism because of the mere appearance of such courses in a catalog, the reaction is often one of amazement. But, however measured, Chinese culture is not something that can be conveyed in a one-semester course, much less in something devoted to all the cultures of Asia. To the extent that the complaint is registered by students who really want a dialogue, however, reasonable justifications can be given. Within anthropology, there are courses relating to American culture; outside, there is sometimes a program of American studies that gives courses similar in scale and scope to the one mentioned about China, as well as others that could be cited. In any event, older anthropologists worry about younger ones, wishing them to receive as much information as possible about world cultures past and present. To be sure, the information is there, at least within certain limits, if one has the inclination to seek it in the library. But the inclination is easily channeled elsewhere, when it is not completely thwarted. At this writing, some students are extraordinarily knowledgeable about Vietnam and Southeast Asia. Queried about Korea, the level of information drops close to zero. Because anthropologists do not necessarily have to be current in their devotion to anthropological problems, the point of this may not be apparent. The anthropologist, broadly conceived, is interested in the ramifications of culture. If he is expert in a particular area, good; but this expertise is developed essentially to enable him to get at another kind of problem for which his local expertise merely forms a *background*. Stripped of his ability to make cross-cultural checks and comparisons, the anthropologist soon becomes something else—a sociologist, a local historian—and forgoes his greatest task, which is to deal with culture in broad terms.

Beyond the survey level is a cluster of courses that supply highly specialized or intricately detailed materials. Gone is the continent- or culture area-wide scope. Concentration in ethnography is on a particular society or segment of a society, usually one in which the instructor has been involved as fieldworker. The actual subject may be a cluster of New Guinea villages, a Polynesian atoll, a Taiwanese peasant village, a Cleveland suburb, an African mining town. The instructor may organize his materials around one or more problems, such as the effects of the impingement of the international market on local economy and social organization, or the thrust of the course may be directed at the useful organization of the multiplex materials, giving practice in synthesizing institutions out of raw behavioral data. Unfortunately, such courses sometimes fare poorly, avoided by all but the very few whose research interests fall almost totally congruent to the areal specificity of the course. Yielding to pressure, a department sometimes discourages the offering of such courses, preferring that the faculty give the much larger scale areal survey courses. Lost sight of in such exigencies is the fact that the course offering a "microscopic" approach is totally different from that based on a macroscopic view. Attempts to combine the two approaches in a single course by taking a broad view of a very large region and then focusing down to a village are more likely to accomplish neither end with much success, mainly because inevitable compression will create lacunae and distortions. What is more, and what must be faced, is the realization that macroscopic courses are basically not of the graduate level in their conception. Their contents are almost as readily available in a reasonably structured bibliography. On the other hand, a detailed course about a specific place, even if the monograph has already been published and presents the instructor's own work, makes available information that can be gotten nowhere else. The instructor is there to answer questions and to participate in dialogue, almost as if he were an informant from the culture in question. Such a course, utilized skillfully by instructor and students, can develop into a proseminar, a stage intermediate between lecture course and seminar, capable of enriching much of the seminar work that will be undertaken by the student in following semesters.

Properly handled, the courses previously described are quite evidently graduate in design and function. They lead into the seminars which prepare the candidate for his final predegree work. If successful, the dissertation should be fully professional; it may be the best thing of its kind the candidate will ever do. That being the case, it is in the seminars that the student becomes the master of his subject and rises to professional level.

If this insistence on professionalism strikes the reader as misplaced, he should consider once again the relation between undergraduate and graduate schools and curricula. The latter, as I have indicated, are not attuned to the problems of general education and would be wasted if they had to devote themselves to such a problem. The purpose of graduate school is to develop and train certain abilities and talents for a range of tasks including, hopefully, some that are not yet known. Very much part of the goal, whether it be in cultural or any other part of anthropology, is development of the ability to convey clearly in speech or writing even complicated concepts, descriptions, or analyses. Accomplished early, much trauma may be removed from the arduous process of producing the dissertation. The intent of these remarks should be considered most carefully by those students who resent being criticized on the mechanics of their various presentations, believing instead that the instructor should devote himself almost exclusively to intellectual substance. Yet, if anything, it is likely that problems of clarity of expression and communication are neglected in graduate work. Many instructors seem inured to ungrammatical presentations or poor word choice in written work. On the level of verbal presentation, lapse of the critical function is particularly widespread. This is part of a broader failure of most graduate departments to deal with the preparation of students for the teaching role.

While the role of the instructor can be crucial in determining the character of a seminar, real success, defined in terms of productivity, excitement, and enjoyment, is a product of cooperation among the members. A monologue by the instructor or by one or a few dominant students can kill a seminar dead. The instructor can help avoid this fate by screening participants in advance and by asking noncooperative seminar members to leave. My own practice has been to refuse free riders access to my seminars. Let me explain that "free" means to have no paper-writing responsibility. Every student who sits in on seminar discussions, it seems to me, should be working on a problem with the responsibility of presenting a paper. Otherwise, attendance can be spotty and criticism irresponsible. Similarly, reading can fall off with no commensurate rise in humility. It is not a way to increase popularity, but insistence upon having seminar participants register with the understanding that failure to produce may lead to a failing grade has produced some fine seminars. Other instructors have their own methods.

We have come this far in a discussion of the graduate curriculum in anthropology having mentioned hardly any specifics about the courses offered. Given the present diversity of course offerings, it could scarcely be otherwise without converting this chapter into a catalog. During the academic year 1969–70, for example, there were eighty-two distinct courses at the graduate level offered by the Columbia department.

Even with such proliferation of courses within the department of anthropology, and with the degree of diversity that necessarily attends such proliferation, students often are not satisfied with the offerings of their own department and request greater license to take courses outside. Such courses may be mentioned by the adviser as useful, or they may even be listed in the catalog in conjunction with appropriate departmental courses. In many schools there is no problem in obtaining access to such courses, even when they take a student to the medical school, or to journalism, or to a school of social work. (Much more difficult to obtain is the crediting of work done in a completely different institution. Summer session transfers of credit provide substantial precedents. During normal semester work, however, most universities prefer that the resources they offer be exhausted before a student looks abroad.) Not infrequently, the departmental adviser is helpful and cooperative when a student wishes to range outside the home department. The rub comes, of course, in the context of the department's examination requirements. In other words, it little avails the student to have a friendly adviser, if the department lurks in wait with a massive examination protocol that can be passed only by taking extensive course work in the department. Unfortunately, the contrast between seeming permissiveness and the reality of examination requirements is seen by some students as evidence of the hypocrisy of the Establishment—in this case, their department. Meanwhile, many faculty members have never looked at the situation this way, are constitutionally unable to see themselves as an establishment, and the rift widens to their perpetual mystification.

Once again the solution raises a question that has plagued us repeatedly in this and preceding chapters, that of the degree of control of information that the student will be responsible for, the contest being between knowledge of general anthropology and knowledge of a tightly defined specialization. If favor is shown to the latter, then relatively few restrictions in the form of counterdemands will be placed on the student. Presumably, a department favoring such an approach will have some arrangement whereby it can advise and approve (or disapprove) of a student's concept of major interest. At Columbia we have been asking each student, in consultation with one or more advisers, to evolve a list of three subjects in which he wishes to specialize *and be examined*. The department has a suggested list of subjects, including many quite conventional ones (psychological anthropology, ecology, sociology of kinship, paleolithic archeology, and primatology, to name a few), plus consideration of areal interests (China, East Africa, Brazil, American communities, for example) and some newer (for us) but rapidly developing categories, such as colonialism and imperialism (or comparable categories). Once the student has come up with his three subjects, which may be related but should not be so close as to represent merely different aspects of a single problem, he must fashion bibliographies in each. These are gone over with various faculty members, as many as may be helpful. The bibliographies are crucial, since written examinations for the Ph.D. will be based upon them to a considerable extent. It is therefore imperative that faculty members who feel that certain books or articles are indispensable to the subject in question make their feelings known early enough so that the student has ample opportunity to read the book, assimilate it to his thinking, or prepare his critique. To those faculty members who feel that one purpose of an examination is to see how widely a student has sampled a body of literature on his own, two things may be said. First, in this day of tremendously proliferating publication, how fair or reasonable is it to treat a body of literature in such fashion? And, on the heels of that, it may be noted that the predoctoral oral examination (which is different from the thesis defense) continues to provide the opportunity to check on a candidate's breadth of knowledge although, hopefully, in a constructive rather than punitive way.

Plus ça change. The graduate curriculum has been in flux since its inception. Mainly, until now, the trend has been toward multiplication. Few if any courses ever seem to be dropped, except very specialized ones associated with a particular instructor who has moved on, retired, or died. In the present climate of higher education, this may change. For a little while, now, there has been a subtle trend toward the devaluation of lecture courses as such in favor of more participatory courses, especially research seminars. (As the earlier remarks of Eggan about Boas show, this is nothing new. Actually, as indicated in the remarks about the origins of general education in Chapter 5, the initiation of the graduate school in America was on the German model and has much in common with the new trend.) This trend may be reinforced by economic recession. Even if not, the financial situation of the universities is such as to encourage any trend to reduce course proliferation, although it does favor the multiplication of courses capable of attracting and sustaining mass audiences. Although this prognosis applies most directly to undergraduate teaching, some comparable trends are expectable in graduate education if its growth continues.

The role of the research course should continue to enlarge as graduate education in anthropology improves. That being the case, let us see what presently exists, and what might be, in the realm of research as seen by the graduate student.

11

RESEARCH AND THE GRADUATE STUDENT

> It isn't in his possibilities, but in man
> himself that we must study mankind. It
> isn't a matter of imagining what man
> might have done or should have done,
> but of looking at what he does.
> —De Brosses (1760)[1]

Graduate students expect to carry out research projects on at least two levels before getting their degrees; they will do papers for courses and a major work for their doctoral dissertation. Some will do a third, presenting an essay for the M.A. Setting aside theses and dissertations, let's begin this brief consideration of the place of research in the graduate program with some remarks about course papers.

There is no sharp distinction between the papers turned in by undergraduates and by graduate students, just as the papers received in an advanced seminar may not be qualitatively distinct from those turned in for an ordinary course. Yet, from undergraduate to graduate paper, from seminar report to M.A. thesis and thence to the doctoral dissertation, there is a marked gradient of rising expectations. A paper returned to an undergraduate with the grade of A might be considered worth a substantially lesser grade if submitted by a graduate student. The principle underlying the distinction is simple and clear enough, yet, unfortunately, there is something less than agreement on it. The matter of grading is one of the most discussed and least rational aspects of our culture, from grade school through university. This is not the context in which to attempt a thorough discussion of this problem, but it is very relevant to the question of encouraging and developing research abilities. In the present instance, some instructors maintain what they consider absolute standards, grading the same way regardless of the level of the student. Like many colleagues, however, I prefer to make individual distinctions, even when undergraduates and graduate students share the same class. I believe that the primary function of the course paper is to extend the learning situation; criticism of the paper is more important than the grade. In any case, I feel that both justice

---

[1] *Merci à Georges Condominas (1965:237).*

195

and the students are best served if a high degree of discretion is preserved.

Against this background, consider the reasons for applying a more demanding set of standards to the graduate paper. First, it is obvious that the graduate student has embarked on a career commitment while the undergraduate is still in the process of choice. Both need sympathy and understanding, of course, but in different ways. The graduate student is in the throes of making the major lifetime decision that still lies one or more years in the future of the undergraduate. To lead poor graduate students on, falsely, encouraging them to expend their time, energy, and treasure on a goal that will never elude them more than when they seem to grasp it—plugging through to a degree only to be locked into a career they find themselves unsuited for and hating—is not a kindness. We have made enough, perhaps too much, of this theme; but it is deeply related to the ability to carry out independent research and to the instructor's obligation to criticize the research efforts that are tendered. To that end, the reader, even if a graduate student, is urged to read the chapter (6) on undergraduate research. What follows takes off from what has been said there.

There are several practical reasons for applying higher standards to the assessing of papers contributed for course work by graduate students. The graduate course usually comprises one-third fewer hours than its undergraduate equivalent on the frequently overlooked assumption that the subtracted hours will be utilized in a heavier program of readings. It is also assumed that as a natural product of the narrower specialization of their education, there is a tighter fit among the courses taken by graduate students. Accordingly, there should be more overlap among their courses, more exchange among their readings. For reasons such as this, it seems reasonable for an instructor to expect that the graduate student is able and ready to put more time and effort into papers than should be expected from all but the most outstanding undergraduates.

Even if the candidate has not had much anthropology as an undergraduate, it is presumed that the screening process attending admission to the graduate department has indicated the possession of some degree of that critical intelligence which is indispensable in the conduct of research. This is usually manifested in the decline in graduate-level papers of dependence upon sources of information far removed from the phenomena being studied. Concomitantly, there is increased expectation that statements will not be taken as fact simply because they appear in print. Graduate papers should display a critical attitude toward the information used; they should reveal the interest of the student in the methods used to obtain the original data, and some curiosity about the logical tools employed in manipulating them. One expects to find an awareness of theoretical sets, whether apparent or latent. In other words, graduate students, much more than undergraduates, must show sophistication in assessing the biases that produced the work on which their papers rely. (This is certainly not to say that undergraduates are incapable of the highest degree of critical analysis. Some of the very best research that I have seen on the structure of the United States economy and its relation to American society and on that society's world posture has been put together by undergraduates. On the other hand, I have also seen much that simply repeats with absolutely no critical appraisal the cant and drivel of one or another political camp. And, lest this be misunderstood, let me add that self-serving propaganda can be found as often among centrists as among ideologues of right or left.) One way of accomplishing this, as suggested earlier, is to do research on the critical statements found in the work of others that supplies the main basis of the paper in question. This means digging into learned journals to find reviews or critiques of that work, checking out the author's sources, trying to find other accounts of the same phenomenon. Even if the student still lacks the expertise needed to make an authoritative decision about truth, it is possible to indicate the basis for acceptance or rejection of the statements in concern.

Another aspect of paper writing in which higher demands are placed on graduate students has to do with the nature of the problem underlying the paper. What has the student undertaken as the subject of research? Is it one of the grandiose riddles of the ages, as exemplified in Chapter 6? I hope that these comments are not taken as evidence that I would suppress imagination and creativity; on the contrary, I very much agree with Marvin Harris when he says that "to deprive science of speculation altogether is to deprive it of its very life blood" (Harris 1968:286). There is a touchy and delicate sense of proportion that is called for, especially on the training level, in advancing subjects for research. Not all topics are manageable, particularly when deadlines are short and other courses require their share of attention.

A good topic for a paper is one that is treated in a reasonable amount of literature, one that can be tackled in a reasonable space, and one that provides some opportunity for students to show their own creative abilities, either by uncovering some new data (although this is unlikely, given the limitations under which they are likely to be working) or by coming up with a fresh synthesis. For some personalities, the easiest way to frame a viable topic is to take some more or less current theoretical argument and jump on one of the contributors, taking that position apart. This may be hard on the victim, but it is a fine way of learning how to strip arguments bare and requires a certain amount of back-checking and collateral reading to establish the strengths and weaknesses of the opponent's arguments. Indeed, in the end, the theory and its framer may be triumphantly vindicated. Such a paper also has the virtue of offering a prestructured hypothesis for testing. For example, a widely held conclusion among students of social organization is that Crow kin terminological systems show a high degree of correlation with matrilineality and postmarital residence of the uxorimatrilocal type (i.e., the new couple lives with the bride's mother and her matrilineal relatives). It is pointless for a young graduate student working on a course deadline to begin to comb hundreds of monographs to check up on this asserted correlation. That work has been done, and the student should instantly know by whom, in what book, and where to locate the follow-up.[2] Instead, using a growing knowledge of the literature and the bibliographical suggestions usually advanced by the instructor (and the bibliographical suggestions that are in Chapter 7), the student may select a few societies to represent a range of matrilineal-cum-uxorimatrilocal societies, obtain the monographic publications dealing with these cultures, and check the hypothesis against the actual details of their organization, residence, and descent rules. Although it will not be possible to do so in most of the older monographs, the student carrying out such a project would be well advised to keep a wary eye out for clues to behavior in contrast to the rules—postmarital residence or instances of inheritance that take different shape from that prescribed.

I am perhaps overly concerned that graduate students may be put off by being lectured about choosing research topics for term papers and given encouragement to do only boring problems of dubious relevance. I admit that the topic of kinship terminology may be so classified. On the other hand, there are few topics that stand closer to the heart of cultural (or social) anthropology; whether or not they wish to do such studies themselves, students who cannot see this are probably not really plugged into the discipline. Either that, or what we are facing is a premature desire to leave the nest. There is a substantial body of theory, method, and information that must be assimilated before fledgling anthropologists are ready to make an independent way in research. One of the better ways of mastering what has already been contributed is to take it in manageable, representative parts, and do it again, albeit secondhand and in reduced scale. Of course, anyone who continued to do this kind of thing throughout an entire career might be foolishly wasting time. There is a time for learning and a time for original research; the fact that a few fortunate and gifted students manage to combine the two should not lead others to jeopardize their

[2] *The answers to these questions: George Peter Murdock,* Social Structure *(New York: Macmillan, 1949); the "Ethnographic Atlas" in* Ethnography.

early graduate education by setting impossible and destructive standards for themselves.

Another area in which instructors' expectations undergo a great leap forward has to do with what may be called, somewhat euphemistically, nonsense. Plagiarism falls into that category. I am not talking about ghost-written papers, which seem even more monstrously idiotic in graduate school than in college, but about the practice of encysting shorter or longer passages from the work of another in one's own, without proper identification and attribution of the appropriated remarks. Once again, I believe penalties for such an intellectual offense should be severe among undergraduates; if the offense is detected in a graduate paper, it calls for nothing less than a direct confrontation between the teacher and the offending student. I would argue that a second, clearly proven, offense of plagiarism in term papers provides ground for dismissal from candidacy, if for no reason other than the difficulty of ever trusting the work that such a person would do in the field, where there are almost no limits to the extent to which materials can be falsified.

Plagiarism, thank goodness, does not seem a big problem in graduate school. In over twenty years of teaching graduate students, I am aware of relatively few cases, although some of these have been egregious. Actually, most graduate students tend to sin on the other side, making direct quotes with full citation for the most routine and obvious remarks.[3] One purpose behind writing papers is precisely to develop control in this area. (This is an excellent instance of the value of writing such papers as an undergraduate, working out problems of technique before graduate school.)

One other matter I should like to take up as "nonsense." Without getting too deeply enmeshed in clinical psychology or in Freudian theory about slips and errors, let us note that one assumption dividing the evaluation of papers from the evaluation of in-class exams is that errors have no justification in the former. Having access to all his materials, a student's mistakes in a paper can be taken only as evidence of inferior ability or poor attitude. A proliferation of errors in a paper in a field the candidate has declared to be his lifetime professional

---

[3] *Although fashions and tastes vary, as well as instructors' standards, it is usually agreed that direct citation should be particularly apt and cogent. In many cases, it is possible to summarize the gist of the desired remarks, noting that as so-and-so says, and so on. Even when direct quotes are useful, adding to your case, or putting the matter so brilliantly and economically, or with so much authority that such use is justified, they should be trimmed as much as possible, without altering meaning, and reproduced absolutely verbatim, except for indicated ellipses.*

career interest is direct evidence of incompatibility between candidate and subject. The interference of sentimentality with such a judgment will ultimately penalize the student rather than the well-meaning but ill-advised instructor who overlooks such symptomatology.

This brings us to a final matter in this particular section, the general level of craftsmanship displayed by the candidate at successive stages of his training. As indicated elsewhere, there is a feeling encountered among all sorts of students that a paper submitted in an anthropology course should be criticized for its anthropology and not for anything else. "Anything else" usually includes the general appearance of the paper, its prose, choice of vocabulary, grammatical structure, and all other details of presentation. I will not pause here to comment on the soundness of such an attitude on the undergraduate level; in graduate school it should not be tolerated. There is no reason why even newly admitted graduate students should not be held to the style requirements of the major professional journal in their own subdisciplinary field, or to that of the *American Anthropologist,* since a single unified model is more appropriate. Although the journal is easy to come by and certainly should be read regularly by all such students, Xerox copies can be distributed of sample pages and of the style-sheet (regularly found on the inside front cover of each issue of the *American Anthropologist*). Some faults are harder to work on than others and presumably have defied the attentions of a generation of English teachers. The ministrations of anthropology teachers will presumably not do much, but efforts should not be abandoned by either teachers or students. The goal of professional research includes dissemination of the results. To achieve that end, reports must be literate and comprehensible. Authors must say what they intend, or the rigor of their work will be destroyed. To the end of achieving optimum communication, the student should welcome whatever efforts his instructors make to improve the quality of his written presentations.

If most successful term papers have subjects of limited scope, that scope can be effectively widened for the master's essay and once again for the doctorate. Most M.A.'s in anthropology are associated with an essay involving library rather than field research, although this varies with the field of specialization. It is probably least the case in archeology, where excavation of a local site, or even one more distant, may supply the data. In cultural anthropology, however, the use of field materials occurs in a minority of master's essays. On the other hand, the use of field materials dominates doctoral dissertations in cultural anthropology, and some departments have gone so far as to make it mandatory for this to be the case. Let us talk briefly about research for the master's essay and then conclude the chapter with remarks about the doctorate and beyond.

The M.A. essay usually lies between a major term paper, perhaps one written in conjunction with a seminar, and the doctoral dissertation, not merely in an architectural and chronological sense but with regard to its length, seriousness, and construction. Yet, there are so many variations between departments that simple declarative generalizations may be misleading. Similarly, a list of topics covered by the M.A. essays for even one year reveals such diversity as to make one despair of offering a formula. The candidate faced with the problem of writing an M.A., however, can take advantage of certain simple prescriptions. First, the thesis will be easiest to do, and probably more substantial and convincing, if the topic picked develops or is developed out of the precise interests that previously motivated the candidate. This means that the chosen problem weds theoretical and geographical area interests. Second, candidates should familiarize themselves with the M.A. style at their own institutions. To the extent that the information is available, they should know what sorts of topics have been chosen and they should scan a few finished theses to get some idea of how themes were handled. These suggestions are not made to encourage mechanical repetition and stereotyping of essays; all students should be encouraged to innovate if they can. However, there seems to be no reason to adopt an ostrich attitude, refusing to see what models have been established in the past.

Once a topic has been developed, it is a good idea (and sometimes required) to construct an outline, perhaps adding a précis of the argument in a page or so of text, plus a suggestive bibliography that indicates work done and work contemplated. These can be submitted to an adviser or a committee, whatever practice is followed, for approval and suggestions. During the discussion, it is appropriate to attempt to get additional bibliographic advice from the advisers, including suggestions of persons on campus or off who might be able to assist. This is a matter of considerable delicacy. Properly approached, a scholar in another department or even in a distant university might be of tremendous help in specific cases. The worst way to enlist such help, however, is to ask eminent scholars to tell you what they know about the subject in question. Much more likely to yield favorable results are a limited number of very clearly formulated questions, especially those that get at sources of data, or raise matters of interpretation. The key, it seems to me, is to show your correspondent that you have done a good deal of work already, that you are soliciting aid because you want to understand better, not lighten a routine burden.

When it comes to setting the length of a master's essay, instructors and institutions vary. Like many colleagues, I infuriate students by answering questions about length with statements such as, "Essays should be as long as but no longer than necessary." Frankly, I prefer a short, tight essay, but I know that may take longer to write than a sprawly one. There is no value in length for itself, and much against it. Some topics can be handled with elegance in twenty-five or thirty pages, other topics take a hundred. Candidates who swell their M.A.'s, making them into little doctoral dissertations, may be wasting their own time. On the other hand, if this is done at the insistence of the advisers or the department, I feel sorry for all concerned, but mainly for the misled candidates.

The relation between a master's essay and a doctoral dissertation is also difficult to specify simply. In some disciplines the attempt is made to have the M.A. thesis play the role of kernel for the longer Ph.D. I think, though, that this applies rarely in anthropology, where the dissertation usually takes shape as a completely independent work. Since most M.A.'s are based on library materials while most anthropology dissertations involve field work, one might think that the M.A. could embody a portion of the library research germane to the Ph.D. project, say a preliminary part upon which the field work was later to be shaped. Undoubtedly this does work, although in my own experience the gap between the two enlarges with the years until the final dissertation that may indeed have begun with an M.A. essay shows only the most remote connection to the original theme. Once again, I am not trying to discourage anyone from attempting such a course, but simply to warn that it should not be a compulsion.

A final word about the M.A. essay—what about the actual research on which it is based? As indicated, for most it will be confined to the library and will consist of digging out relevant books and articles and whatever other materials pertain to the case being made. It is possible to base an M.A. essay on new research, depending on the topic. Studies of class or ethnicity as subculture are not only possible but have a high degree of relevance. For example, although it may be old hat by the time these words are read, there is a nice conflict between the late Oscar Lewis and Charles Valentine over the concept of "the culture of poverty." An aspect of this problem can be refined anywhere in the United States out of local conditions of deprivation and can yield a neat, tight but tough subject for investigation. The extra difficulty of doing such research is balanced by its likelihood of having value beyond the training exercise.

Another set of topics on which original research can be performed has to do with the history of anthropology. A brief biography of a particular anthropologist, emphasizing intellectual development, placing the figure in time, and showing how the person's ideas related to those times would be much appreciated in a discipline that still pays relatively little attention to its own history. There are innumerable topics that immediately come to mind and that also relate to the crisis of relevance that has influenced various portions of this book. In an essay previously cited, June Helm (1966) began a discussion of the role of women in the development of American anthropology. While a full-scale biography of any of the women involved would be a much larger undertaking than usually is thought of in terms of the M.A., a portion of the productive life of such a person would make an excellent topic. Such a suggestion leads to others of a different kind, such as research into the relation between certain kinds of interests in academic anthropology and the availability of foundation grant support. Some commentators on the left have raised questions about the workings of the social science establishment in controlling the direction of research through the administration of funds. I think investigation of such topics is difficult but perfectly proper; there is no reason why academic degrees should not be given for such work. Indeed, there is a very good reason for encouraging such work within the disciplines and under the aegis of formal academic structure, for by this means, it may be possible to provide access to persons and materials that would otherwise be uncooperative or forbidden. It ill becomes a field that has made its core the investigation of social structure, of relations between economic and social organization, and the like, to shy away from comparable investigations into the heart of its own society. If we train young anthropologists not to be afraid to work in alien cultures, amid dangers of human hostility and the unknown microbe and parasite, we should also apply similar standards to the study of the danger spots of our own culture, the areas of exploitation, oppression and repression, whether of racial, sexual, economic, social, religious, ethnic, or other constitution.

There is no reason why much of the foregoing should not apply to the Ph.D. dissertation, especially that last part about encouraging work close to home in our own society. In recent years, of course, there has been a marked increase in the number of dissertations about urban subjects, many in our own society, and it is to be hoped that these will now be joined by serious studies of other aspects of our own society. I repeat my belief, spelled out in Chapter 6, that anthropological research within one's own society is more difficult, and may be faced with greater psychological hazards than work abroad. But there are other reasons for expecting a sharp increase in the number of domestically situated research projects. For one thing, unless conditions change drastically, the amount of support available for dissertation research will be inadequate to put into the field abroad all who are qualified to go. For another, there is evidence that the areas of the world to which an American anthropologist may go are slowly but surely diminishing. There may be occasional reversals, like Indonesia, but the trend is definitely against our open access, even where political considerations are not directly involved. Finally, there is the stance that is increasingly encountered among advanced students, the desire to turn the tools of social research on their own society.

Most doctoral theses that I know about in detail present unique convergences of planned and fortuitous factors. Few, if any, dissertations have gone as planned before the field work was undertaken. In some instances, even the country originally selected for the site of research had to be changed for reasons beyond control of the researcher. More usually, the precise location must be determined in the field, and the early stages of field work include surveys and other steps providing the basis for an informed decision about location.

As for the working from a hypothesis, as opposed to the notion of going out to see what's there, much depends upon the nature of the hypothesis. Pelto, for example, notes that some anthropological hypotheses are simply descriptive: "most of the people in the village own land" or "the rate of divorce and separation seems high in this community" (1970:253). There are other kinds of working hypotheses. To continue with examples from Pelto, there are the more or less straight informational queries: "What are the main features of organization in the market system of _____ (town or region)? What is the role of animal husbandry among the _____ (tribe or society)? What kinds of mental illness are found among the _____ (tribe or society)? . . ." There is another category of hypothesis which makes statements about the nature of the relationship between two variables thought to be causally linked: here one of the examples is much the same as the one given earlier (see p. 198):

> Various hypotheses about relationships of particular kinship
> terminological systems and types of residence, descent, and
> marriage systems.   [ibid.: 333]

There are also a number of others, among them the epistemologically very difficult search for causes, as in such examples as:

> What are the causes of mental disorders among the _____
> (tribe)? . . .
> What factors account for cargo cults?   [ibid.]

Quite common are hypotheses that take the opportunity afforded by a breaking situation to set up a test of causal relations between an independent variable and one or more dependent variables. Paraphrasing Pelto's examples: The relocation of a village will have such and such effects on various aspects of its social relations. Or, the introduction of such and such a technological innovation will have such and such effects on various aspects of its social relations. Of course, as Pelto points out, some hypothesis construction combines two or more of

these approaches. Furthermore, the data that are secured will frequently be of various types. Some will be descriptive in the archetypal
sense, while others will be more strictly quantitative. Some data will
be derived from emic inquiries, some from etic; both types may be
useful, depending on the way they are handled.

There is much to be said for the dissertation based upon a set of
hypotheses taken into the field and tested. Such work merits the highest admiration (provided, of course, that the central problem is a reasonable one and not merely another nit-picking example of the triumph
of empirical technique). It makes various contributions to the discipline,
not the least of which is to its scientific aura. The matter thus raised
is of prime significance, since implicit within it is a contrast between
a problem-oriented anthropological research strategy and an eclectic
inductionism, for which Franz Boas and some of his students are the
exemplars. As analyzed by Marvin Harris (1968:285–89), the inductionist
approach is a reaction to "the fragmentary nature of the ethnographic
record and . . . the urgency of obtaining data from fast-disappearing
tribal groups. . . ." What emerged was a "natural history approach,"
marked by opportunism and serendipity. Harris cites Marian Smith with
telling effect: "Masses of data may therefore be worked over with no
clear knowledge of what is to be gained at the end" (Harris 1968:287,
quoting Smith 1959:54).

To the extent that this procedure was elevated to a mind-killing
theoretical position that sought to drive out all forms of speculation,
Harris can be supported in his counterattack. After all, he is not alone
in giving us the warning. Almost twenty years earlier the sociologist
Max Horkheimer wrote:

> The constant warning against premature conclusions and
> foggy generalizations implies, unless properly qualified, a
> possible taboo against all thinking. If every thought has to be
> held in abeyance until it has been completely corroborated,
> no basic approach seems possible and we would limit our-
> selves to the level of mere symptoms. [Cited in Mills 1961:
> 122–23]

What seems wrong here is the presentation of the matter in
either-or terms. Never more than now, when rapid changes are occurring
not only in the rare simple societies but in all societies, there is an absolute need for simple descriptive ethnography. One can agree with Harris
that facts are endless, receding into "higher degrees of infinity." To conclude, therefore, that the problem-oriented study is the answer is to miss
a salient point. Most such studies require a fairly rigorous separation of
data into categories based on a conception of relevance, this time in a
practical rather than political sense (although some influence of the

latter will always be felt in the process of discrimination). Perhaps I am unduly sensitive to this point, because my field work in mainland China in 1947–48 was written up and published in the context of a problem-oriented dissertation ("kin and nonkin in Chinese society"). I used only a fraction of the data I collected to make a case I thought important at the time. Since then, the changes in Chinese society and culture have been great, and I think that a simple descriptive account of what I observed might be more useful to posterity. I was channeled by forces beyond my control (my committee) into making this decision, but if there is guilt in what they did to me, I share it, not merely because I submitted, but because I have since done comparable things to other students. It is a serious matter and one worthy of greater consideration. In a way, the point is neatly summed up in a remark of Isaac Bashevis Singer's: "If Homer had written the *Iliad* and the *Odyssey* in terms of the psychology of his time, we wouldn't be able to read them today. It's a wonderful thing that Homer gave us the story and let others decide the meaning" (Shenker 1970:100. Pertti J. Pelto considers this kind of problem in several excellently presented paragraphs, too lengthy to reproduce here. I urge the concerned reader to read his remarks in full; see Pelto 1970:320–28).

One aspect of evolutionary process seems relatively clear and applies to the matter under discussion. With the exception of relatively few bioforms, like the African lungfish, some insects, and a scattering of others, evolutionary "success"—survival—has depended in crucial periods on the maintenance of a certain degree of flexibility, the conservation of a number of "options." To narrow anthropology, even the production of anthropology dissertations, to a restricted sense of problem and relevance is to take chances on the viability needed in the unknown future. This is a matter to approach with caution and humility.

A word about the dissertation defense. Where it exists, this is the last hurdle to which a candidate is subjected before he obtains his degree. As there are variations among universities in the requirements leading up to this point, so there are various means of handling this particular situation. With no exceptions I know, the protocol for handling the acceptance of dissertations is set primarily by some organ of the university outside of and administratively superior to the department. In other words, the process of granting this degree is not left, except in its details, to the department, but is made uniform throughout the graduate departments in the arts and sciences. (Professional schools, such as in medicine, are distinct.) By and large, there are two main plans. The older one, which is probably still more widespread, calls for a "defense." This is an examination that gathers together the few professors who have advised the candidate along the way, adds one or more members of the sponsoring department who have not yet been involved, and one or more members of other departments, to form a final examining committee. The last named are there to keep the proceedings honest; since they are usually the least competent in the areas under discussion, their actual effect is often muted. Theoretically, as a consequence of the descent of this examination from classical European forebears, the occasion is a public one and anyone may attend and even ask questions. Although this is now rare, most universities protect the candidate by allowing the chairman of the exam to rule out questions as irrelevant. In any event, each questioner takes his turn, usually raising either general or specific points having a finite locus in the work being examined. There is no question of raising extraneous issues. After questioning, the candidate is excused and a discussion ensues, followed by voting. Does the thesis pass, more or less, as is (minor revisions being counted a full pass), or are extensive changes required? If the latter, a subcommittee may be appointed to oversee and approve them. The committee can also reject the thesis in toto. This is a total disaster that inevitably signifies the end of candidacy without degree, since the topic is considered closed. If such a candidate wished to continue, he would have to generate a new thesis topic, which is unlikely under most circumstances and rendered impossible by new rules controlling the amount of time during which a candidate may pursue his goal.

An alternative scheme that is slowly spreading does away with the formal examination. Instead, the candidate satisfies each member of his committee individually, never confronting them all at the same time. At first glance, students might regard this system superior for its elimination of a formal examination. Second thoughts suggest other possibilities. The examination operates according to majority principles; one person dedicated to failing the candidate cannot succeed unless he convinces at least two others (most committees are comprised of five members). The system that operates without exam provides an opportunity for one critic to hold up the degree indefinitely.

A final word about research. There are no statistics that tell how many anthropologists continue to conduct research after receiving their doctorates. Certainly there are some who settle down to teaching and devote themselves completely to it, never even contributing an article on a theoretical subject to a professional journal. My impression, shared by most anthropologists with whom I have discussed this question, is that such retirements from research are in the minority in our profession. Anthropologists not only continue active research careers after obtaining their Ph.D.'s, but do additional field work as well.

There are many problems about the conduct of field research at various stages of an anthropologist's career. Some of these are treated in the final chapter of this book, along with other ethical problems of the discipline. Not all problems are on symbolic, political, or ethical planes. Some are more practical, or simply more mundane. What about conducting field work when one has a nonanthropologist spouse and small children? What problems are faced by women fieldworkers that do not apply to men, or vice versa? What about the reluctance of anthropologists to do field work in truly primitive cultural surroundings, so that suggestions about urgently needed ethnographic research go without takers?[4]

It is quite clear that the need for anthropological and ethnographic research does not vanish with modernization. If anything, recognition of the stresses and strains of a world in various stages of technological development, with a variety of economic systems, political structures, and ideologies, spurs the need for more research. The drive for knowledge merges with the drive toward mastery of the problems of mankind, which are the problems of culture. War, poverty, racism, repression, persecution, discrimination—there is no end to problems, and the anthropologist can contribute to their understanding. Whether understanding can bring a millennium by changing culture is another matter entirely. Most people who are young today seem to believe with unusual intensity in the possibility of transforming their world. Even those of us who take the view of cultural determinism can be found among the strivers for change. Perhaps it is a paradox; if so, its name is life.

[4] *Looking for a dissertation topic? Try reading through the issues of the* Bulletin of the International Committee on Urgent Anthropological and Ethnological Research, *published in Austria by the International Union of Anthropological and Ethnological Sciences. Established in 1958, the earlier issues in particular offered suggestions about possible work in cultures that faced rapid change or extinction. More recent issues present articles about research on dying traditions, but most of these are not on the level of primitivity earlier referred to.*

12

ANTHROPOLOGY AS AN OCCUPATION

> ... he hypothecated an America in which
> almost all the work was done by machines,
> and the only people who could get work
> had three or more Ph.D.'s
> —Kurt Vonnegut, Jr.

Whatever the conditions at the time you are reading this, the fact is that only a short time before these pages were written the demand for anthropologists far exceeded the supply. At that time, departments zealously guarded the names of the outstanding graduates who were ready to take positions; they were passed from one department to another, between friends, as favors. Departments competed for the young Ph.D.'s. They were offered reduced course loads, attractive beginning salaries, research support, small classes, graduate classes, few classes, a wide variety of inducements. Then something happened. The administration decided to try to cool off the inflation, the stock market succumbed to pessimism, Congress withheld funding of crucial higher education bills, foundations became cautious, universities and colleges stared into recession. At first it was the harder sciences that noted decreasing employment, then it was the humanities. Finally, the social sciences reported difficulties, too. Anthropologists in leading departments began to telephone or write close friends elsewhere, "We have this terrific student who's finishing a thesis and needs a job. Any openings in your department?" The tide had turned.

With few exceptions, anthropologists work directly in education, mainly at the college and university level. They are also to be found, of course, on the staffs of museums. Trailing far behind these is employment in some branch of government, mainly federal, although quite a few states support their own staffs of archeologists and some anthropologists for local historical work. The smallest component of anthropologists is that in private noninstitutional employment. The numbers involved are probably not tabulated; in any event, I could not come up with a figure.

Opportunities for private employment as an anthropologist are associated with consultant firms for the most part. People who received training as anthropologists but do not maintain active associations with the discipline, or who left anthropology for business, are not counted. There are any number of cases, some authentic, some part of the mythology of the field. One brilliant student of the American Indian became a victim of McCarthyism and started a taxicab company in a Middle American country. It is said that he became a millionaire, but his success seems to have had nothing to do with his anthropology. Less well founded are rumors of a nameless genius who combined dentistry and anthropology. As the story goes, he located in Southeast Asia (in less troubled times) and made a fortune out of the sale of false dentures—subtly tinted to match the colorations of betel-stained teeth.

The number of trained anthropologists employed as such by private firms is not very great. After exchanging opinions about this with other academic anthropologists, I called two firms that carry on social science research on a fee basis. I cannot say whether the practices of these companies are typical of their field, but both tend not to employ anthropologists permanently, at least not as such. Instead, they recruit with relatively little emphasis on degree specialization, except for the marked interest of one firm in social psychology. An anthropology degree is not regarded as a reason for *not* hiring a candidate, but preference is shown for people who are interdisciplinary, or at least quite flexible with regard to disciplinary interests. This is in accord with the proclaimed mission orientation of such firms.

As noted by Ralph Beals, some anthropologists view commercial, industrial, or other private anthropological employment as unethical per se (1969:142). Beals takes exception to any blanket condemnation of such employment, but notes that there are several grounds for its disrepute in some quarters. For openers, he comments that studies done under private auspices are usually held secret, their data and results never reaching a wider scientific community. Beals says, rather emphatically for him, that such studies "may provide income to scientifically trained persons, but only rarely do they contribute to the advancement of the profession" (*ibid.*). Additional items of criticism note the frequent inadequacy of performance in the private sector, as well as the charge that this sector, more than the academic, is given to the performance of work that may be regarded as unethical by the professional body at large. The question is a complex one, and we will have another look at it in the final chapter. Meanwhile, a cynical note: hitherto the scarcity of anthropologists in such private undertakings may have been more the result of market economics than ethical considerations. The private employment of anthropologists, small as it is, is fairly recent and coincides with the period of optimum demand for anthropologists by colleges and universities. While some of the private firms may be able to offer young graduates or doctoral candidates higher salaries than those of instructors or assistant professors, they cannot offer equivalent rewards in terms of security, advancement in the discipline, or prestige. As long as placement was easy in the academic milieu, private firms could be expected to get the second-raters. What will become of this distribution if economic recession hardens into depression, and teaching jobs, even at lower levels, become fewer than the regular supply of trained persons? What strain will the threat of privation place upon newly emerging ethical standards?

Ethical problems also face anthropologists in government employ. Perhaps the most severe questions pertain to those who use anthropological identity and status to mask the fact that they are spies, sometimes in counterintelligence. Nor is this something new that has emerged with the CIA; Franz Boas complained about it more than half a century ago in a letter to *The Nation* (109 [20 December 1919]:797). Boas's position is described by George W. Stocking, Jr.:

> In it [The Nation *letter*] he attacked four unnamed anthropologists whom he "refused to designate any longer as scientists" for having "prostituted science by using it as a cover for their activities as spies." Introducing themselves as representatives of American scientific institutions sent out for anthropological research in Central America, they had in fact been on secret missions for the American government. Boas was willing to countenance such activities on the part of soldiers, diplomats, politicians, and businessmen who "set patriotic devotion above common everyday decency." Such men, "owing to their callings," would conform to "certain conventional standards of ethics." But the scientist's calling made unique demands; "the very essence" of his life was "the search for truth." What for others was a matter of unthinking adherence to conventional morality was for the scientist a question of "the most fundamental principles of professional ethics." In this instance the violation of these ethics not only undercut belief in the "truthfulness of science," but "raised a new barrier" against international scientific cooperation. [1968:273–74]

The number of anthropologists who carry out such activities or who work for the government directly in various intelligence capacities cannot even be guessed. Equally distressing, there are apparently many individuals without any credentials or training who represent themselves as anthropologists while carrying out intelligence missions abroad. It may be quixotic to get upset about such things, particularly since there is no ready means to check or control them. But of course such practices raise grave ethical problems for us as citizens. Apart from such considerations, these practices threaten to debase all government employment of anthropologists, and, as Boas clearly pointed out, threaten the utility of all social science as well as the delicate structure of international communication. More about this in the next chapter.

According to a survey conducted for the National Science Foundation, in 1967 there were 6668 social scientists employed in the various agencies of the federal government. A little less than a third of the total, about 2000, were in two departments, State and Agriculture. However, very few were anthropologists; 152 were explicitly noted as employed in anthropological sciences. Although I shall deal briefly with the question of the employment of women later in this chapter, it may be noted here that a mere 16 of the 152 anthropologists just mentioned are women. Furthermore, the mean salary of the men so employed was $12,345, while that of the women was $11,586. The latter exceeded the mean for all female government scientific personnel ($10,894), but male anthropologists were under the mean for all male government scientific personnel ($13,198). (National Science Foundation, *Scientific and Technical Personnel in the Federal Government, 1967* [1969]. Summarized in *Newsletter of the American Anthropological Association* 11:2 [1970]:11.)

Employment of anthropologists in government bridges a wide range of statuses. I presume, for example, that among the hundreds of social scientists said to be in the Department of State in 1967 was the anthropologist Elliott P. Skinner, who was on academic leave as Ambassador to Upper Volta (and has since returned to anthropology). Unfortunately, I cannot say who the others were, or what they were doing. I think that it would be quite useful to have such information. Indeed, a study of the use of anthropologists outside of the academic milieu would fill some worrisome gaps in our knowledge of the profession. I regret that I cannot offer such a study as the basis for my comments in this chapter, but I note with relief that a similar recommendation also was forwarded by Beals, who called for a Congressional inquiry into the operations and structure of private social science research organizations (1969:143). Congressional inquiry is not exactly what I have in mind, but a substantial question probably exists as to how far such an inquiry could proceed without the power of subpoena.

Like the private sector, government has operated for some years against a seller's market in anthropologically trained personnel. Some positions, such as those associated with the Smithsonian Institution, competed at par with academic institutions. Indeed, such association was deemed academic by most anthropologists, quite the same as association with any of the major museums in the country not directly encapsulated in a university structure. It seems likely that as far as anthropologists are concerned, the attractions of government employment decrease as the job description varies more and more from what is obtainable in an academic setting. Once more, there is good reason to wonder how such a correlation may be affected by trends in the larger economy. Previous depressions have seen sharp contests among highly trained persons for positions that would be totally ignored by today's graduates. That was the state of affairs when the number of post-doctoral anthropologists did not exceed a few hundred. What will the situation be when a major economic recession finds mounting unemployment in a world of thousands of specialists?

The tone of the preceding remarks is clearly that of the Grand-father in *Peter and the Wolf:* "If the wolf hadn't been caught, what then?" Grandpa, of course, had lived through the Great Depression, and it colored his thinking about everything. He was not to be put off by optimism, not even when it came from high places, such as a study made for the National Institute of Mental Health, published in 1969, indicating that when all factors were considered, there would still be a high demand for anthropologists in the foreseeable future.

According to the NIMH study, the largest single group of employed anthropologists are those in graduate departments of anthropology—close to half of the total of employed anthropologists in the country (Public Health Service 1969:13). The proportion can be enlarged if anthropologists working in combined departments of sociology and anthropology are included. It is interesting to note that this makes anthropology far more a graduate, specialized department-centered discipline than, for instance, sociology, whose total was approximately 39 percent as revealed in the same study (*ibid.*). It is not surprising that for anthropologists the next most important sources of employment were to be found in teaching at the undergraduate level in liberal arts colleges (15.4 percent) and in junior colleges (8.4 percent), with a smaller representation in teachers colleges (4.3 percent). To these can be added the scattering of anthropologists teaching in schools of theology, social work, public health, and nursing, all of these "other" institutions of higher learning combined offering employment to 7.2 percent, as of October 1965. The grand total of employed anthropologists to be found in education, represented as a proportion, comes to a whopping 99 percent, according to this study. While the data collection of the study was such as to skew results in favor of accurate reporting for the academic sector and underreporting for the nonacademic sector, the disparity is obviously tremendous and reflects the actual proclivity of anthropologists to seek academic employment.

Approximately 87 percent of the anthropologists employed in October 1965 were identified by the survey; a questionnaire developed information about a number of variables. In the population covered (1773), about 56 percent had completed the Ph.D., about 30 percent held the M.A. as highest degree, and approximately 13 percent had the B.A. only. A handful (5, or 0.3 percent) held no degree. (The same study offers a basis for comparison with the distribution found among sociologists: about 49 percent with Ph.D.'s, 42 percent with M.A.'s, about 9 percent with B.A.'s, and a mere 0.1 percent with no degree [*ibid.*:8–9, 35].) It should be noted that more than 85 percent of those teaching anthropology with only a bachelor's degree are to be found in graduate departments. As the study remarks, this "probably reflects the practice of employing graduate students on a part-time basis while pursuing graduate study" (*ibid.*:15). In any event, the correlation between advancement and higher degrees is quickly manifested. A Ph.D. was held by about two thirds of assistant professors, almost 89 percent of associate professors, and over 97 percent of full professors.

As might be expected, most anthropologists reported their primary activity as teaching. Of 1225 anthropologists responding to the NIMH questionnaire, 48 percent were engaged in teaching only, and some 43 percent in teaching and research. Somewhat surprising to me was the statement, "As in the case of sociologists, a very small proportion of the anthropologists was engaged solely in research, slightly more than 6 percent" (*ibid.*:14).

The questionnaire used by NIMH was distributed to department heads and applied to their entire staffs. It asked for identification by specialty, limiting each respondent to two choices per staff member to be made from a prepared list of two columns, each with nine items. On the left the possibilities were more or less conventional, although many familiar headings, such as political or economic anthropology, or musicology, or folklore, or religion, were absent. On the other hand, some categories overlapped or presented fuzzy images, and must have troubled some respondents. The right-hand column offered eight specialties within the domain of the varied interests in mental health. Apart from the separation of the columns there was no conspicuous clue to indicate that all specialties were not of equivalent order. A final item in the right-hand column provided space for listing any other specialty; only 45 entries were made in that space out of a total return of 3209 items.

I offer this much detail not as a backhanded way of criticizing this study, but to indicate its limitations and warping as a source of information about what anthropologists do. (An alternative might be to analyze the Fourth International Directory of Anthropologists [*Current Anthropology* 8:5 (1967)], which gives a wider range of explicit specialties. Unfortunately, I lacked the resources for such a task.) For what it is worth, however, Table 6 shows the order of frequency of specialties within anthropology as determined by the NIMH survey. (The total number of specialties reported was 3209 [not including 26 responses pertaining to persons in nonacademic employment]. A number of respondents offered only one specialty per person, rather than the two permitted.)

TABLE 6[1]

	Percent
Anthropology, general	23.8
Ethnology and social anthropology	18.3
Mental health	15.2
Archeology	10.7
Social organization	6.6
Culture and personality	6.4
Physical anthropology	6.1
Applied anthropology	4.1
Scientific linguistics	3.7
Ethnohistory	3.6
Other	1.5

[1] *This table derived from Table B-10 of the NIMH study (Public Health Service 1969:98).*

No category "mental health" appeared in the questionnaire as such. The category as represented in the table above comprises the total of all responses to specialties in the right-hand column of the questionnaire, not including "other."

The NIMH study determined that the median salary of anthropologists employed full time in all types of institutions of higher learning in 1965 was $10,000. A fairly wide range was indicated between the median in graduate departments of anthropology ($11,600) and in undergraduate colleges ($8,300). The summary table is sufficiently interesting to reproduce here (Table 7).

Another table showed substantial salary differentials by region within the United States, but was too spotty to reproduce here. The leading indications, however, were that salaries tended to be highest in the North Atlantic states, lowest in the Southeast, with the Midwest, West, and Southwest tending to be intermediate (*ibid.*:17).

TABLE 7

Rank	Graduate Dpts. of Anthropology	Graduate Dpts. of Sociology, and Sociology and Anthropology	Liberal Arts Colleges
Full Professor	$17,000	$14,300[1]	$13,100[1]
Associate Professor	11,800	11,000	10,000
Assistant Professor	8,800	8,500	8,000
Instructor	7,500[1]	7,000[1]	6,600[1]

[1] *Subject to selective sampling variability estimated to be up to 20 percent (1 chance in 3) because of limited number of institutions reporting (ibid.: 17).*

We have already referred to the main findings of the NIMH study, pertaining to the present conditions of supply and demand of trained anthropological personnel and estimating future demand (see p. 213). The significant conclusion, based, of course, on the situation in 1965, was that there would continue to be a high demand for anthropologists (*ibid.*:20). The study predicted that in 1970–71 the total number of academically employed anthropologists would jump to 4198, an increase of almost 100 percent over the 1965 figure of 2117. The main increases, however, were calculated to occur in teachers colleges and liberal arts (undergraduate) colleges. Lesser increases were predicted for graduate departments (*ibid.*:21). A comparison with statistics from the 1970–71 *Guide to Departments of Anthropology* indicates that the NIMH forecast was much too optimistic. Although the 1970–71 *Guide* was admittedly incomplete, it was by far the most extensive listing of the series, dipping more deeply into undergraduate departments and museums. (Also, it includes colleagues in Canada and Mexico.) The grand total of academic and museum jobs according to that source comes to approximately 2750.

In 1965, conditions were such that many institutions seeking anthropologists failed to find qualified candidates. Of 254 institutions reporting difficulties in hiring, 106 indicated that the major drawback was the inadequacy of the conditions of employment they had to offer. In particular, low salary scales placed them at a marked competitive disadvantage. But schools in the South, or in isolated locations, had special troubles, as did those with heavy course loads, insufficient opportunities for research, or various other handicaps (*ibid.*:24).

If deepening economic recession continues, more anthropologists will be taking positions in the face of undesirable working conditions. These conditions will probably also force anthropologists to seek positions at lower academic levels than they have previously except during graduate training or in unusual instances. As a result, it is predicted that trained anthropological personnel will be found more and more commonly in junior colleges, in high schools, and perhaps even on the elementary level. While such a trend might be viewed with apprehension by a job seeker, it would have clear social advantages if it brought increased opportunities for students to have contact with trained anthropologists at lower levels in the general curriculum. However, there is reason to be pessimistic even about this possibility. For one thing, the recession that has struck higher education is perhaps even more virulent in elementary and high schools. Not only has there been general slackening of the rate of increase in the teaching force at those levels, but some areas, such as New York City, have been visited by periods of absolute contraction. Under such conditions, it must be said with considerable regret that arguments will be heard advising against the hiring of anthropologically trained Ph.D.'s on the grounds of over-qualification, with fear of attendant dissatisfaction with the teaching role at lower educational levels.

It is possible that some of the slack in the job market will be taken up by increased demand for anthropologists in junior colleges and in conjunction with academic programs associated with open-admission policies. One implication of these speculations is that even under conditions of economic depression there is likely to be employment for the trained anthropologist who is willing to accept conditions more fortunate predecessors were able to avoid. On the other hand, should the Southeast Asian war be brought to a conclusion or fade away, and if the economic conditions of the middle 'sixties return, anthropology would probably again become a scarce and desirable discipline from the viewpoint of the academic marketplace.

Considering the economic factors of supply and demand, it might be thought that the dearth of trained anthropologists in recent years would have encouraged the widest possible distribution of women and men whose ethnic identities or origins were associated with populations subject to discrimination. This is patently not the case with respect to persons identified (by self or others) as black, Negro, Puerto Rican, American Indian, or Chicano. There are some anthropologists of each such origin or identity, but their absolute numbers are small. This is a matter for consideration again later in this chapter. On the basis of the numbers of various other ethnic or religious sorting groups, such as Jews and many of the so-called hyphenated groups—Greek-, Irish-, Italian-, or Polish-Americans, for example—I would say that they have had variable success in entering anthropology as a profession. Too, there are subtle problems about Catholic and WASP anthropologists. One well-known anthropologist from the hills of Appalachia has been heard to remark, partly in jest, partly out of bitterness, that he had to learn to suppress his normal manner of speech in order to get a job and be taken seriously in the profession.

It is somewhat curious that raising such questions and telling such anecdotes seems to embarrass some anthropologists. I say curious because it is anthropologists who usually raise precisely such questions about others. Anti-Semitism, for instance, is a phenomenon of first-rate anthropological interest, yet some anthropologists shy away from asking whether there has been, or for that matter still is, any discrimination against Jews in anthropology. Certainly the question is legitimate. Before coming to these questions and others pertaining to ethnic, racial, and religious minorities, it is important to look into the matter of sexual discrimination and consider the position of women in anthropological employment.

A question was raised some paragraphs back: Is there a noticeable differential in the employment of women on a regional basis or in terms of the size of the department? While I am not in position to answer this question with finality, I have developed some suggestive figures. Let us take three groups of five departments each. Group I comprises five departments in deep South institutions: Alabama, Mississippi, Louisiana State, Georgia, and Arkansas. Group II comprises the middle five of the 15 selected smaller departments discussed in Chapter 9 (see Table 4, p. 172). Group III includes the five largest departments as presented in Chapter 9 (see Table 2, p. 166). Using the *Guide to Departments of Anthropology 1969–70* as data source, no significant differences in the employment of women anthropologists are discovered relating to location or size of department, as Table 8 shows.

TABLE 8

Group	Number of Full-time Positions	Number Held by Women	Percent (approx.)	Total Tenure Positions	Number Held by Women	Percent (approx.)
I	48	6	12.5	22	2	9
II	75	11	14.5	43	4	9
III	165	20	12	104	10	9.5

The question of how women fare in the profession of anthropology is a most interesting one in this time of renewed interest in the movement for women's rights. It is sometimes naïvely assumed that because some of the women held up as models of success in American life, Margaret Mead and Ruth Benedict to mention only two, have been identified as anthropologists, anthropology as a profession must be relatively free of sexual discrimination. I regret to say that this assumption is unfounded. As the previous table hints, there is evidence that despite the fact that some women have scaled the heights of the anthropological profession, the profession as a whole is not hospitable to women. It may well be that anthropology is relatively more accessible to women than many other professions, but there is still enough of a problem of equal female participation in the field to dispel any pride in anthropologists' achievement in this area.

Consider the picture that may be derived by analysis of the raw data provided in the *Guide to Departments of Anthropology 1969–70*. My own scrutiny indicated that there were some 1511 full-time positions listed in conjunction with graduate departments of anthropology and combined departments of anthropology and sociology for the year in question. (This is a crude figure, including some visiting people and others on leave. It also includes "anthropologists in other departments," as the *Guide* puts it.) Of this grand total, 201 positions were held by women, coming to 13.3 percent. We note immediately the close relation of this figure to those indicated in the previous table, having to do with distributions affecting three selected groups of institutions.

One of the things mentioned in connection with discrimination against women in our field is that they are likely to be found in part-time rather than full-time positions. It can be demonstrated, although I will not do so here, that the rate of pay associated with part-time teaching is usually, and on the average, far below the rate of full-time pay, computed on hourly equivalency basis. Of course, the most common rationalization advanced to justify the assumed higher frequency of women in part-time teaching slots has to do with the marital and family responsibilities of females. This is not the context in which to argue such issues. Anthropologists in particular should be wary of accepting the self-serving ideological statements of informants at face value. Yet as anthropologists we are aware of the reality of culture, especially in the form of traditions of class relations of an exploitative kind. In other words, the anthropologist should be able to perceive that there are tremendous possibilities for change, while at the same time recognizing that cultural barriers may be as formidable as once were the physiological or psychological factors that no longer apply.

Retreating from the political debate, I note with some surprise that the impression that women are shunted into part-time employment in anthropology is confirmed in one sense, but debunked in another. My reading of the 1969–70 *Guide* indicates listings of 161 part-time positions, of which 35 were held by women. Thus I compute the percentage of part-time positions held by women at 21.8, considerably larger than the proportion of full-time positions held by women, but not as high as is usually thought. It is necessary, however, for me to call attention to a parallel study reporting somewhat different findings, perhaps as a consequence of the difficulty of precisely rendering the data supplied in the Guide. At any rate, Carole Vance estimated that during the same period some 30 percent of part-time jobs in academic anthropology were held by women (1970:2–3).

According to Vance, her analysis of the 1969–70 *Guide* reveals that 14 percent of all full-time positions were held by women (*ibid.*:8). The distribution of ranks within these full-time positions, however, shows great disparity, with very heavy concentration at the lower end, clearly disproportionate in contrast with the distribution of male-held full-time positions.

My analysis of the 1969–70 *Guide* came up with a figure for full-time positions held by women that is very close to Vance's; as previously indicated, my figure is 13.3 percent. By my count in the same *Guide,* the total number of tenure positions in anthropology in 1969–70 came to 808. (This is possibly the weakest figure in my repertory of statistics. Rules of tenure vary, and in many institutions there is no necessary relationship between rank and tenure. Nonetheless, I applied the simple assumption that full and associate professors had tenure, while all other positions did not. Thus I excluded from my tenure count all emeritus, adjunct, assistant, and visiting professors, research associates, and the like.) Of this total 78 are women, or 9.65 percent. Considering the number of women holding full-time appointments, about 39 percent of these positions are tenured. Compare this with the equivalent situation among men. Of 1310 men with full-time appointments, I estimate that about 730 (56 percent) have tenure.

According to the 1969–70 *Guide*, six women were serving as heads of departments. If this information is placed alongside that given above, a most interesting progression seems to emerge. In percentages, the proportion of positions held by women is highest with respect to part-time appointments (21.8 percent according to my own study, 30 percent according to Vance). Considerably lower is the proportion of full-time appointments held by women (13.3 percent). Next in declining order is the estimated proportion of tenure positions held by women (9.65 percent), and finally, the proportion of department heads who are women (5 percent). The regularity of the decline shown by these figures can be read as an indictment. I realize that the figures are approximations, but some corroboration is obtained from the similarity between my figures and those obtained independently by Carole Vance. Both of us urge further research along these lines. We should like to know, for example, what proportion of living anthropologists with the doctorate are women. Vance indicates that this might be on the order of 14 percent (*ibid.*:2–3). On the other hand, scrutiny of the recent dissertations listed in the 1970–71 *Guide* (pp. 228–36) indicates that of 237 recent (i.e., 1968, 1969, 1970; all years incomplete) doctorates, about 24 percent (54) went to women. The reasons for female Ph.D.'s being considerably fewer than expectable on demographic grounds are quite complex and have not received adequate attention, although some interesting contributions are already available (Fischer and Golde 1968; Graham 1970; Rossi 1970; Simon, Clark, and Galway 1967; Harris 1970).

There is also a historical question here. We need a better picture of the situation that existed in past decades. Cynthia Irwin-Williams reacted angrily in 1970 to "ill-considered resolutions from tiny, noisy pressure groups" agitating for women's rights. In her experience, wrote archeologist Irwin-Williams,

> the anthropological profession probably exhibits much less prejudice toward women than many others. This is principally because our battles were fought for us in the 1930s, '40s, and '50s by professional women anthropologists whose unquestioned excellence compelled and justified their acceptance (eg, Wormington, Underhill, Mead, Hawley, Du Bois, de Laguna, Benedict, etc) [1970:6]

This remark attracted Vance's attention and she offered a partial refutation on the basis of comparison with women in sociology (1970:9). She concludes that "the dogma that women fare better in anthropology compared to other disciplines" is a myth. Vance might have added that the illustrious Ruth Benedict, whose career is cited by Irwin-Williams, was promoted to the rank of full professor at Columbia a scant year before her death, after long service. Although some colleagues have already indicated their displeasure at my remarks on this subject (which appeared in the *Newsletter of the American Anthropological Association*, 12:2 [1970]:6–7), I find it necessary to repeat that until more reliable data are in hand, we shall have to assume that the charges feminists are currently making against academic anthropology are true. What is more, we must begin immediately to correct the imbalances.

In attempting to determine whether there are also discernible patterns of racial, ethnic, or religious discrimination within the profession of anthropology, we raise a very hard question indeed. First, the difficulties of ascertaining the sex of an individual through the analysis of names pale beside those which arise in attempting to use names to sort individuals into ethnic, racial, or religious groups. What makes such a question even more formidable is its intimate association with some of the most fundamental theoretical positions of modern anthropology. The question of identity, of sorting individuals into groups on the basis of racial characteristics, gives laymen little or no reason for concern but is overwhelmingly complicated for anthropologists. For the anthropologists to drop their own highly technical approach to such schemes of classification and adopt the easy hasty conclusion of the layman would destroy a substantial part of the discipline's accomplishments to date.

Yet in the contemporary climate the pressures to do exactly this are almost overwhelming. It is frequently charged, for example, that refusal to take account of racial or ethnic differences is a technique of overlooking or concealing discrimination, or even actively furthering it. The matter is one of utmost seriousness. It will not simply go away. If anthropologists do not want to be carried on the racist or discriminatory tides that most of us profess to abhor, we had better take some positive steps to dissociate ourselves from such currents.

Very few members (however identified) of the minorities suffering the greatest and most prolonged discrimination in our society are to be found in the ranks of professional anthropologists. This state of affairs must be due in part to the very high cost, until recently, of obtaining the advanced education required for taking a position in anthropology. However, such reasoning only goes part way. It fails, for example, to deal adequately with the paucity of black anthropologists produced with the assistance of the G.I. Bill and other subsidization that has been in such good supply since World War II. The question then is not that of a small discipline and a particular exploited population, but one of the entire structure of a society that forces everybody into racist and discriminatory postures, often by default or omission, where intentions are the purest, or deepest ideological convictions to the contrary.

This is not the context, however, in which to pursue issues of such overwhelming magnitude and complexity. Let me instead ask if prejudice and discrimination exist within academic anthropology. Does access to positions hinge in any degree upon factors other than ability?

The processes of job getting, particularly in the case of the first appointment obtained after completing the Ph.D., often involve extensive personal interactions, hence must implicate qualities other than simple ability. The best way to spot discriminatory and prejudicial policies and procedures is to seek out the hard evidence of their results. That is what we did with reference to the conditions in feminine employment. Unfortunately, it is not possible to develop similar data with respect to other minority groups without a major research project that would require site visits to a good many anthropology departments, and extensive interviewing. To check various kinds of name lists and catalogs will simply not produce the kind of evidence we require. What is left is anecdotal and impressionistic.

There is widespread belief in some quarters that it is easy to get a good job in anthropology today if one is black, or has other minority status, and a Ph.D. Some black colleagues insist indignantly that this is not so, while members of other depressed minority groups point scornfully to the absence of their members from professional ranks. It is true, however, that pressure from black student associations and black community activists did create at least a flurry of activity in the field of hiring and, although largely opportunistic, it is likely that colleges and universities will continue to place a premium on locating qualified personnel, especially blacks, for a variety of programs. The coupling of such appointments to the needs of newly launched Black Studies programs, or Afro-American institutes, implicitly raises questions of racism, sometimes in reverse form. Beyond the obvious opportunism, however, lies a variety of invidious and sometimes blatantly discriminatory procedures. A brilliant ethnohistorian may be wooed because of his long and successful teaching career, but the institutions seeking to get him make it clear that he should be working on "more realistic" problems. Justified in terms of the very same concepts of relevance discussed earlier, the sometimes handsome financial offers made to such a scholar are often accompanied by blatant pressures that would be almost unthinkable in connection with regular appointments.

I believe that my own cohort of anthropologists, during its years of training and early employment, was much disturbed by problems of prejudice. This group of colleagues did not view anthropology as a discipline free of discrimination. We were aware that few of our numbers were black, and we became even more painfully aware that the very occasional Negro who gained his Ph.D. disappeared into a kind of oblivion. Certainly there were no black professors in any of the departments we knew. We also heard rumors of other kinds of discrimination. So far as we could tell, for example, there were a number of departments, including one of the largest and most famous, that had never appointed a Jew to the faculty.

Whatever conditions were twenty years ago, the present situation is relatively favorable with regard to an absolute decline in discriminatory hiring procedures. Clearly women and members of certain minorities, such as blacks and Puerto Ricans, still enjoy limited access to unrestricted employment opportunities. In the cases of blacks and Puerto Ricans, the number of candidates remains very low, although efforts are being made to increase it. There is still a long way to go, but there has been change.

What has changed little, if at all, is the way in which jobs are obtained. Anthropology is not unique but shares much of its social structure with academia in general. But anthropology is small compared to such teeming fields as English or history, or even political science and sociology. Most senior professional anthropologists in the United States know each other; at a minimum, they have heard of each other and have mutual friends. Within the lifetime of anthropologists of middle age, the profession was tiny. Even today much of the business of the discipline is carried out interpersonally. The anthropologists are amused —they are aware that their own profession tends to be organized along gemeinschaft lines. It was not long ago that it resembled a small community. But here, as elsewhere, the folk organization is imperiled by population expansion, the communications revolution, and changes in the encapsulating larger world.

For several years, at such professional meetings as the annual one held by the American Anthropological Association, the United States Employment Service, usually in conjunction with the employment service of the state where the meeting was held, organized job-locating services and registry for those who sought positions. Actually, in 1969, for budgetary reasons, the USES declined any longer to provide these services of placement and registry. The secretariat of the Association thereupon began to provide these services and expected to continue to improve and expand these facilities in the future.

The decision to enlarge the employment services of the Association is in line with another service provided by the Association. For a modest fee an anthropologist, whether a Fellow of the AAA or not, may advertise that he is looking for a position. For a larger but still relatively modest fee an institution may advertise for candidates. While the "Positions Wanted" usually outnumber the "Positions Open," that is not always the case, even in these economically parlous times.

The advertisements seeking applicants have displayed an interesting diversity over the past few years. While the majority seem to ask for responses by cultural anthropologists (including social anthropologists and ethnographers or ethnologists), almost all varieties of anthropologists have been called for by name. A number of ads have not indicated specializations and some note that this is not a major matter —other criteria, such as willingness to participate in a general education program, being considered more important. The same seems to be generally true of areal specialization. Sometimes the area is closely specified and is obviously intended either to conform to a major existing research orientation or to fill a gap. More usually, no areal specifications are listed. The "positions open" ads usually seek teachers, or mention a combination of teaching and research. In the latter case, it is generally obvious that the research encouragements are mentioned to attract a certain kind of respondent. In some cases, however, the emphasis is explicitly on research with teaching ancillary or absent. Ranks and salaries may be closely specified, but more frequently wide ranges are indicated, with final determination depending on qualifications. Absolutely clear is the preliminary nature of the advertisements. No positions will be filled on the basis of immediate responses. Instead, names of candidates and their vitae are solicited, references requested, and in many cases it is stressed that negotiations will be concluded only after a personal visit has been arranged.

When these advertisements do specify a particular rank, it is quite often the higher levels that are mentioned. Specific requests for applications for full professorships are relatively abundant, as are openings for departmental chairmanships. This is readily understood in conjunction with the intersection of two trends already discussed: the relatively low rate of production of anthropology Ph.D.'s until the 1950's, and the spurt thereafter in the formation of graduate departments of anthropology. This "room at the top" phenomenon will, presumably, level off in the next decade unless there is dramatic reinvestment in higher education such as was contemplated among the congressmen who vainly introduced the International Education Bill during the Johnson administration. Passage of such a bill would create exceptionally favorable employment demands for various kinds of social scientists, none more than anthropologists.

In addition to seeking candidates for teaching posts, ads present other possibilities. Some are research oriented, as was one that appeared in March 1969:

RESEARCH ASSOCIATE. Participate in and help execute large-scale research project on problems of adjustment to urban environment. Emphasis on comprehensive health is-

*sues with sociopsychological perspective. To be conducted
in a tri-ethnic setting. Opportunity to innovate; should have
imagination and drive, interdisciplinary interests, and quantitative orientations.*

The advertisement concluded by asking that vitae be sent to a medical
doctor at a medical college at a prominent university in the Southwest.
In December 1969 the Encyclopaedia Britannica advertised in the *Newsletter* for an associate editor specializing either in cultural or physical
anthropology but able to handle both. The job required an M.A. and
preference for a Ph. D. was stated.

None of the job advertisements in the *Newsletter* has evoked unfavorable public comment. This was not the case when, in December
1968, the subscribers to the *American Anthropologist* received their
regular issues and discovered therein (70:4:852) a full-page advertisement placed by the Overseas Employment Office of the U.S. Navy, seeking a research anthropologist for military and paramilitary work in Vietnam. Consternation was the immediate and widespread reaction. At
least one group of anthropologists circulated a letter of protest directed
against the editorial judgment that had accepted the ad, and many individual responses expressed critical views. This led to some rallying of
an opposition, or at least of those who believed that the editor had
acted wisely and within his competence to accept and publish such an
advertisement. There were further consequences, although there has
been no repetition nor any similar event. The problem of that ad, however, is part of a much larger set of questions pertaining to ethics, so
I shall set it aside temporarily for consideration in the next chapter.

Before leaving the topic of "positions open" advertisements, a few
additional comments may be especially interesting to beginners. First,
these notices are frequently inserted by institutions outside the United
States. While Canada, Australia, and New Zealand have clear predominance in this category, there are occasional insertions from other
countries as well. Second, in the columns of the *Newsletter* can be
found possibilities of summer employment, sometimes teaching, occasionally research or some other activity linked to anthropology.
Finally, there is no mention of sexual distinctions in any of these notices and, of course, absolutely nothing relating to any racial, ethnic,
religious, or other group identity characteristic.

Similar ambiguity marks the "positions wanted" advertisements.
These have appeared at the rate of forty to fifty notices per year in
recent times. Although placed by persons with a wide range of education, experience, and subject or areal specializations, the main body
seems to represent applicants who have not yet completed their doctorates. Reading between the lines, one large portion seems to be com-

prised of those who are actually on the verge of completing their degrees and seek their first major appointments. Another large category, again reading by implications, comprises an older group of people who are still sincerely pursuing their Ph.D.'s but are somewhat vaguer about their prospects for completion. To compensate, anthropologists in this category offer teaching experience and some publications.

Which takes us to the interesting question of publishing or perishing. It is certainly true, particularly in the large departments, that the extent of a candidate's written contributions is a critical factor in the determination of hiring, promotion, and rise to tenure. Almost no one speaks of firing; it is a matter of the unrenewed option, or more usually the "terminal year." A great deal of paper and ink, not to mention heated voices, has been devoted to the pros and cons of relying heavily upon publications records; I will not enter the argument here. Whatever the ideal procedures, the fact is that sharp interest is taken in the quantity, quality, frequency, placement, and reaction to an upwardly mobile colleague's printed output, particularly when the appointment concerns graduate teaching. (Pressures are considerably less in undergraduate departments, although many exceptions can be cited. Furthermore, demands and allowances change with shifting conditions; when the supply of qualified candidates goes up, so then may the standards of qualification.)

I will not say that there are no institutions relying solely on the publications record of an applicant for appointment or a candidate for promotion. Most institutions, however, are concerned also about teaching and they may be concerned about other things as well. We have already seen that women become fewer in the higher and tenured ranks. Questions have been raised also about employment and political beliefs and associations. Like other disciplines and professions, anthropology has had its quota of cases of political repression. A number of well-known anthropologists, some of outstanding brilliance, were driven from employment in the United States during the late 1940's and early 1950's. At the time of writing, the outstanding case was a Canadian one. Dr. Kathleen Gough Aberle was denied tenure at Simon Fraser University in Burnaby, British Columbia. A popular teacher (as described in the Simon Fraser University student newspaper, The Peak), Dr. Aberle is an anthropologist of international reputation and quite extensive personal bibliography. At her request, the American Anthropological Association appointed an ad hoc committee to study the case and report if a violation of the principles of academic freedom had occurred. Based upon the preliminary report of that committee, the Executive Board of the AAA expressed to the president of Simon Fraser University the recommendation that dismissal procedures against Dr. Aberle be withdrawn until the completion of thorough investigations. The AAA requested the Canadian Association of University

Teachers and the Canadian Sociology and Anthropology Association to set up a commission to inquire not merely into the immediate circumstances of the denial of tenure to Aberle, but into the general and special conditions at Simon Fraser which led to the existing denouement. The AAA committee made clear that grounds did not exist for denial of tenure to Aberle on the basis of scholarship. It also declared that the complications surrounding the case and arising out of a student and faculty strike at SFU, in which Aberle played a role to the evident dismay of the administration, "appear to the committee to be far less serious than those involved in the inadequacy of the tenure review" (*Newsletter of the American Anthropological Association* 11:6 [1970]:11).

Insidious problems of academic freedom relating to employment will be further complicated in coming years if the present job freeze or contraction continues. At the root will be the system whereby a department takes on more people at the junior level than can possibly be moved into senior posts or given budgetary tenure. Actually, such a system operated throughout the period of great departmental expansion, but with negligible consequences as many new posts were opened in the department of the candidate or equivalent posts could be found elsewhere without too much difficulty (particularly if the candidate was male). In recession and with retrenchment, each promotion, especially one involving tenure, becomes a major battlefield. If an aspirant is refused and if he is known as a controversial or difficult personality, if he is involved in certain political activities or causes, then whatever may be said of his teaching or publications, it will probably be charged that he was let go for political reasons. There are no sure remedies for such problems, but some guidelines are available. There is inherent conflict in the juxtaposition of the rules supporting the objective application of universalistic criteria of ability and the special exemptions that are claimed in the light of the handicaps of previous injustice. What will happen in this area of potential discord will be less a matter of solutions than the evolution of a new *modus vivendi*—the usual means by which society copes with its difficulties and creates new ones.

A few last comments for beginners seeking positions. If it is at all possible, delay taking a full-time position until you have your dissertation virtually in hand. The first years of teaching are particularly demanding. Although some people have been able to write fine theses while teaching nine-hour (or even heavier) loads, a lot more have either had to suspend work on their doctorates or have suffered unpleasant consequences. Talk the situation over thoroughly with your adviser before taking a fateful step, if only to give your prospective students a decent break.

In seeking a position, prepare a vita, giving all significant information about yourself, stressing your education and academic accomplishments and honors, if any. Indicate what courses you are prepared to teach, the lines of specialization you hope to develop in research. Couple the vita with a brief letter explaining your availability and send it off to as many institutions as you wish. Don't be discouraged by the high rate of negative responses or the frequent failure to get any answer or even acknowledgment. All you need is one really good nibble. There are still fewer trained anthropologists than positions requiring anthropological skills. Edward J. Lehman, Executive Director of the American Anthropological Association, states that during the 1969 annual meeting of that association there were four positions open to anthropologists with Ph.D.'s for every available candidate who was qualified. As long as such conditions prevail, it would seem that anthropologists will not be able to complain about the wolf at the door (although some salaries have failed to keep pace with inflationary rises in the cost of living, but this constitutes a different kind of problem).

ETHICS

I sat in the sunset shade of their Bastille, the Pentagon,
... and heard, alas, more speeches
—Robert Lowell

It is the nature of any discussion of ethics to be a speech. I prefer to say it that way. Influenced by Lowell's lines, I might have written that it is the nature of any discussion of ethics to be, *alas,* a speech. But the added word implies an alternative that I think does not exist. May and Abraham Edel remark about ethics that

> we do not find specialized groups to carry it out, nothing to correspond to a priesthood or a police force. There are no buildings for ethics, nor visible tokens of it like shell money or a witch's herbal bag. Apart from education, it is hard to find common institutional forms peculiarly dedicated to it. [1968:7]

Ethics, then, is manifest in speeches, in finger-pointing, in gossip, in sublime poetry and irritating doggerel. It concerns decisions about good and bad, about the desirable and undesirable, and above all relates exclusively to human relations. A dog that takes another's bone or chases a cat or messes on the rug cannot by any stretch of the imagination be said to have committed an unethical act, no more or less than a breach of ethics is to be seen in a guppy eating its young.

The study of moral and ethical systems formerly pertained, for the most part, to philosophy, and indeed, philosophers are still to be found who make this their prime area of concern. But certain aspects of the inquiry into moral and ethical questions have become more closely associated with social scientists and anthropologists in particular. Dorothy Emmet (1968:157), a specialist in these areas, tells us, for example, that the attempt to distinguish ethical components of a socio-cultural system, as distinct from political, religious, or legal aspects, or even from etiquette, crested in the late nineteenth and early twentieth centuries in the work of anthropologists like Edward Westermarck (1862–1939). In more recent decades, however, the primary interest of anthropologists in a technical sense has been devoted to the comparative

229

study of values, including moral and ethical concepts and precepts. Paralleling this to some degree is strong sociological interest in the analysis of ethical codes as the normative charters of specialized sectors of a larger society. Thus, in the work of Talcott Parsons, ethical codes are seen as the strictures controlling role playing among such professionals as doctors and lawyers, both in terms of relations among themselves and between themselves as professionals and other portions of the larger society (e.g., patients, technicians, drug salesmen, clients, and so on). Beals, in his survey of ethical problems in contemporary anthropology, calls attention to Parsons' suggestion "that ethical problems in science arise primarily at the intersection of the various subsystems in which the individual scientist participates" (Beals 1969: n. 8, p. 82, citing Parsons 1967). Beals then goes on to identify three loci at which ethical questions appear in conjunction with professional problems: (1) with regard to professional responsibility—maintaining integrity and high working standards; (2) observing one's responsibility to others—proper treatment of associates, fellows, informants, nonprofessional associates, the subjects of research, the public; and (3) observing a responsibility to oneself—"considering one's personal background and psychological needs" (Beals 1969:83). I think that the sharpest attack on Beals could be expected to develop from left activists. I suspect that they would find that with these strictures he would have covered the waterfront—that in providing for just about everything, he has provided for nothing; he has, instead, avoided the biggest question. We encountered that question back in Chapter 2, in association with A. G. Frank's statements about what anthropologists should be doing, where it was most sharply stated by the Habers, who frankly declare for a "revolutionary ethic."

Having staked out some of the difficult terrain we will have to traverse in this chapter, let us move first to the easiest ground, to speak briefly about matters of an ethical nature relating to anthropology, yet of such nature as to be minimally controversial or universally accepted. There is, for example, the ethical matter of standards that cuts across all subdivisions.

Whether one is linguist or archeologist, physical or cultural anthropologist, there is a presumption of craftsmanship that has ethical overtones. Most obvious are the restraints on misrepresenting credentials. The Ph.D. must be in hand before it is appended symbolically to one's name. Obvious as this may be, it is unfortunate that there have been tragic cases to the contrary. Furthermore, there is a certain low frequency of semimisrepresentations, for example, in the tendency of candidates to present themselves (or be presented by their departments) as having completed their doctorates when they are still pending. To assume, as sometimes is done, that this matter of the Ph.D. is mere elitist snobbery is to completely miss the point of the certification of competence. It is obvious, however, that concepts of competence, its standard, and the means of assessing it are subject to continual review. In the past, it has been common for students to be excluded from the process of standard setting. During the height of student activism in 1968 and 1969, there seemed to be movement in some departments toward greater student participation at this level of determination of professional competence. In the subsequent period, however, interest in such reform seems to have waned, although some examination changes were accomplished at certain institutions.

There is a set of ethical problems that have to do with the initial determination of certain types of competence and with the maintenance of a previously demonstrated competence. The latter refers to the difficulty of ascertaining in advance whether any particular individual will be a reasonably good teacher. As we have seen (p. 213 f.), the overwhelming majority of anthropologists are engaged in teaching as their primary activity. Yet, as we have also seen, little effort is expended during their periods of training to make them competent instructors. Indeed, we have only rather haphazard and primitive means of determining how good a teacher someone is. Some of the means have dubious ethical overtones by our present values—I refer to the visits to a junior colleague's classroom of some inspector or group of inspectors (whatever they may be called). On the other hand, using the evaluations of students, a very necessary part of determining the competence of a teacher, brings up another batch of ethical questions, such as the relations beween differential standards of grading and student reaction to a teacher's personality. It is evident, however, that such a problem touches anthropology only as one of many academic subjects and is exacerbated only to the degree that anthropologists are capable of looking objectively at their own social structure, however painful that may be.

Even in such relatively mild ethical considerations one finds the materials of very deep and difficult problems. There is an acceptance of a certain very general pattern of social organization in the larger society which embodies formal hierarchy, the cultivation of esoteric specializations, and elitism. There is an alternative that deplores all of these things and asserts that a counterculture can be built on opposite principles. The contrast between these systems is usually discussed in ethical as well as political terms. It is appropriate to note here that a major complication facing anthropologists who consider such problems is the latent, and frequently manifest, conflict between their moral preference for one set of solutions, and the professional ideology of objectivity.

Comparable in difficulty to the detecting of teaching competence in the young instructor is the determination of continued competence in older ones. A common method of attempting this has disturbed several generations of students and young professionals. Usually referred to as "publish or perish," placing great reliance on the volume of published work has obvious ethical implications in addition to practical drawbacks. Consider merely two aspects: the draining of some instructors' energies such that they shortchange their students in order to maintain certain levels of publication, and the burden of such publication on their science as the volume of junk and trivia swells to flood proportions. Yet, alternatives for assessing competence later in the development of a career have potentially alarming ethical consequences, particularly in suggesting some form of "thought police," or intellectual coercion.

Moving to a more general consideration of ethical problems in anthropology at large, it seems to me from my vantage point in the cultural portion of the discipline that linguists have the fewest problems of professional ethics. (This is not to say that linguists may not play vanguard roles in the moral and ethical struggles of their day, as the activities of Noam Chomsky so brilliantly illustrate.) However, even linguistics has sometimes been placed in the service of colonialist and racist ideology, as when theories of the evolutionary superiority or functional superiority of certain languages have been offered.

Archeologists have somewhat more frequent possibilities of encountering ethical problems. To suggest just one or two, let us take the once common situation in which the ancient treasures of a defenseless society were removed with neither consultation nor permission from their native locales and placed in a museum in Europe or North America. Many of the countries in which international archeological projects are carried out have since placed an embargo on the export of antiquities. Yet, there is a substantial residue of heritage materials, ranging from such famous objects as the so-called Elgin Marbles to the uncounted precious objects of art from China, which are held in public and private collections around the world. A new case has come to the pressure point. Representatives of at least a portion of the Iroquois people (Onondaga), plus Indian leaders representing a wider spectrum of peoples, have successfully demanded the return from New York State of an extensive collection of wampum gathered into the custody of the Regents of the University of the State of New York by donation and purchase about three quarters of a century ago. In line with the ongoing political revival among American Indians is a religious revival, and the wampum is being demanded on grounds similar to those being presented the government in the case of the sacred Blue Lake near Taos Pueblo in New Mexico. Anthropologists and archeologists are becoming involved, pro and con, in such demands and are finding that what started out as professional questions are becoming more and more entangled in ethical considerations.

Archeologists also become enmeshed in ethical problems through their conduct surrounding a dig. I cannot erase from my mind a certain film supplied graciously and gratuitously to me by the French consulate for use in a class many years ago. I was teaching a survey of the cultures of Southeast Asia, and the film showed the temples of Angkor. In one segment, running perhaps a couple of minutes, an old, white-bearded, and very dignified, if anonymous, professor was shown conducting another seemingly academic person about a portion of the ruins. A fallen piece of sculpture attracted the older man's eye and he brought it to the attention of his companion. Unfortunately, at that very moment a Khmer workman was bending in front of the object, possibly at some task. Without thought or hesitation, the old archeologist poked the Cambodian away with a long fan he was carrying. So commonplace was the event that it obviously never occurred to anybody in the French information service to excise that bit of colonialist by-play.

The day has gone by, in some countries at least, when the archeologist was the great white god with clean, soft hands. My archeologist friends assure me that this image never really applied to the anthropological archeologist, who has always (it is said) been accustomed to come into first-hand (sic) contact with the dirt. In any event, labor relations can present problems with ethical reverberations, just as can the proper securing of legal rights to dig at particular sites.

A final note about archeological matters that have ethical aspects. The archeologist is no longer involved in abstruse affairs. Some of his digs are seized upon for political significance, perhaps as an additional source of legitimacy for a new or shaky state, or to place or refute some territorial claim. One example must suffice:

Archeologists have been under attack in Rhodesia for their findings at Zimbabwe and similar ruins near Salisbury. Zimbabwe has been identified as the remains of a medieval Bantu city, dated by radiocarbon between the 11th and 15th centuries with occupation possibly as late as the 17th. These dates have undercut previous held beliefs that the city was a settlement of Egyptians, Phoenicians or Indians rather than the creation of the immediate ancestors of Rhodesia's black population.

Recent discovery of a similar ruin at Bindura in the same area has stimulated attacks on the archeologists and even an Information Department pamphlet by white citizens of a new nation dedicated politically to white supremacy. It is psychologically almost impossible in the present intellectual environment for the white critics to ascribe to native Bantu technical skills that could produce the masonry buildings, gold figures, sculptures and pottery that are un-

covered at the ruins. Rather, it is more comfortable to view
such suggestions as black African nationalist movement
propaganda.   [Newsletter of the American Anthropological
Association 11:2 (1970):11]

The ethical involvements of physical anthropology are related to
those implied in the paragraphs just cited. They are also among the
oldest and best known of those faced in the anthropological discipline.
It is instructive and perhaps a source of relief to realize that physical
anthropology played an important role in one of the decisive moral
turns in the history of not only Western but world civilization. I refer,
of course, to the place of physical anthropology in demonstrating the
soundness of the evolutionary approach, in producing the evidence of
man's evolutionary ancestry, and in driving religion and supernatural-
ism from this area of knowledge. But equally old, if less decisive, have
been the ethical implications of the physical anthropological study of
race.

Although there is no dearth of racist literature that seems to have
emanated from physical anthropologists, very little of the current crop
has actually been produced by scholars who have specialized in physical
anthropology. Yet there are a few such specialists who join a hetero-
geneous group of anthropological amateurs in spreading a compost of
old and new lies, half truths, innuendos, and hypotheses about race.
Some physical anthropologists, who easily could do otherwise, make
little or no effort to limit the use of their work by others for patently
antisocial ends. Indeed, I think the most important ethical issue that
faces physical anthropology concerns the basic question of the social
responsibility of the scientist. I see no reason to revise an indictment
that I offered some years ago. I began by noting that excellent work
had already been done for years by scientists to counter what I call the
pseudoscientific proclamations about race:

> *I do not say that they failed in their intentions; certain ame-*
> *liorations have occurred. But one thing they did not do is*
> *stop the nonsense. The pseudo studies go right on. What is*
> *more, some fine scientific journals throw open their pages to*
> *serious discussion of this nonsense. Those who oppose the*
> *pseudo study of race are called "equalitarians," and this term*
> *has been skillfully manipulated to make it appear as if there*
> *are two valid camps participating in a normal scientific ex-*
> *change. But this is not a question of digging the "Mohole" or*
> *not, or whether* Homo habilis *is or is not an* Australopithecus.
> *It is more like dividing on the question of whether or not to*
> *exterminate six million Jews: one side says no and presents*
> *its arguments, and the other side says yes and presents its*

*arguments, and this too becomes a debatable scientific
question. . . .*

*Science has no social responsibilities, but scientists
must accept social responsibility or face the consequences.
Racial problems are as fraught with danger and potential
disaster as problems of nuclear proliferation. . . . What I am
suggesting is only a slight extension of the element of social
responsibility from the individual subject to the larger social
aggregates whose futures are just as much influenced by this
work.   [Fried 1968:129–130]*

The mounting gradient of ethical responsibility in anthropological
work crests in the various subfields of cultural anthropology. Here
ethical problems become so abundant and are so pressing that the
present brief chapter cannot hope to do justice to them. We have, however, already gotten a look at some of the problems in Chapter 2. Before
taking a final plunge into the most serious and controversial, we should
briefly consider some of the less complex questions that arise.

Consider first the ethical problems that beset relations with informants. We already warned about potential cruelties that might
arise in dealing with aged informants from whom we obtain historical,
biographical, or other kinds of information. The return to the informant
is likely to be limited to the transient companionship that such interviews bring. What happens when the interviews are concluded? The
young and busy anthropologist goes off and forgets; the old person has
been deserted yet again. Nor are such problems confined to relations
across generational chasms. Most informants come to believe that they
are developing a viable human relationship when they spill out con-
fidences or help gather materials. Some make elaborate plans to use the
relationship for other social purposes. After all, the anthropologist is
frequently regarded as a representative of the ruling class, or the powerful metropolitan country. Usually, the anthropologist is correctly considered to be wealthy beyond local dreams. Surely such a friend will
help in various emergencies throughout life. Yet, at the time of departure
from the field, the anthropologist frequently disappears into a void and
is never heard from again.

I have no sure remedies for these types of situations. Different
anthropologists handle the matter in different ways. Let this mention of
the problems, however, stand as a warning. The ethnographer had better
do some thinking about these possibilities before he is swamped by
events that may damage others and leave very heavy psychological
burdens of guilt.

There are so many problems that revolve about the relation of
anthropologists with their informants that several volumes could be

devoted to them. Consider, for example, the word "informant," which carries an unwanted freight, not the least portion of which is its tendency to convert persons into things. But there are other aspects as well. Few go deeper into the ethical morass of our field than the problem of maintaining scientific verity while protecting real people from the dangers of exposure. It is commonplace now to remark that the day is long past when the anthropologists' monographs existed in a completely different world from the one in which lived their sources of information, their subjects. Now literacy is growing and communications approach the instantaneous. Write about a Minnan community in any portion of Taiwan and the people will soon know exactly what is in the book. What may be worse, the government will also know about it. In many cases this will not matter, but what if sections of the book deal candidly with political values and raise questions about the loyalty of some Taiwanese to the existing Nationalist Government? What complicates matters further is the fact that the anthropologist cannot know what may become a sensitive issue. His book may be a time bomb for decades. To avoid this possibility, or to reduce its potential, a variety of devices of concealment are utilized. But concealment is a form of secrecy and, as we shall see, anthropologists are usually opposed to secrecy and have held secrecy against various sponsoring agencies, particularly those associated with the military. Of course, it is a big leap from obfuscation to preserve privacy to total classification that leads a study to be withheld indefinitely from the scrutiny of other scientists and from the public at large.

There is also a problem concerning financial arrangements between an anthropologist and those whose information he must utilize. There are a few instances, very few, in which the anthropologist has made rather considerable sums from the books that have resulted. Should the author split the profits with his informants? To determine how equity is to be arrived at in such cases remains essentially a matter of ethics involving the conscience of the principal researcher. As we have seen, however, suggestions have been made that amounts equal in size to the grant supporting the research should be paid to the community being studied (cf. p. 70). This might be contrasted with a once rather prevalent view that condemned the paying of informants as a source of corruption in field work.

Additional ethical problems concern the relation of the anthropologist with the government of the society he chooses to study. From one point of view, the anthropologist must be considered a guest of the country he journeys to in carrying out his research. He is, of course, legally bound to observe the laws of that country. Does he have additional obligations? Some anthropologists seem to think not; they perceive their obligations to lie with some segment of the society other than the government. Many who hold such views are never called upon to translate them into any kind of action. Their field experiences pass without friction or at least without overt manifestations of such friction. There are some, though, whose activities openly fly in the face of the host government's desires. Whatever value such activities may have for whatever constituencies, the fact that they are associated with an anthropologist is likely to have decided effect on subsequent anthropological work in that country. The most obvious, of course, is that anthropologists applying to do work in that society in the future are liable to be turned away or receive less than full cooperation. It is the threat of the former eventuality that concerns so many anthropologists, raising, as it does, serious ethical questions requiring some balancing of obligations within the discipline of those that individual practitioners feel they have as citizens, or simply as members of the human race. It reminds us of Talcott Parsons' suggestion (see p. 230) that the ethical bind is to be found precisely at the point where the individual is subjected to the clash of codes for two or more of the subsystems in which he is involved.

Since this is not a book about ethical problems in anthropology, but merely a chapter, it is time to get into some of the major controversial issues. None is more central than the question of selecting a focus of interest for anthropological teaching and research. Involved, on the one hand, is the entire battery of problems known as relevance. On the other are fundamental questions of individual decision, still very much a part of the culture in which this book will take its place.

As we have seen, one bit of advice is that anthropologists should abandon, at least for the time being (until the revolutionary transformation), all ideas about working in other cultures. They are advised, instead, to stick to their own and, in fact, concentrate even there on revolutionary activities. I am not sure how beneficial this scheme may be for any practically based concept of revolution, but it would be the death of anthropology. Anthropology came close to dying in the Soviet Union when this attitude prevailed there. Now there is some anthropology, but it is not synonymous with Marxist-Leninist theory. Similarly, in Cuba there remains an independent anthropology, although its role and contributions are not quite clear. Anthropology, however, can scarcely be said to exist in the People's Republic of China, although it is too early to consider its demise permanent. (I will argue in the sequel that at certain levels of sociocultural complexity the social sciences, and anthropology in particular, will be reintroduced, even reinvented, many times, each time in response to the need for real information as opposed to ideological eyewash.)

Concentrating once again on selecting a focus for anthropological work, let us note that the discipline is somewhat more relaxed in its attitudes about area specialization than some of its relatives, especially in adjacent social sciences. To some extent, however, it is true that the biggest kudos is reserved for those whose reputation is primarily associated with anthropological theory in general; it does not hurt to be associated *also* with some particular culture or culture area. Eric R. Wolf, pointing out that the more talented fieldworker, Malinowski, lost out in influence to the greater theoretician, A. R. Radcliffe-Brown, nonetheless underlines the significance of ethnography to the anthropologist who thereby "has escaped from the humdrum world of his civilization to walk among headhunters, cannibals, and peyote-worshippers, to concern himself with talking drums, magic, and divine kings" (1964:11). What must be added, because it enhances contrast, is that this has been done in cold blood, without patronization. As Radcliffe-Brown commented:

> the anthropologist is not concerned, as an anthropologist, with whether such things as slavery and cannibalism, or the institutions of the United States or Russia, are or are not right, good, reasonable, or just.   [1949:321]

It must be realized that there were many who disagreed with that stand at the time of its writing, as there are today. Before we return to consider the dispute that this position entails, a few more remarks about the issue of problem selection in its ethical setting may be appropriate.

Let us consider first the recommendation that anthropologists place a moratorium on working in foreign cultures until the problems of their own cultures are solved. Most particularly, this stricture is aimed at anthropologists in the United States, although it is applied to those coming from other metropolitan and colonialist or imperialistic powers as well. Earlier in this chapter I wrote that observance of this stricture would destroy anthropology. A colleague, reading the draft, noted at first that if this were so, he would have no regrets. Then he continued, reflecting that a "new anthropology" might arise from the wreckage, an anthropology that had severed its links with the exploitative past. What is more, my friend suggests, the limitation of the purview of United States anthropologists to their own country does not necessarily herald the destruction of cross-cultural methods and studies, since this country contains a variety of cultures within its borders.

I can agree with my colleague, but only up to a point. I change my charge from "destroy" to "cripple." The limitation of anthropologists' research purview to the bounds of their native countries would cripple anthropology, possibly to such an extent that it would cease to exist as we know it, although not necessarily perishing as a demarcated area of knowledge and inquiry, if that were a goal in itself. What is more, there are grounds for believing that the restriction of inquiry to one country is but the leading edge of a larger restraint. We have already heard assertions that only members of a particular subculture are competent to study it.

The essence of cultural anthropological discipline is cross-cultural analysis. Since, as we have seen, one aspect of ethical behavior is conformity with high standards of technical competence, the suggestion that we abandon work in alien settings is tantamount to a professionally unethical proposal. Anthropology requires a cross-cultural setting for its most basic theoretical operations. Rather than urging anthropologists to dwell within their own cultures, the needs of the discipline are best served by encouraging all anthropologists to maximize their experiences outside their own cultures. This obviously requires that optimum support be given to ventures that would place foreign anthropologists in sensitive research niches in the United States. It also requires that anthropologists continue to press for frequent and easy international exchange of qualified research persons. But these things in turn require some understanding of the real world in which, on the one hand, codes of ethics are proposed to increase trust, and conversely, governments regard all citizens as servitors, thereby vitiating the effects of such formal ethical statements. Although this theme will reappear before the end of this chapter, let me say here simply that the matter is completely open and unresolved and a veritable cockpit of struggle. As the struggle is waged, however, it will be helpful to keep in mind the words of the 1967 Statement on Problems of Anthropological Research and Ethics by the Fellows of the American Anthropological Association:

> The human condition, past and present, is the concern of anthropologists throughout the world. The study of mankind in varying social, cultural, and ecological situations is essential to our understanding of human nature, of culture, and of society.
>
> Our present knowledge of the range of human behavior is admittedly incomplete. Expansion and refinement of this knowledge depend heavily on international understanding and cooperation in scientific and scholarly inquiry. To maintain the independence and integrity of anthropology as a science, it is necessary that scholars have full opportunity to study peoples and their culture. . . .

We must recognize, however, that the choice of subject made by an anthropologist in the United States, while free in certain respects, is often the result of certain subtle pressures. Outstanding among these are the sources and quantity of available funds for research support.

The matter is given fairly extensive treatment in the recent book by Ralph L. Beals (1969:85–146, *passim*); let us take up a few of the main points and one question not raised by Beals.

Treating the last matter first, it should be noted that legitimate efforts of scholars to delve into the workings of the foundation world (e.g., the Ford Foundation, Foreign Area Fellowship Program, Social Science Research Council, and the like) have sometimes been rebuffed. Quite often, the refusal to cooperate has been based upon an implicitly ethical response: the files to which access is requested contain information relating to the evaluation of individual scholars and their projects, evaluations that are usually collected with the explicit proviso that their contents will not be divulged. The matter is both sticky and sensitive. The reason for the investigations I have in mind is the fear in certain circles that the foundations have acted deliberately to direct the development of United States scholarship along certain lines while keeping it away from others; this, it is asserted, has been done by careful selection of projects for funding not so much by merit as by the conformity of projects with the desires of the foundation in question.

Those of us who have served on various boards and panels connected with the making of research grants are often baffled by such charges. They do not conform to our experience, which tells us that, indeed, individual merit of researcher and proposal is the outstanding, if not the only, focus of judgment. Yet none of us has experience of more than a limited arc of the total spectrum of grants. On the other hand, it seems possible to erect certain procedures that would make public a great deal of the inner workings of foundations, including the details of their grant-bestowal machinery, without violating the privacy of individuals. Since this is a problem that torments cultural anthropology at large, there is no reason for avoiding it at home in our own operations.

Taking another tack, the fellows of the AAA have recommended that "when queried by individuals representing either host countries or groups being studied, anthropologists should willingly supply evidence of . . . their sponsorship and source of funds." The phrasing of 1967 now seems a bit narrow. One of the main constituencies that wish to know such details consists of the students who attend such researchers' classes. I can see no reason why they, and the researcher's colleagues, and indeed his public, should not also be granted such information if they desire it.

Left untouched is the question of accepting government funds for any particular research. There is a wide range of such support. We assume that large sums are available for espionage and that some anthropologists will join others in claiming them. I don't think that anything can be done to stop such activities. Traditionally, when such individuals have been exposed, the government concerned has denied any connection with them. Can any self-respecting, organized discipline do less?

What we are concerned with, however, usually comes in more complex packages, such as in the shape of a Project Camelot.[1] There are still quite a number of social scientists who feel that the mistake was in the stopping of Camelot, which they believe put the brakes on the development of "big social science" in the United States. Most recently the center of attention has been on certain aspects of anthropological research in Thailand and elsewhere in Southeast Asia. Indeed, it was the previously mentioned advertisement placed by the U.S. Navy Overseas Employment Office (see p. 225) that gave the additional impetus to demands in some anthropological circles for an explicitly worded code of ethics for the profession, plus various kinds of watchdog committees to police it.

When the advertisement appeared, it sparked a flow of critical letters and a campaign that produced a counter-ad in the *American Anthropologist* (70:1968:852). In January 1968, the Executive Board of the Association accepted a report of the newly formed Committee on Ethics, and endorsed the view "that the Navy ad is not in keeping with the positions taken by the Association with regard to problems of modern war" (*Newsletter of the American Anthropological Association* 10:3 [1969]:1). The Board declared it would not accept advertisements involving end products that would not be made public to the scientific community in a usual way. In case of doubt, the possibly offending material would be scrutinized by the Ethics Committee before acceptance for publication.

Eventually, a polling by mail of the entire membership of the AAA on this and other questions revealed that a majority of respondents opposed official secrecy with regard to anthropological work. The vote, however, was a fairly close one. Without exhausting the categories of voters who did not wish the association to take a formal stand on the matter of secrecy, we can note several camps. One of these comprised anthropologists already involved in precisely such projects. Another included those who were not themselves involved in such projects and might never be, but who opposed the condemnation of secrecy on what they considered to be principled grounds. It seems fair to say that some of these see any such restriction as an infringement on their civil rights; others frankly gave first priority to scientific activity above any other activity, and obviously did not believe that secrecy in itself was an impairment of that scientific activity. It is probable that some were confused or unable to deal with a critical ambiguity—the fact is that many anthropologists, for a variety of reasons, have concealed the

---

[1] *We have mentioned Camelot before. See p. 41.*

identities of informants or even the site of their study, or have repressed data in order to protect the privacy of individuals or groups in a hostile social or political environment. People facing such problems are sometimes unable to draw clear distinctions among various competing motives for secrecy. Finally, a theme to be encountered and reencountered: some respondents are indignant on cultural anthropological grounds, asserting that what is involved is an ethnocentric placing of one particular set of ethical concepts to the fore. Any particular respondent, of course, might have his own blend of these elements and might have others as well. Indeed, one additional element, frequently expressed, relates to the closeness of the vote. Some members of the minority continually protest that their rights are trampled when the course of action approved by a small margin is adopted, or when a particular position, passed in referendum by a majority of responding voters who may be a minority of the total membership of the professional society, is proclaimed as the policy of the membership at large. These, however, are commonplace complaints about the workings of democratic procedures in general. Professional concern over aspects of the conduct of anthropological research in Thailand peaked in 1970 and led to the formation of a special ad hoc committee of inquiry into the charges and countercharges in this matter. The committee report, which tread quite lightly in treating anthropological work in Thailand, was subsequently rejected by the Council of the Association.

Although the American Anthropological Association is perhaps more deeply riven over such matters than ever in the past, this is not the first time that such issues have arisen. We have already seen that half a century ago Franz Boas denounced the use of the anthropological research role as a cover for espionage. Subsequently, additional issues of an ethical nature occupied the attention of the profession. World War II, however, saw a general diminution of sensitivity. Anthropologists were called upon to serve the war effort by placing their distinctive skills at the service of the military. With few, if any, exceptions, they responded with pride and proved eager to assist in the conduct of the war, whether by serving directly in intelligence, compiling area background handbooks, or providing other applications of the discipline. After the war, sentiment remained high for assistance to certain kinds of projects, particularly those associated with the United Nations, especially in such subdivisions as UNESCO. Quite soon after the end of the war, the Executive Board of the AAA was given a mandate by the membership to draft a Statement on Human Rights. It appeared in 1947 (*American Anthropologist* 49:539–43), but by this time opposition was again more vocal and the publication of the Statement precipitated an interesting although inconclusive debate. Homer G. Barnett summed up one view when he wrote:

The import of the statement is that anthropologists, as trained students of human relations who maintain a disciplined atti- tude toward their materials, have something scientific to say about the requirements for a charter of human rights. Un- fortunately this is not so; and the reason is as obvious as it is well known; namely, that there is no scientific approach to the question of human rights, nor to any other problem that calls for an appraisal of human relations in terms of some absolute value system.   [1948:352]

Julian H. Steward offered similar views and expressed them more forcibly:

The conclusion seems inescapable that we have gotten out of our scientific role and are struggling with contradictions. Dur- ing the war, we gladly used our professional techniques and knowledge to advance a cause, but I hope that no one be- lieves that he had a scientific justification for doing so. As individual citizens, members of the Association have every right to pass value judgments, and there are some pretty obvious things that we would all agree on. As a scientific organization, the Association has no business dealing with the rights of man. I am sure that we shall serve science better, and I daresay we shall eventually serve humanity better, if we stick to our purpose. Even now a declaration about human rights can come perilously close to advocacy of American ideological imperialism.   [1948:352]

For another side of the argument we can deliberately take an anachronistic jump of twenty years, to the words of Gutorm Gjessing:

Ethically, the social sciences should serve humanity—no more, no less; but in a world filled with conflict between classes, ethnic groups, nations, etc., it would seem to be im- possible to serve the interests of all simultaneously. If we must choose between the immediate interests of the op- pressed and those of the oppressor, there can be no doubt that our responsibility is first and foremost to the former; for it is here that our special competence lies.   [1968:402]

Leo S. Klejn, a Soviet anthropologist, applauds the view that "a neutral science is an illusion, cultivated because of its advantages for the ruling circles of capitalist society" (1968:415). Klejn reminds us that "the scientific truth is not always easy to discover," and is sometimes perceived differently by different scientists because of the differences in their social positions. Klejn is amused by Gjessing's tendency to seek truth through self-searching. Instead, he points out, "The Marxists believe that the most progressive scientific position . . . , that the most fruitful methodological conception is dialectical materialism" (ibid.).

To pursue the implications of Klejn's remarks, I will jump to a very interesting book, one that Kathleen Gough has mentioned on several occasions as favorable to the "newer socialisms," and which she says has consequently suffered the fate of being "neglected or scoffed at in the United States" (1968:404). I refer to William Hinton's Fanshen, a well-written, detailed, and by no means entirely uncritical account of the coming of the Chinese revolution to one particular village. There is no question, however, of Hinton's involvement in what he is describing. One of the main things that disturbed him was the demand of the poorest peasants for egalitarian distribution of just about everything that could be divided. Although quite understandable, such demands threatened the development of a viable socialist economy. The problem, however, was that egalitarian demands were viewed by the Chinese Communist Party as appropriate in certain contexts, but counterrevolutionary in others. Hinton discussed the matter with one Comrade Lai, the Subregional Communist Party Secretary. The peasants could not understand, complained Secretary Lai, that egalitarianism "was revolutionary when applied against the power and the property of the landlords and the rich peasants, but it became reactionary as soon as it was applied against the middle peasants" (Hinton 1966:606). Comrade Lai continued his analysis, "Many peasants do not understand about this turning point, and so they make mistakes. . . . It is just for this reason that the peasants need proletarian leadership" (ibid.:606–607). It is Hinton's comment at this juncture that deserves our sharpest consideration, for at its heart is every question relating to determinations of truth in all of social science, including anthropology:

> Obviously one aspect of "proletarian leadership" was an
> ability to define and anticipate turning points. The Chinese
> Communist Party, through a grasp of history as process,
> through diligent study of all pertinent social phenomena,
> through never-ending analysis and review of all actions
> undertaken, had developed this to a remarkable degree. It
> was therefore able to prepare its adherents in advance for
> major shifts in the spiral of events or to adjust policies
> quickly whenever events outran foresight. [Ibid.:607]

Whatever lies within Hinton's remark, it is not science. To me it sounds like some not altogether unfamiliar blend of religion and politics. At the least, it is a surrender of the essential responsibility of individuals to make their own determinations, as far as that is possible, given access to data and theory. It may be anticlimactic on my part to suggest that the Chinese Communist Party, that very same organization which Hinton clearly believes had developed "to a remarkable degree" the "ability to define and anticipate turning points," was caught completely off balance by the Red Guards and was almost destroyed in the middle 1960's during the Great Proletarian Cultural Revolution.

I certainly have no intention of denying the generally coercive character of a specific sociocultural setup, much less of the institution we know as the state, which evolved as an instrument of political repression. It is with full recognition of the forms and degrees of compulsion that may be brought to bear in matters of this kind that a contrary statement must be made. In making such a statement, I am painfully aware, to paraphrase the recently quoted remark of Julian Steward, that I have no scientific justification for doing so. Nonetheless, I exist as citizen as well as scientist, worker as well as anthropologist, in short a human being. Hopefully, it is in the last-mentioned role that I would like to say that one should not voluntarily resign the initiative in making crucial decisions, and it does not matter if such relinquishments are made to a political party or to a religious organization or body.

On the other hand, there is no quibble about the reality of racism, exploitation, and war. What is more, not to oppose these phenomena and the societal and cultural institutions which maintain and reinforce them is tacitly to support them. The political events of our own century have forced many of us to bite into another apple of knowledge, and with that bite we have lost every claim to innocence. The numbing truth is that neutrality has been abolished and everyone is seen to lean to one side. Given this burdensome vision, what should an anthropologist do? At this point the field is wide; nonetheless, though some anthropologists tend to be much more active than others, out and out revolutionaries are very few among them.

At present, anthropologists in large numbers, considering the yet small size of the profession, are vocal in protest, as behavior at recent annual meetings shows. In a break with the past, resolutions bearing on current social problems are passed on with increasing frequency to the Executive Board for appropriate action. Activity has not stopped there. In growing numbers anthropologists are becoming increasingly cautious about participation in various types of programs. Not all options are open, it is true, nor is there anything like agreement on proper courses of action. Wherever choices appear, the ethical questions are reasserted and take predominance. Into the breach have stepped some volunteers who would show the way. Gerald Berreman, for instance, puts it this way:

> we must demand of ourselves and our colleagues a sensitive, responsible interest in the ecology of scholarship; a conserva-

*tionist point of view and behavior consistent with that view.
Herein lies the ultimate commitment to the scholarly profession. Its essential ingredients are a deep respect and concern
for the people we study, responsiveness to their values,
claims and perspectives, trust in them, and commitment to
the truth as we discover it. This means avoiding even the
appearance of mission-oriented, politically or economically
colonialist research. A crucial step in achieving this is to
avoid all funds from mission-oriented agencies of government
or neo-colonialist private agencies, to avoid any hint of secret
or clandestine activity, and to coordinate closely and recipro-
cate fully with [foreign] colleagues at every step of the way.
[1970:9]*

When I first wrote this portion of the book, I intended to close
with these words of Berreman, allowing him to express shared feelings
of disgust and revulsion against unwanted war, racism, and complicity
with a social system and an economy that mandate such atrocities. But
neither the world nor the issues are that simple. Berreman's ideas, like
many of those expressed by Kathleen Gough, Gutorm Gjessing, and
others who have cried out to our consciences, are rich in humanity and
good feeling, but romantic and enmeshed in philosophical idealism. For-
get the unadjudicated claim of the culturologists, that the cultural
process brooks no interference by the actors, that humans' assertions
of control over culture are boastful and illusory. What remains inescapable is the realization that Berreman's notions are never so true as
when we agree with them, when we as anthropologists see eye to eye
with the people whose culture we are studying. But seeing eye to eye
with the people an anthropologist studies is not a prerequisite for nor a
necessary accompaniment of good anthropology. It may lead to the
worst kind of anthropology imaginable.

At the heart, the core, of anthropology is the requirement that
people and their cultures be viewed dispassionately. Anthropologists
must be able to see their own culture for what it is, but they must also
see other cultures for what they are. Anthropologists may not be un-
flinching, but they cannot turn away their gaze if they see human sacrifice, slavery, a cult of torture, the glorification of war, degradation of
women and men, racism, exploitation, or a thousand other garden-
variety cultural predilections. This does not mean that they approve of
what they see, but they should not confuse their task of analysis with
the act of judgment. Nor does this discrimination in any way curtail the
anthropologist's personal exercise of ethical decision in rejecting certain
kinds of research, certain kinds of funding, certain kinds of employment.

Anthropologists must confront the distribution of realities. In today's world, this means that they cannot attribute all the evil to one social system, one form of economic organization. More basically, anthropologists, as anthropologists, cannot transfer their scholarly responsibilities to anyone else, not to the president of their country, or the chairman of their party, or the head of their department or even their research assistant. One cannot, as an anthropologist, subscribe to a code of ethics that vacillates between science and politics. Just as it is true that science is never neutral in a political sense, so politics can never be objective in a scientific sense. I said earlier that a basic incompatibility exists between the roles of anthropologist and revolutionist. No one can carry out both simultaneously without betraying one or the other.

Whatever it may be for others, ethics for the anthropologist turns out to be a miserably charted sea in which one makes a personal way, like a frail craft that lacks slick navigational devices. Terrifyingly enough, there is no infallible helmsman at the wheel. In lieu of precise azimuths, we lecture each other, interminably. Alas! This puts us back to where we started at the beginning of the chapter. Unfortunately, that's exactly where I think it is. You take it.

BIBLIOGRAPHY OF CITATIONS

Alland, Alexander, Jr.
1970   *Adaptation in Cultural Evolution: An Approach to Medical Anthro-pology.* New York: Columbia University Press.

Almond, Gabriel A., and James S. Coleman (eds.)
1960   *The Politics of Developing Areas.* Princeton: Princeton University Press.

Aristotle
1941   *The Basic Works of Aristotle.* Edited and with introduction by Rich-ard McKeon. New York: Random House.

Avorn, Jerry L., et al.
1969   *Up against the Ivy Wall: A History of the Columbia Crisis.* New York: Atheneum.

Barnett, Homer G.
1948   "On Science and Human Rights." *American Anthropologist* 50:352–355.

Beals, Ralph L.
1968   "Comment [in Social Responsibilities Symposium]." *Current Anthro-pology* 9:407–408.
1969   *Politics of Social Research. An Inquiry into the Ethics and Respon-sibilities of Social Scientists.* Chicago: Aldine.

Bean, Robert Bennett
1932   *The Races of Man; Differentiation and Dispersal of Man.* New York: The Universal Society.

Beattie, John H. M.
1963   "Techniques of Graduate Training." In Mandelbaum, Lasker, and Albert 1963:439–453.

Bender, Donald
1965   "The Development of French Anthropology." *Journal of the History of the Behavioral Sciences* 1:139–151.

Berreman, Gerald M.
1968   "Is Anthropology Alive? Social Responsibility in Social Anthropol-ogy." *Current Anthropology* 9:391–396.
1970   "Ethics, Responsibility and the Funding of Asian Research." Ex-panded version of "The Funding of Asian Studies: Needs, Oppor-tunities, and Ethics." Paper presented to Presidential Panel: 22nd Annual Meeting, Association for Asian Studies. Mimeographed.

Binford, Lewis R.
1968   "Archeological Perspectives." In Binford and Binford 1970:5–32.

Binford, Sally R., and Lewis R. Binford, (eds.)
1968   *New Perspectives in Archeology.* Chicago: Aldine.

Boas, Franz
  1901 "The Mind of Primitive Man." *The Journal of American Folklore*
         14:1–11.
  1911 *The Mind of Primitive Man.* New York: Macmillan.
  1919 "Scientists as Spies." *The Nation* 109:797.
  1938 *The Mind of Primitive Man,* rev. ed. New York: Macmillan.
Braestrup, Peter
  1967 "Researchers Aid Thai Rebel Fight: U.S. Defense Unit Develops
         Anti-guerrilla Devices." *The New York Times* 20 March 1967:17.
Bruner, Edward M.
  1970 "Graduate Record Exam Considered by Board: Statement by
         Bruner." *Newsletter of the American Anthropological Association*
         11:3 (March 1970):11–12.
Carroll, Sophie C.
  1970 "Discrimination in Fieldwork." *Newsletter of the American Anthro-
         pological Association* 11:6 (June 1970):2, 15.
Cartter, Allan M.
  1966 *An Assessment of Quality in Graduate Education.* Washington, D.C.:
         American Council on Education.
Cohn, Werner
  1969 "Review [of Michael Banton, *Race Relations.* (New York: Basic
         Books. 1968)]." *Current Anthropology* 10:203.
Condominas, Georges
  1965 *L'exotique est quotidien.* Paris: Plon.
Cox Commission
  1968 *Crisis at Columbia; Report of the Fact-Finding Commission Ap-
         pointed to Investigate the Disturbances at Columbia University in
         April and May, 1968.* New York: Vintage Books.
Deloria, Vine, Jr.
  1969 *Custer Died for Your Sins; An Indian Manifesto.* New York: Macmil-
         lan.
Du Bois, Cora
  1963 "The Curriculum in Cultural Anthropology." In Mandelbaum, Lasker,
         and Albert 1963:27–38.
Edel, May, and Abraham Edel
  1968 *Anthropology and Ethics; The Quest for Moral Understanding,* rev.
         ed. Cleveland: Press of Case Western Reserve University.
Eggan, Fred
  1963 "The Graduate Program." In Mandelbaum, Lasker, and Albert 1963:
         409–419.
Eliot, T. S.
  1935 *Collected Poems 1909–1935.* New York: Harcourt, Brace.
Emmet, Dorothy
  1968 "Ethics: Ethical Systems and Social Structures." *International En-
         cyclopedia of the Social Sciences* 5:157–160.
Engler, Robert
  1968 "Social Science and Social Consciousness: The Shame of the Uni-
         versities." In Roszak 1968:182–207.
Evans-Pritchard, E. E.
  1940 *The Nuer.* Oxford: Clarendon Press.

Featherstone, Joseph
  1969 "Who's Fit to Teach?" *New Republic* 161, No. 24, Issue 2868 (13 December 1969):19–21.

Fischer, Ann, and Peggy Golde
  1968 "The Position of Women in Anthropology." *American Anthropologist* 70:337–344.

Fortes, Meyer
  1963 "Graduate Study and Research." In Mandelbaum, Lasker, and Albert 1963:421–438.

Frank, Andre Gunder
  1968 "Comments [in 'Social Responsibilities Symposium']." *Current Anthropology* 9:412–414.

Freeman, John F.
  1965 "University Anthropology: Early Developments in the United States." *Kroeber Anthropological Society Papers* 32:78–90.

Fried, Morton H.
  1967 *The Evolution of Political Society.* New York: Random House.
  1968 "The Need to End the Pseudoscientific Investigation of Race." In Margaret Mead, Theodosius Dobzhansky, Ethel Tobach, and Robert E. Light (eds.), *Science and the Concept of Race.* New York: Columbia University Press, 122–131.

Friedl, Ernestine, and Robbins Burling
  1970 "Graduate Record Exam Considered by Board: Statement by Friedl and Burling." *Newsletter of the American Anthropological Association* 11:3 (March 1970):10–11.

Gjessing, Gutorm
  1968 "The Social Responsibility of the Social Scientist." *Current Anthropology* 9:397–402.

Goldman, Irving
  1955 "Status Rivalry and Cultural Evolution in Polynesia." *American Anthropologist* 57:680–697.

Gossett, Thomas F.
  1963 *Race: The History of an Idea in America.* Dallas: Southern Methodist University Press.

Gough, Kathleen
  1968 "New Proposals for Anthropologists." *Current Anthropology* 9:403–407, 428–431.

Graham, Patricia Albjerg
  1970 "Women in Academe." *Science* 169, No. 3952:1284–1290.

Haber, Barbara, and Alan Haber
  1967 "Getting By with a Little Help from Our Friends." *Our Generation* 5:83–101.

Haldane, J. B. S.
  1956 "The Argument from Animals to Men: An Examination of Its Validity for Anthropology." *Journal of the Royal Anthropological Institute* 86:2:1–14.

Hallowell, A. Irving
  1960 "The Beginnings of Anthropology in America." In Frederica deLaguna (ed.), *Selected Papers from the American Anthropologist 1888–1920.* Evanston: Row, Peterson, 1–96.

Harris, Ann Sutherland
  1970 "The Second Sex in Academe." *Bulletin, American Association of University Professors* 56:283–295.
Harris, Marvin
  1964 *The Nature of Cultural Things.* New York: Random House.
  1968 *The Rise of Anthropological Theory.* New York: Thomas Y. Crowell.
  1971 *Culture, Man, and Nature: An Introduction to General Anthropology.* New York: Thomas Y. Crowell.
Harvard University. Committee on the Objectives of a General Education in a Free Society
  1945 *General Education in a Free Society.* Cambridge: Harvard University Press.
Hays, H. R.
  1958 *From Ape to Angel.* New York: Knopf.
Helm, June
  1966 *Pioneers of American Anthropology; The Uses of Biography.* American Ethnological Society, Monograph 43. Seattle: University of Washington Press.
Herskovits, Melville J.
  1941 *The Myth of the Negro Past.* New York: Harper.
Hinton, William
  1966 *Fanshen; A Documentary of Revolution in a Chinese Village.* New York: Monthly Review Press.
Hitchcock, James
  1969 "Comes the Cultural Revolution." *The New York Times Magazine* 27 July 1969:4–5, 40, 50, 52.
Horowitz, Irving Louis
  1965 "The Life and Death of Project Camelot." *Trans-action* 3:3–7, 44–47.
  1967 *The Rise and Fall of Project Camelot: Studies in the Relationship between Social Sciences and Practical Politics.* Cambridge: MIT Press.
Hulse, Frederic S.
  1963 "Objectives and Methods." In Mandelbaum, Lasker, and Albert 1963: 69–79.
Hymes, Dell H.
  1963 "Objectives and Concepts of Linguistic Anthropology." In Mandelbaum, Lasker, and Albert 1963:275–302.
Irwin-Williams, Cynthia
  1970 "Letter." *Newsletter of the American Anthropological Association* 11:5 (May 1970):6.
Keniston, Haywood
  1959 *Graduate Study and Research in the Arts and Sciences at the University of Pennsylvania.* Philadelphia: University of Pennsylvania Press.
Klejn, Leo S.
  1968 "Comments [in 'Social Responsibilities Symposium']." *Current Anthropology* 9:415–417.
Kroeber, Alfred L.
  1939 *Cultural and Natural Areas of Native North America.* Publications in American Archaeology and Anthropology, Vol. 38. Berkeley: University of California Press.

1953   "Introduction." In A. L. Kroeber, et al., *Anthropology Today*. Chicago: University of Chicago Press, xiii–xv.

Lasker, Gabriel W.
1963   "The Introductory Course." In Mandelbaum, Lasker, and Albert 1963:99–110
1963a "Advanced Courses." In Mandelbaum, Lasker, and Albert 1963: 111–121.

Lasker, Gabriel W., Zenon Pohorecky, and Lewis Klein
1963   "A Survey of Catalog Listings in Anthropology." In Mandelbaum, Lasker, and Albert 1963a:7–21.

Lehman-Hartleben, Karl
1943   "Thomas Jefferson, Archeologist." *American Journal of Archeology* 47:161–163.

Lévi-Strauss, Claude
1966   "Anthropology: Its Achievements and Future." *Current Anthropology* 7:124–127.

Lewis, Oscar
1959   *Five Families: Mexican Case Studies in the Culture of Poverty*. New York: Basic Books.
1966   "The Culture of Poverty." *Scientific American* 215:16, 19–25.

Lynd, Robert S.
1939   *Knowledge for What? The Place of Social Science in American Culture*. Princeton: Princeton University Press.

Lynd, Robert S., and Helen M. Lynd
1929   *Middletown: A Study in Contemporary American Culture*. New York: Harcourt, Brace.
1937   *Middletown in Transition: A Study in Culture Conflicts*. New York: Harcourt, Brace.

Mandelbaum, David G.
1963   "A Design for an Anthropology Curriculum." In Mandelbaum, Lasker, and Albert 1963:49–64.

Mandelbaum, David G., Gabriel W. Lasker, and Ethel M. Albert
1963   *The Teaching of Anthropology*. American Anthropological Association, Memoir 94.
1963a *Resources for the Teaching of Anthropology*. American Anthropological Association, Memoir 95.

Mao Tse-tung
1964   "On Correcting Mistaken Ideas in the Party." In *Selected Works of Mao Tse-tung*, Vol. 2. Peking: Foreign Languages Press, 105–116. (Orig. 1929.)
1965   "Preface and Postscript to Rural Surveys." In *Selected Works of Mao Tse-tung*, Vol. 3. Peking: Foreign Languages Press, 11–16. (Orig. 1941.)
1965a "Combat Liberalism." In *Selected Works of Mao Tse-tung*, Vol. 2. Peking: Foreign Languages Press, 31–33. (Orig. 1937.)

Mauss, Marcel
1913   "L'ethnographie en France et à l'étranger." *La Revue de Paris* (September–October 1913): 537–560, 815–937.

Mering, Otto von
1968   "Comments [in 'Social Responsibilities Symposium']" *Current Anthropology* 9:421.

Merriam-Webster
    1961 *Webster's New Collegiate Dictionary.* Springfield, Mass.: G. & C.
          Merriam.
Mills, C. Wright
    1961 *The Sociological Imagination.* New York: Evergreen. (Orig. 1959.)
Moos, Elizabeth
    1967 *Soviet Education: Achievements and Goals.* New York: National
          Council of American-Soviet Friendship.
Morgan, Lewis Henry
    1877 *Ancient Society.* New York: Henry Holt.
Nisbet, Robert
    1970 "Subjective Si! Objective No!" *The New York Times Book Review*
          5 April 1970: 1–2, 36–37.
Parsons, Talcott
    1967 "The editor's column." *American Sociologist* 2:138–140.
Pelto, Pertti J.
    1970 *Anthropological Research; The Structure of Inquiry.* New York:
          Harper & Row.
Powell, John Wesley
    1888 "Competition as a Factor in Human Evolution." *American Anthro-
          pologist* 1:297–323.
Public Health Service
    1969 *Sociologists and Anthropologists: Supply and Demand in Educa-
          tional Institutions.* Public Health Service Publication No. 1884.
          Washington, D.C.: U.S. Government Printing Office.
Radcliffe-Brown, A. R.
    1949 "Functionalism: A Protest." *American Anthropologist* 51:320–323.
Resek, Carl
    1960 *Lewis Henry Morgan, American Scholar.* Chicago: University of
          Chicago Press.
Richards, Cara
    1968 "Comments [in 'Social Responsibilities Symposium']," *Current An-
          thropology* 9:423–424.
Robinson, Armstead L., et al. (eds.)
    1969 *Black Studies in the University.* New York: Bantam.
Roche, Marcel
    1970 "Notes on Science in Cuba." *Science* 169 (24 July 1970):344–349.
Roose, Kenneth D., and Charles J. Anderson
    1970 *A Rating of Graduate Programs.* Washington, D.C.: American Coun-
          cil on Education.
Rosen, Sumner M.
    1968 "Keynes Without Gadflies." In Roszak 1968:62–91.
Rossi, Alice
    1970 "Status of Women in Graduate Departments of Sociology." *Amer-
          ican Sociologist* 5:1–12.
Rossman, Jack
    1968 "Patterns of Interest Among Anthropologists." *Newsletter of the
          American Anthropological Association* 9:10 (December 1968): 7–8.
Roszak, Theodore (ed.)
    1968 *The Dissenting Academy.* New York: Vintage. (Orig. 1967.)

Ruchames, Louis
1969 *Racial Thought in America; A Documentary History.* Amherst: University of Massachusetts Press.

Sapir, Edward
1924 "Culture, Genuine and Spurious." *American Journal of Sociology* 29:401–429.
1963 "The Unconscious Patterning of Behavior in Society." In David G. Mandelbaum (ed.), *Selected Writings of Edward Sapir in Language, Culture and Personality.* Berkeley: University of California Press, 544–559. (Orig. 1927.)

Sills, David L.
1968 "Introduction." *International Encyclopedia of the Social Sciences* I:xix–xxx.

Shenker, Israel (ed.)
1970 "Isaac Bashevis Singer Scoffs." *Atlantic* 226 (July 1970):98–100.

Simon, Rita James, Shirley Merritt Clark, and Kathleen Galway
1967 "The Woman Ph.D.: A Recent Profile." *Social Problems* 15:221–236.

Sorenson, John L.
1970 "Mobility of Academic Anthropologists." *Newsletter of the American Anthropological Association* 11:4 (April 1970):4–5.

Spaulding, Alfred
1968 "Explanation in Archeology." In Binford and Binford 1968:33–39.

Spindler, George D.
1955 "Anthropology and Education: An Overview." In George D. Spindler (ed.), *Education and Anthropology.* Stanford: Stanford University Press, 5–23.

Stalin, J. V.
1954 "The Foundations of Leninism." *Problems of Leninism.* Moscow: Foreign Languages Publishing House, 15–111. (Orig. 1924.)

Steward, Julian H.
1948 "Comments on the Statement on Human Rights." *American Anthropologist* 50:351–352.
1955 *Theory of Culture Change.* Urbana: University of Illinois Press.

Stocking, George W., Jr.
1965 "On the Limits of 'Presentism' and 'Historicism' in the Historiography of the Behavioral Sciences." *Journal of the History of the Behavioral Sciences* 1:211–218.
1965a "From Physics to Ethnology: Franz Boas' Arctic Expedition as a Problem in the Historiography of the Behavioral Sciences." *Journal of the History of the Behavioral Sciences* 1:53–66.
1966 "The History of Anthropology: Where, Whence, Whither?" *Journal of the History of the Behavioral Sciences* 2:281–290.
1968 "Tylor, Edward Burnett." *International Encyclopedia of the Social Sciences* 16:170–177.

Tax, Sol
1964 "The Setting of the Science of Man." In Sol Tax (ed.), *Horizons of Anthropology.* Chicago: Aldine, 15–24.

Tylor, Edward B.
1871 *Primitive Culture; Researches into the Development of Mythology, Philosophy, Religion, Language, Art, and Customs.* London: John Murray.

1881   *Anthropology; An Introduction to the Study of Man and Civilization.*
       New York: D. Appleton.

Valentine, Charles A.
1968   *Culture and Poverty. Critique and Counter-Proposals.* Chicago: University of Chicago Press.

Vance, Carole
1970   "Sexual Stratification in Academic Anthropology." Paper presented at the 69th Annual Meeting of the American Anthropological Association. Mimeographed.

Vogelin, Erminie
1950   "Anthropology in American Universities." *American Anthropologist* 52:350–391.

Wagner, Philip L., and Marvin W. Mikesell (eds.)
1962   *Readings in Cultural Geography.* Chicago: University of Chicago Press.

Weiner, J. S.
1958   "Courses and Training in Physical Anthropology and Human Biology." In D. F. Roberts and J. S. Weiner (eds.), *The Scope of Physical Anthropology and Its Place in Academic Studies.* New York: The Wenner-Gren Foundation for Anthropological Research, 43–50.

Welling, James C.
1888   "The Law of Malthus." *American Anthropologist* 1:1–21.

White, Leslie A.
1937–38 "Some Suggestions for a Program in Anthropology in China." *The Chinese Social and Political Science Review* 21:120–134.
1948   "Man's Control Over Civilization: An Anthropocentric Illusion." *The Scientific Monthly* 66:235–247.

Williams, Bobby Jo
1968   "Establishing Cultural Heterogeneities in Settlement Patterns: An Ethnographic Example." In Binford and Binford 1968:161–170.

Willis, William S., Jr.
1970   "Anthropology and Negroes on the Southern Cultural Frontier." In James Curtis and Lewis Gould (eds.), *The Black Experience in America: Selected Essays.* Austin: University of Texas Press, 33–50.

Wissler, Clark
1917   *The American Indian; An Introduction to the Anthropology of the New World.* New York: D. C. McMurtrie.
1943   "The American Indian and the American Philosophical Society." *Proceedings of the American Philosophical Society* 86:189–204.

Wolf, Eric R.
1964   *Anthropology.* Englewood Cliffs: Prentice-Hall.

Woodbury, Nathalie F. S. (ed.)
1969   *Guide to Departments of Anthropology 1969–70.* Bulletins of the American Anthropological Association 2:2 Washington, D.C.: American Anthropological Association.
1970   *Guide to Departments of Anthropology 1970–71.* Bulletins of the American Anthropological Association 3:2. Washingon, D.C.: American Anthropological Association.

INDEX

ABD students (all but the dissertation), 161
Aberle, Kathleen Gough, 47, 48, 73, 226–27, 244, 246
ABS Guide to Recent Publications in the Social and Behavioral Sciences, 134
academic freedom, 39–40, 226–27
ACE questionnaire (American Council on Education), 165–66
Advanced Anthropology Test, 168–69, 180, 181, 183
Advanced Sociology Test, 181
advocacy anthropology, 48–49
aesthetics: anthropology and, 12
Africa (publication), 135
American Anthropologist (magazine), 66, 67, 133, 188, 225, 241, 242
American Indians: ethics and wampum of, 233; legislation to help, 51; Morgan and, 65–66; as preferential subjects of investigation, 68–71
Anglo-American General Encyclopedias (Walsh), 137
anthropological archeology ("dirt" archeology), 32
Anthropological Index to Current Periodicals in the Library of the Royal Anthropological Institute, 134
anthropological linguistics, 32–33
anthropology: defined, 5–6; themes of study in, 20–21
anthropometry, 25–26
anti-Semitism among scientists, 217, 223
application fees: graduate school, 149
applied anthropology, 51–52
archeology: area of concern of, 28–30; cultural anthropology and, 31–32; data of, 109; data collection in, 117–19; ethical problems in, 232–34; excavation and, 31; graduate schools for, 179
"archetyping": errors of, 30–31
Aristotle, 59
Atlas for Anthropology (Spencer and Johnson), 136

australopithecine fossils, 105

Banton, Michael, 63, 64
Barnett, Homer G., 242–43
Beals, Ralph L., 64, 210, 212, 230, 240
Bean, Robert Bennett, 60
behavioral approach to politics, 19
Benedict, Ruth, 5, 123
Beran, Shirley, 159
Bergson, Henri, 16
Berreman, Gerald, 245–46
bibliographical materials, 131–36; reading lists, 139–40
Bibliography of Asian Studies, 135–36
Bibliography of the Peoples and Cultures of Mainland Southeast Asia (Embree and Dotson), 136
Bibliography on Southwestern Asia (Field), 135
Bibliotheca Sinica (Cordier), 134
Biennial Review of Anthropology, 133
Biological Abstracts, 132
biological race: human variation and, 27. *See also* race
biology: anthropology and, 5–12; time and, 78, 79; usefulness of anthropology courses for majors in, 102
Black Panthers, 42, 83
black students, 42–45
Black Studies movement, 44, 83, 222; major system and, 145
blacks. *See* Negroes
Bloomfield, Leonard, 140
Boas, Franz, 5, 14, 63, 186, 205, 242; on cultural relativism, 72–73; racism of, 61–62; on scientists as spies, 211–12
Book Review Digest, 139
Book Review Index, 139
Boulding, Kenneth, 16
bourgeoisie: dominance of, 38
Brixham Cave, 57
Broca, Paul, 74
Burling, Robbins, 181–82
business: anthropologists in, 209–11
Butterfield, Herbert, 56

Caesar, Julius, 59
Camelot project, 41, 44, 52, 241
capitalism: anthropology as product of, 67–68; anthropology textbooks and, 88; ethnic minorities and, 51; racism and, 38, 62–63
careers: in anthropology, 159–60. *See also* occupation; placement
Carribbeana 1900–1965, 134
cataclysmic emergence, 16
Chin Hsun-hua, 41–42
China: A Critical Bibliography (Hucker), 135
Clark, George, 69
"classical" archeology ("fine arts" archeology), 32. *See also* archeology
Cohn, Werner, 63–64
Columbia University: academic freedom and, 39–40; disturbances at (1968), 45, 46, 143; racism of, 40
Comitas, Lambros, 134
commonsense, science vs., 61–62
comparative method: as tool, 22–23
comparative sociology: social anthropology and, 33, 34
competitive grading, 145, 146
componential analysis of language, 32, 33
computerization of behavior, 99
contraception, 79
counterinsurgency, 40–41, 52
courses: length of anthropology, 11–12. *See also* curriculum
Cox Commission, 45, 143
Crisis at Columbia (Cox Commission report), 143
Cro-Magnon man, 29–30
cultural anthropology: achievements of, 71–72; archeology and, 31–32; as by-product of colonialism, 67; data collection in, 120–21; essence of, 239; ethical problems in, 235–36; field work technique of, 22; graduate schools for, 179; output of books in, 130–31; racism and textbooks of, 88; social anthropology compared with, 33–34; sociology and, 20
cultural determinism, 49–51
cultural ecology, 15
cultural evolution, 13
cultural relativism, 5; concept of, 72–73; grasp of concept, 87
culture: defined, 5
culture concept: presenting, 79; purpose of, 7–8; sociology major and courses in, 94–95
culture shock: described, 34–35, 124–25

Cumulated Index Medicus, 133
Current Anthropology, 133
curriculum: centrality of anthropology in, 81–83; cost-accounting system in determining, 149–50; social classes and changes in, 81–83. *See also* graduate curriculum; introductory anthropology courses; undergraduate minor
Custer Died for Your Sins (Deloria), 70

Darwin, Charles, 140
Dawes Severalty Act (1887), 51
Debray, Régis, 152
de Gaulle, Charles, 138
degrees: employment and, 213–14; graduate schools (1968–70), 160, 162, 169–70, 174. *See also* occupation
DeLeon, Daniel, 40
Deloria, Vine, Jr., 70, 113
demography: usefulness of courses in, 101
departmentalization of subject matter, 143–45. *See also* major system
departments: leading, by placement of graduates, 175, 176
determinism: cultural, 49–51; geographical, 14, 15
dictionaries: useful, 138–39
Dictionary of Anthropology (Winick), 138
Dictionary Catalog of the National Agricultural Library, 139
discrimination (prejudice) in anthropology, 217–23. *See also* racism
Dissenting Academy, The (Roszak), 54
dissertations, 161, 202–7; completing, 163; hypotheses for, 204–5; relation between master's essay and, 202
Dorsey, George A., 73
Driver, Samuel R., 78n
DuBois, Cora, 87, 155, 156
Durkheim, Émile, 23, 74, 123

eclecticism in scientific thought, 156–57
ecology: cultural, 15; problems of, in anthropology courses, 85
economic anthropology, 17; courses in, 95–97; "subjectivists" and "formalists" of, 19
economics: anthropology and, 14, 16–17; defined, 18
Edel, Abraham, 229
Edel, May, 229
Eggan, Fred, 184